THE DISENCHANTED ISLES

ALSO BY THEON WRIGHT

The Voyage of The Herman
Rape in Paradise
The Open Door

The Disenchanted Isles

The Story of the Second Revolution in Hawaii

Theon Wright

THE DIAL PRESS NEW YORK

1972

Library of Congress Cataloging in Publication Data

Wright, Theon.
The disenchanted isles.

Includes bibliographical references.
1. Hawaii—Politics and government—1900–1959.
2. Hawaii—Politics and government—1959–
I. Title.
DU627.W75   320.9'969   77-37452

Printed in the United States of America

First Printing

Contents

Photographs follow page 146

Foreword   vii

PART I: 1893–1920

"SUGAR IS KING"

1. The First Revolution   5
2. Annexation of Paradise   14
3. Rulers of Paradise   22
4. Signs of Discontent   32

PART II: 1921–1940

THE MELTING POT

5. The Pot Begins to Boil   45
6. The Dividing Line   64
7. Straws in the Wind   75
8. "Tokyo High"   87

PART III: 1941–1955

REVOLT IN PARADISE

9. The Inside Wave   101
10. "Go for Broke!"   114
11. The "Second-Class Citizen"   129
12. The "Red Menace"   140
13. The Turning Point   150

PART IV: 1956–1960

THE FIFTIETH STATE

14. Changing the Guard   167
15. Sugar and Statehood   179
16. Strategy for Statehood   192
17. The End of an Era   202

PART V: 1960–1970

THE NEW FRONTIER

18. The Politics of Change   221
19. The New Establishment   236
20. The Takabuki Incident   252
21. The Emerging Races   264

PART VI

HAWAII 2000

22. Hawaii's 30-Year Plan   277
23. "Aloha"   286

Notes   294
Index   297

In the years just before World War II there were a number of prophets of doom in this country of the type who consistently view things with alarm who warned that the United States was harboring in the middle of the Pacific Ocean an explosive mixture—a bomb. At any moment, given the necessary ingredients and proper fuse, this bomb might blow up in the face of the American people, with disastrous results.

The bomb, of course, was Hawaii. Among its explosive ingredients were about 270,000 people of Asiatic origin who lived in the Territory. Of these, approximately 160,000 were of Japanese blood, and among the latter were more than 100,000 second-generation Japanese, or *nisei*, who had been born in Hawaii and therefore were American citizens. They presented a peculiarly sensitive situation since, as American citizens, they had certain inalienable rights common to all Americans. One of the more apocalyptic prophesies stated: "Hawaii is facing an international threat. It is the logistic key to future wars in the Pacific. Long a social test tube where race motivation can be studied clinically, Hawaii shows signs of developing an explosive mixture which may not only disturb the internal security of America's most important Pacific outpost, but is capable of throwing out of focus our aims in the Pacific."

Just how "clinically" these matters were studied at the time may be subject to some question, but at any rate the warnings can now be reviewed objectively and with less passion than might have been expected when they were first uttered. The "explosive mixture" has failed to explode. Hawaii, once an almost feudal regime existing under the control of a small group of revolutionaries who had overthrown the ruling monarch of the island kingdom in the Revolution of 1893, has passed

Foreword

through several phases, including a "second revolution," and has become a full-fledged American state. It is an aggressive, highly industrialized, and economically flourishing society, quite peaceful and wholly American. The question that immediately suggests itself is, What happened to the racial tensions and the "bomb"?

There are certain situations in which the personality of a single man may portray the soul of a people. This was true of Winston Churchill whose bulldog tenacity after Dunkirk is often taken as reflecting the English character. In the case of Hawaii, that kind of symbolism would be difficult to apply. The new State has a conglomerate of a dozen ethnic origins and twice as many crossbreedings, not to mention multiple social, political, and economic backgrounds and a religious mix of Polynesian idol worshippers, Congregational missionaries, Catholics, Mormons, Jews, and an admixture of Buddhists, Taoists, Confucians, and Zoroastrians, with a bit of Moslem faith supplied by a scattering of Malaysians and Pakistanis, as well as a few Arabs.

In spite of this mixture of races, religions, and other elements, it might be possible to single out one person who conceivably would represent the "soul of Hawaii" as it is today. If one were required to make such a selection, the man who would best fit the role is a one-armed American war hero born in Hawaii of Japanese parents, the grandson of a plantation field worker imported to the Islands in 1899 as a contract laborer. That man is Daniel Ken Inouye, and he is the junior United States Senator from Hawaii.

The reason for selecting Inouye as the symbol of Hawaii, as Churchill was of England, obviously is not his appearance. Churchill looked like a typical Englishman, whereas Inouye bears little resemblance to a typical Hawaiian. He is short and stocky, swarthy rather than brown, and is not Polynesian. The true prototype of the Hawaiian would be a tall, bronze-colored warrior with a feather helmet and cloak, looking very much like a sunburned Roman soldier. Inouye was not cut along any such lines. As a boy in the Japanese ghetto he wore blue denim pants, sports shirts, and no shoes, customary attire for nonwhite boys living in the slums of Honolulu. He is a *nisei*—a first-generation

American of Japanese ancestry—and when Japan's war planes dropped bombs on Pearl Harbor on December 7, 1941, Dan Inouye suffered, as did all other *nisei* in Hawaii, from the stigma of being of Japanese blood.

He was seventeen at the time and a senior in high school. A year later the 442nd Regimental Combat Team was activated in Hawaii at the urging of Hawaiian-born Japanese who wanted to prove they were loyal Americans. Dan Inouye enlisted, and his record as well as the heroics of the unit, composed almost entirely of *nisei,* became a legend in Hawaii. Two weeks before the war ended in Europe, Dan Inouye's right arm was shot off by a rifle grenade.

He returned from the war a hero, but sadly disillusioned about the business of being an American citizen of Japanese ancestry. They refused to cut his hair in a barber shop in San Francisco because he was a "Jap" even though he had only one arm left from the war. He came home to Honolulu fired not only with anger and resentment, but a determination to drive home the point he and other *nisei* had tried to make with the 442nd RCT: that being of alien antecedents did not necessarily preclude a *nisei* from being a loyal American, any more than it barred American citizens of German, Italian, Scandinavian, or any other foreign ancestry. He decided that the best way to make his point was to get into politics, and he telephoned Jack Burns, a former Honolulu police detective, then one of the leading independent Democrats in Hawaii, to say that he would like to do anything, including stuffing envelopes with political leaflets, just to help out.

Burns needed help, and he needed it badly. He had embarked almost single-handed on a crusade to restructure the political system of Hawaii, which had been ruled for a half-century by a small group of sugar planters and Honolulu businessmen, many of them descendants of missionaries. This group had seized the Islands in 1893 after overthrowing Queen Liliuokalani, the last monarch of Hawaii, annexed them to the United States in 1898, and governed the place as a baronial fiefdom since that time. Burns was trying to do to them what they did to Liliuokalani.

Dan Inouye joined the crusade in 1947. Eight years later the Democratic Party in Hawaii, under Burns's guidance, had won control of the territorial Legislature for the first time since Annexation in 1898, and Inouye sat in the Hawaiian Legislature as majority leader of the House. Four years after that he became the first Congressman from Hawaii and the first of Japanese blood ever to sit in the House of Representatives. Today he is in the Senate, the foremost political spokesman for the new State of Hawaii.

This is not a story of the political career of Dan Inouye. It is an account of the transformation of a society—Hawaii's second revolution that occurred some sixty years after the first Hawaiian Revolution in 1893. It concerns Dan Inouye only to the extent that he became one of the principal architects of the new Hawaii and a symbol of its renascence.

In order to place this second revolution, which was more in the nature of an evolution, in historical perspective, it is necessary to go back to the time when the missionaries, whose descendants seized control of the Islands, first arrived in the year 1820. This is a well-worn theme and has been covered from various points of view by many writers; yet the beginnings of *Hawaii Nei* (old Hawaii) must be understood if the new Hawaii is to be understood.

Hawaii was a tropical paradise in the early years of the nineteenth century, with the brawling little port of Honolulu as its trading center. Whaling had just been discovered in the Western Pacific and a cluster of whalers and American, English, and Russian merchantmen lay at anchor in the tiny harbor that had been opened only a few years earlier when the English sealer *Jackal* found a break in the reef. Sailors roamed the waterfront, passing out trinkets—and also gonorrhea and syphilis— to the dark-haired, dark-eyed native girls who wore flowers in their hair and gaily colored cloth wrapped around their centers of gravitation. Hawaiian hospitality in those days involved sharing sex as well as breadfruit, raw fish, and *poi.*

The seafarers brought Hawaii its first taste of white civilization. Then, in the year 1820, came the missionaries. They brought bibles, long dresses known as *holokuus* and other accouterments of Christian morality; and they also brought a taste for acquiring arable lands.

The first missionaries who arrived in the brig *Thaddeus* in April of 1820 were sincere if somewhat austere zealots in the service of the Lord, wholly dedicated to saving the souls of the benighted heathen of the Sandwich Isles. There were nineteen aboard—seven men, seven women, and five children—and they were followed shortly by others. Many of the names are still well known in Hawaii today: Thurston, Bingham, Holman, Whitney, Richards, Ellis, Judd, and later Castle, Cooke, Damon, Shipman, Alexander, and Baldwin.

During the first years the missionaries battled valiantly for the souls of the kindly, hospitable people of the Islands, whom they sometimes referred to as savages, and the sailors fought just as hard, sometimes in the streets, for special favors of the dark-skinned Polynesian girls. These aspirations often worked at cross-purposes. As the Reverend Asa Thurston, whose descendant, Lorrin Thurston, was a leader of the Revolution of 1893, noted: "We [the missionaries] need men who have their eyes fixed on the glory of God in the salvation of the heathen."

Since the manner in which this "salvation" was achieved forms much of the burden of this book, it may be well to point out that not all members of the missionary band were brothers of the cloth; some were bookkeepers, physicians, and other lay members of the group, who did not always follow the admonition to "open your hearts wide and set your marks high," as instructed by the Congregational Board of Foreign Missions in Boston. "You are to aim at nothing less than covering these islands with fruitful farms and pleasant dwellings and schools and churches, raising the whole people to a state of Christian civilization," the Board said, and particularly warned against "being betrayed into a spirit of worldliness and acquiring property." A few did not heed this warning. Amos Starr Cooke, a bookkeeper from Connecticut and a lay member of the group, wrote in his diary in 1851,

> The foreigners are creeping in among the natives, getting the largest and best lands. The Lord seems to be allowing such things

to take place. . . . Honolulu never looked so green and pleasant. Our large plain of sand is now covered with vegetation and is laid out in lots. I am proposing ere long to purchase some. . . .[1]

He did. In partnership with Samuel N. Castle, another lay missionary who also knew the value of land, he bought some of the lots and they founded Castle & Cooke, Ltd., built a store, and went into business. A hundred years later Castle & Cooke was the most powerful business concern in Hawaii, controlling sugar plantations, steamship lines, hotels, and all manner of worldly things.

Some of the land-seekers were not missionaries. In 1826 a Yankee skipper out of Boston, Captain Charles Brewer, left his ship in Honolulu and with James Hunniwell formed a trading company called C. Brewer & Co., Ltd. In 1848 a young Welshman, Theophilus H. Davies, bought out a bankrupt store for which he worked and formed Theo. H. Davies, Ltd. Another seaman, Captain Henry Hackfeld, of Hamburg, Germany, decided to leave his ship in Honolulu in 1849 and establish a mercantile firm which he called H. Hackfeld & Co., which later became American Factors. On the island of Maui two sons of missionary families, Henry P. Baldwin and Samuel T. Alexander, devised a way to dig an irrigation ditch from rain-soaked upper lands to a dry plateau and grow sugar cane. The "Hamakua Ditch" created a sugar empire, and the two young engineers formed Alexander & Baldwin, Ltd.

These were the Big Five. By the end of the nineteenth century they had acquired by loans, purchase, and other means the most fertile of the lands for growing sugar cane and had formed agencies in Honolulu to act for the plantations. They were all white foreigners, called *haoles* or "strangers" by the Hawaiians; and they insinuated themselves into the councils of the *alii* (chiefs) and kings. There were disputes between the rulers and the commoners, and as one historian noted, "the kings and chiefs, for self-protection, had to rely increasingly on the missionaries, and then friends (and sons) of the missionaries; and quietly, imperceptibly political offices and judgeships began to fall into Caucasian hands."

In 1847 a small Honolulu paper, *The Sandwich Island News,* stated editorially, "The king [Kamehameha III] is king in name only, all executive prerogatives and functions of the king having been assumed by individuals constituting themselves a Privy Council. . . . Either Dr. Judd [a missionary] or Mr. Richards [a missionary] presides at the legislative council and explains the law, then raises his hand to vote for final adoption, and they all vote with him."

In 1849 Dr. Gerrit P. Judd, a missionary doctor, was also Minister of the Interior, Secretary of State, and Treasurer of the kingdom under Kamehameha III. This was the year of the "Great Mahele" or distribution of land, promulgated by the King at Dr. Judd's suggestion, under which the King held land in name only and had "no more rights therein." Under the division the King retained for the crown 984,000 acres, the chiefs received 1,619,000 acres and the government owned 1,495,000 acres. "The people" received 28,000 acres, and the law did not even provide a means by which they could claim these acres. Foreigners, however, were able to buy lands from the chiefs, and by 1862 it was estimated that three-fourths of the land was under control of white foreigners.

This was the beginning of a process by which most of the fertile sugar cane lands in Hawaii passed into the hands of the *haoles,* chiefly Americans. This chain of events is worth recording. King Kamehameha III, who was friendly to Americans to the extent of wanting Hawaii annexed to the United States, died unexpectedly in 1854 while the diplomatic negotiations were in progress. Kamehameha IV, who suceeded him, was more partial to the British; but fortunately for the Americans he died in 1863 and his elder brother, Prince Lot, became King Kamehameha V and died leaving no heirs. Prince Lunalilo, the leading *alii,* called for an election of a House of Nobles who promptly elected him King. This marked the beginning of the end for the rule of Hawaiians in their own land. Lunalilo reigned only thirteen months and when he died early in 1874 the electoral process was in full force. Dowager Queen Emma, widow of Kamehameha IV, tried to gain the throne but was defeated in the House of Nobles by Kalakaua, High Chief of Kauai, who was supported by the American *haoles*. This firmed up the influence of the *haoles*, who by this time controlled most of the sugar-growing lands in Hawaii.

It required a revolution to make the control effective. Queen Liliuokalani, who succeeded Kalakaua in 1891, was ousted from her throne two years later, and five years after that Hawaii was annexed to the United States as a territory.

For the next fifty years these tropical islands, once ruled by Polynesian kings and known as "the melting pot of the Pacific" where many races lived in harmony, existed under a feudal regime of the Big Five, descendants of missionaries, merchants, and sea captains. During most of this period the *haole* rulers lived in splendid insularity on plantation estates and palatial homes in Honolulu, controlling not only the sugar plantations but the agencies that operated them from Honolulu. They also owned the steamship lines that carried sugar to the mainland and brought goods to Hawaii. They owned the stores and ran the tourist bureau, and owned the hotels that accommodated the tourists. The latter, of course, had come to Hawaii to bask in tropical sunshine and absorb the romantic glamour of this Paradise of the Pacific, untroubled by what had happened to the Hawaiians who used to own the place.

THE DISENCHANTED ISLES

Part I / 1893-1920
"Sugar is King"

It was about two o'clock in the afternoon of January 17, 1893, a warm sunny day in Honolulu, not much different from any other day. Spots of rain appeared here and there, falling from the fleecy white clouds that drifted down from the Nuuanu Pali, wetting one side of a street and leaving the other side dry. This was a peculiarity of weather known as "liquid sunshine" in the tropics.

A wagon driven by a man named John Good had just turned from King Street into an alley beside E. O. Hall & Son's hardware store. Several dark-skinned policemen wearing khaki shirts and high bowler hats, much like those worn by English bobbies, watched it disappear into the alley. When it rumbled out of the alley a few minutes later with several boxes piled in back, one of the Hawaiian policemen walked over and grabbed the reins.

"What you got in them boxes?" he demanded. As it later developed, they were filled with guns.

John Good did not answer. He snatched the reins from the policeman, larruped his horse, and the wagon went clattering into King Street and headed toward the intersection at Fort Street. Another policeman jerked out a whistle and blew it, but John Good kept on. A dray had pulled up alongside a horse-drawn streetcar at the intersection and this momentarily blocked Good's progress. He turned, with a pistol in his hand, and fired at the policeman who had grabbed the reins, a man named Leialoha, wounding him in the leg.

This was the actual beginning of the Hawaiian Revolution, and as a matter of historical record, it was the only shot fired. But it was heard, if not around the world, at least around the Pacific.

Queen Liliuokalani was sitting in her royal chambers at

1

The First Revolution

Iolani Palace at the time, awaiting a reply to a note she had sent to the American minister, the Honorable John L. Stevens. In the note she deplored certain events taking place, including threats she said had been made against her throne by a group of rebellious citizens, mostly Americans, who were members of the Reform Party and called themselves the Citizens' Committee for Safety. She asked Mr. Stevens to respect friendly relations between Hawaii and the United States and if possible send troops. The note was sent at eleven o'clock in the morning, but the American minister was "indisposed" and did not reply.

Meanwhile the dissident citizens had been meeting at the office of W. O. Smith, a lawyer, a block down from E. O. Hall's store on Fort Street. They had been meeting at various localities around the city since the previous Saturday, January 14, and inasmuch as the timing of these meetings and of the events of January 17 were particularly significant, they will be covered in more detail than might ordinarily be expected.

On the morning of January 14, John F. Colburn, a swarthy part-Hawaiian, had rushed into the office of Lorrin A. Thurston, a descendant of the Reverend Asa Thurston, one of the members of the little missionary band that had arrived on the *Thaddeus* some seventy years before. He said, "All hell is breaking loose at the Palace! The Queen is going to promulgate a new constitution!"

Mr. Colburn evidently was well-informed. He was the Queen's Minister of the Interior—a position Lorrin Thurston once held—and as a member of the Cabinet was privy to goings-on at the Palace. The subject of a new constitution was a sensitive one among the *haoles* of Honolulu, since the current constitution, known as the Bayonet Constitution, had been virtually rammed down the throat of King Kalakaua in 1887 by a small group of Americans and other foreigners in Honolulu known as the Annexationists.

The Annexationists suspected that the King might seize the lands acquired for sugar plantations after the Great Mahele of 1849. Led by Thurston and Judge Sanford Ballard Dole, Chief Justice of the Hawaiian Supreme Court, they had at that time demanded a new constitution and dismissal of the chief of Kalakaua's Cabinet, Walter Murray Gibson, a former Mormon who had been expelled from that church for allegedly expropriating some of its funds. They offered evidence indicating that Kalakaua, at the urging of Gibson, had sold a concession for importing opium and was mixed up in various other malfeasances, supposedly contrived by Gibson. The King, fearful of losing his throne, had agreed to the new constitution that reduced his authority, revised the voting laws by establishing property and income qualifications—thus disenfranchising most Hawaiians, who had little property or income—and eliminated the King's veto power, which had been absolute under previous constitutions established in 1840 and amended in 1852 and 1864.

The Annexationists' demands were supported by a group known as the Hawaiian Riflemen, chiefly *haoles*, which gave the new set of laws rigorous support as well as the name of "the Bayonet Constitution." The last five years of Kalakaua's reign were virtually under the domination of the foreigners. He died of diabetes in 1891 while in San Francisco, and his sister, Liliuokalani, succeeded him. Her announced determination to restore some of the former monarchial powers of the rulers of Hawaii was now the cause of increasing concern among the foreign element.

Colburn's news hinted of a crisis for the *haoles*, who had formed their Citizens' Committee for Safety to meet just such a contingency. The new constitution, opposed by most of the Cabinet, would enable the Queen to dismiss Cabinet members at her pleasure, appoint *alii* for life, and voting would be limited to male subjects (i.e., Hawaiian-born or naturalized citizens). It would wipe out fifty years of effort on the part of the *haole* sugar planters and Honolulu businessmen to take control of the affairs of the monarchy.

Thurston immediately went to the office of Judge Alfred Hartwell, a former Attorney General, and together they went to see Attorney General Arthur P. Peterson, who confirmed what Colburn had said. They then went to Lawyer Smith's office on Fort Street where Thurston drafted a proclamation declaring that the Queen, by her action, had vacated the throne.

The Committee for Safety decided to hold a mass meeting

the following Monday and announce the Queen's intentions to the foreign community. Meanwhile Thurston, W. C. Wilder of the Wilder Steamship Company, and H. F. Glade, the German consul, who was also a member of the Committee for Safety, called on the American Minister, Mr. Stevens, to determine his position. Stevens agreed to call out Marines from the U.S.S. *Boston*, which was at anchor in Honolulu harbor for just such an emergency, to "protect American lives and property."

The following day, Sunday, Thurston met with Colburn and Peterson and told them the foreign community had decided "the Queen must go," but no public announcement of this was made. Then they went back to Thurston's office and discussed how they would go about dethroning her. The Queen's Marshal, C. B. Wilson, whose son later became Mayor of Honolulu, came to the door of the office, shouted for Thurston to come out and explain what was going on, and received no answer. Later in the day the Governor of Oahu, A. S. Cleghorn, also came to Thurston's office and suggested that Cleghorn's daughter, the Princess Kaiulani, be accepted as Queen in case Liliuokalani was willing to resign. Thurston answered him, yelling through the door: "No—it has gone too far!"

Monday afternoon the Committee for Safety held a mass meeting of *haoles* at two o'clock, still withholding an announcement of their intention to dethrone the Queen; and at four o'clock the royal supporters, not to be outdone, called a meeting of their own, warning the Hawaiians that "the *haoles*" were making trouble. Captain C. G. Wiltse of the *Boston* sent word to both groups that American Marines would be landed that night to "preserve order." At seven thirty that evening the Committee for Safety met at the home of Henry Waterhouse and agreed that on the following day they would form a Provisional Government. At this point the time sequence becomes critical, since it indicates the pattern under which the Kingdom of Hawaii would finally become an American Territory.

The men who gathered at Lawyer Smith's office on January 17 had just finished their meeting and were walking out into the street when they heard the shot fired on Fort Street. The group included Thurston, Henry Cooper, chairman of the Committee,

Judge Dole, Smith, W. R. Castle, and others of the Committee for Safety. When the shot was heard, the members of the Committee promptly scattered, some going down Merchant Street and others along Queen Street. Both routes fetched up at the Government House, across from Iolani Palace.

At two thirty they met at the Government House with Col. John A. Soper, a member of the Committee for Safety, who had been assigned to command four volunteer companies of the future Provisional Government. About a hundred men finally assembled at the Government House but unfortunately they had no guns. That was the purpose of John Good's mission to E. O. Hall & Son's—to get guns.

About a half hour earlier four members of the Queen's Cabinet, Foreign Minister Samuel Parker, Finance Minister William Cornwall, and Colburn and Peterson—all part-Hawaiians —had called on Mr. Stevens to get an answer to the Queen's note in which, as the ruler of a friendly power, she not only asked for the protection of American troops but at the very least that they remain neutral. She also assured him that she had no intention of promulgating a new constitution. Mr. Stevens consented to see two of the Cabinet ministers, Parker and Peterson, in his bedroom. He was told by Peterson that the Queen's Government was the legal government of Hawaii and might properly ask for help of United States forces.

Mr. Stevens replied, "Gentlemen, these men were landed for one purpose only—to protect American lives and property, and not to take part in any contest for power. I cannot use force to sustain the Queen or anyone else."

Whether the American Minister planned to help "anyone else" was not clear but he was generally considered "favorable" to American members of the Committee for Safety. Meanwhile Samuel Damon, who was not a member of the Committee for Safety, went to the station house to ask Marshal Wilson to plead with the Queen to surrender "to avoid bloodshed." Mr. Stevens apparently decided upon the need for protecting someone, because by the time members of the Committee for Safety arrived at the Government House to proclaim the Provisional Government, U. S. Marines from the *Boston* commanded by Lieutenant

Herbert Draper were already drawn up *behind* the four companies of revolutionary troops under Colonel Soper.

In the light of later claims of the revolutionary junta that the dethronement of Queen Liliuokalani and subsequent annexation of Hawaii to the United States was desired by the Hawaiian people—a point echoed by President McKinley seven years later when he requested Congress to take over the Islands—it is interesting to note the words of some leaders of the rebellion on this subject. William A. Russ, Jr., in *The Hawaiian Revolution, 1893–4,* says, "Dole, who ought to know, wrote later that the Government House was deserted except for a few clerks" when members of the Committee for Safety arrived. Dole was quoted as saying, "We got to the Courthouse (Government House) and the only 'force' we saw was Oscar White, carrying a gun." Sam Damon, who tried to get the Queen to abdicate to "avoid bloodshed" later said: "I was perfectly non-plussed by not receiving any support." More insurgents arrived later, but at the time the leaders reached the scene there were only a few committee members and American troops standing beside their stacked arms near a picket fence at the rear of the Government House.

This deployment was significant. Most of the royal forces were at the station house and barracks, about a quarter of a mile from the Palace, but about sixty-five of the Queen's soldiers were at the Palace, armed with a Gatling gun, some small artillery, and rifles. If they had fired in the direction of Colonel Soper's men, the troops from the *Boston* would have been in the line of fire. Thus the royal soldiers would have been shooting at U. S. troops.

As noted, this was approximately 2:30 P.M., a half hour after the members of the Queen's Cabinet had called on Mr. Stevens to ask for help for the Queen. Between 2:40 and 3:10 P.M., the proclamation of the Provisional Government was read. It is therefore evident that the Queen *had not surrendered her throne at that time.* If it was the intention of the Marines from the *Boston* to protect Americans at the Government House, they would have had to shoot them in the back because they were behind them. The alternative explanation is that they were there to prevent the Queen's soldiers from shooting in her defense and perhaps hitting the *Boston* troops, thus provoking retaliatory action by U. S. troops.

The circumstances of the landing of troops also were quite interesting. The previous afternoon, after the two mass meetings, a representative of the Committee for Safety, for some reason that was never adequately explained, visited the *Boston* and asked Captain Wiltse to delay landing troops, but Wiltse replied that the troops "will be landed this afternoon at 5 o'clock, whether you are ready or not."

They were landed and marched in formation through the streets, much to the astonishment of the citizenry. A small patrol proceeded up Nuuanu Street to the American legation while the remainder—162 men fully armed—were quartered at Arion Hall, just behind the Government House. Governor Cleghorn, on behalf of the Queen, protested their landing at this time, since she believed it was to intimidate her, but his protest was ignored.

The Government Building was virtually deserted at the time of the proclamation Tuesday afternoon, and no resistance was offered the scattering of revolutionary "troops" hastily assembled from the streets by Colonel Soper, who admittedly had no previous military experience. It appears in retrospect that the Queen's royal troops could readily have put down any insurrection had it not been for the presence of the American Marines. There were nearly five hundred soldiers available for the Queen's defense, all armed, against about one hundred insurgents, untrained and virtually without arms.

At about five o'clock that afternoon the Queen, a gracious, full-bodied lady, rather short and plump but with a regal bearing characteristic of Hawaiian women, decided she could not resist the insurgents with American forces behind them, and so the last monarch of Hawaii abdicated her throne. In her announcement she wrote,

> I, Liliuokalani, by the grace of God and under the constitution of the Kingdom of Hawaii, Queen, do hereby solemnly protest against any and all acts done against myself and the constitutional government. . . . That I yield to the superior force of the United

States of America, whose minister plenipotentiary, His Excellency
John L. Stevens, has caused United States troops to be landed at
Honolulu and declared he would support the Provisional Government . . . I do, under protest, and impelled by said force yield my
authority until such time as the Government of the United States
shall, upon facts presented to it, undo the action of its representatives, and reinstate me in authority which I claim as the constitutional sovereign of the Hawaiian Islands. Done at Honolulu, this
17th day of January, A. D. 1893.
Liliuokalani, R.[2]

The Queen's statement, somewhat obscured in later historical accounts of the revolution, amounted to an indictment of
the United States, or at least its official representative, Mr. Stevens, for connivance in her dethronement; but this has seldom
been emphasized in historical records.

The only physical casualty of the revolution was the policeman, Leialoha, who had been shot by John Good. He was taken
to the police station and his wound was treated; it ultimately
healed. The real casualty was the Hawaiian people, who never
recovered from the dethronement of Queen Liliuokalani.

The Provisional Government took over following her abdi-
cation and established a *de facto* regime under Judge Dole, a tall,
bearded man whose father, the Reverend David Dole, had been
a founder of Punahou Academy (then Oahu College), a school
for children of missionaries. Judge Dole left no question as to
the intentions of the revolutionary junta with respect to the
United States. In a statement issued immediately after the takeover he said the Provisional Government would exist "only until
terms of union with the United States have been agreed upon."

The purposes of the Provisional Government, as set forth
by President Dole, were: (1) abolition of the monarchy; (2) establishment of a Provisional Government to rule the Islands
until annexation; and (3) selection of officers, including Dole as
President, Damon as Vice President, James A. King as Minister
of the Interior, and W. O. Smith as Attorney General. There was
an Advisory Council of fourteen members, including the four
officers, and it is noteworthy that there was not one person of
Hawaiian blood among them and more than half were not even
Hawaiian citizens.

It is also noteworthy that of the members of the Council, eight owned shares of sugar plantation stock, including the following major stockholders: W. R. Castle, $86,500; C. Bolte, formerly a German, $38,000; Ed Suhr, a German, $26,100; W. O. Smith, $22,900, and Thurston, $9,200. W. C. Wilder owned no sugar stocks but was principal owner of the Wilder Steamship Company, which shipped sugar, and others had business interests in Honolulu. Six of the Council were Hawaiian citizens, five were Americans, one was English, and two were German.[3]

At the time of the revolution in Hawaii President Benjamin Harrison, a Republican, was in the White House in Washington, but his successor, Grover Cleveland, a Democrat, had already been elected to succeed him. Two months later he took office, which materially changed the situation in the Islands.

Shortly after the Provisional Government had been established a delegation was sent to Washington to discuss annexation. The group included such prominent members of the Committee for Safety as Lorrin Thurston, descendant of the first missionary group to arrive in Hawaii; W.R. Castle, of the powerful missionary family that formed Castle & Cooke; and W.C. Wilder, the Honolulu shipowner. Thurston had been born in Hawaii and was therefore a Hawaiian citizen; Castle was a citizen of Hawaii who later became an American Under Secretary of State, and Wilder was a naturalized citizen of Hawaii.

These men conferred with Secretary of State John W. Foster in February, 1893, in an effort to obtain action on the annexation of Hawaii before President Harrison turned his administration over to Cleveland on March 3. Foster advised the delegation to accept annexation as a Territory, which would be acted on quickly, rather than introduce a bill in Congress for statehood which might not be passed before Congress adjourned.

Unfortunately time ran out, and when Cleveland took office he became suspicious of the whole affair and sent Colonel John H. Blount to Hawaii to inquire into the means by which Queen Liliuokalani had been dethroned.

Thurston had expected a favorable report from Blount; and in fact he wrote home, "As a Southerner [Blount was a former Congressman from Georgia] he is thoroughly familiar with the

2

Annexation of Paradise

difficulties attendant upon a government with an ignorant majority in the electorate." The latter reference might be regarded as some indication of the attitude prevalent among members of the revolutionary junta toward the Hawaiian electorate whose Islands they had taken over.

Blount's report was not favorable. He described in detail the manner in which United States troops had been deployed so that shots fired by royalist troops, directed toward the forces of the Provisional Government, would also have the troops from the *Boston* in the line of fire. He also reported that six members of the Provisional Government were citizens of Hawaii, not American citizens; and that as such they were not entitled to protection by American troops any more than the Queen, who by treaty was the head of government of a friendly nation.

Hawaii at that time had a Treaty of Reciprocity with the United States, negotiated in 1876 by King Kalakaua and extended ten years later; and this was the only binding agreement between the two countries. It gave Hawaii a quota of sugar free of import duties, and also rice import benefits; it did not give the American minister authority to land troops to assist a contingent of revolutionaries, nearly half of them of Hawaiian citizenship, in ousting the Queen from her throne.

Colonel Blount also interviewed a number of people involved in the activities of January 17 to determine when recognition of the Provisional Government by the American minister actually occurred. He noted that those questioned used such expressions as "I cannot remember" or "It might have been so," when pressed for details. Among the people interviewed were Samuel Damon, son of a missionary and Vice President of the new government, and C. Bolte, the former German who became a naturalized citizen of Hawaii and was a member of the Committee for Safety. Damon, who conferred with the Queen's Marshal just before she abdicated, said, according to Blount's report, "I was under the impression when we went into conference that recognition had taken place." This was before 5 P.M. Bolte said, "I cannot say what time of day Mr. Stevens sent his recognition [of the new Provisional Government]. I think it was after sunset." Stevens said he had recognized the revolutionary regime "not far from 5 P.M.—I did not think to look at my watch." Dole, who headed the new Provisional Government, had no idea when it had been recognized.

Members of the Queen's Cabinet said the American minister had actually recognized the new government at 3:10 P.M. after Dole finished reading his proclamation, and before the Queen finally agreed to surrender. The position of the United States representative, as well as the position of the *Boston* troops, was the reason she had abdicated, according to Blount's report. Thus it was fairly definite that the United States had recognized the new government *before* the purpose of the revolution had been achieved—unseating the old regime. In effect, the Provisional Government had been officially recognized by the United States before it was a government.

President Cleveland, after receiving Blount's report, immediately took steps to investigate the situation and to rectify what he regarded as an injustice. The record of these events is so beclouded with conflicting reports by various historians, however, that it seems advisable to look into the matter in some detail. Shortly after the Provisional Government was established, Minister Stevens was recalled on the basis of Blount's statement that he was implicated in a "prearranged plan to overthrow the Queen."

According to Blount's account, the Queen's minister, Colburn, had at one point asked Stevens point-blank, "Do you intend to annex Hawaii to the United States?" and Stevens said, "No." When he was asked to rescind the order to Captain Wiltse to land troops from the *Boston,* he was reported to have said, "Put your request in writing." Both Sam Parker, the Foreign Minister, and Cleghorn, as Governor of Oahu, presented this request in writing but Stevens' written replies were described as "even more ambiguous and impractical than his oral replies."

On Monday evening, the night before the revolution, Colonel Soper, a precise sort of man with a bristling beard, more military in appearance than experience, was given a message by Dole to be handed to Stevens, announcing that the revolt would take place the following day, and the American minister was reported to have told Soper, "I think you have a great opportunity."

According to Professor W. D. Alexander's report—the most authentic account written at the time—a note from the Queen to the American minister was delivered at the legation shortly before noon by Charles L. Hopkins, a messenger, and was received by Stevens' daughter. Liliuokalani agreed in the note not to promulgate a new constitution. At 3:10 P.M., the exact minute Dole completed reading the proclamation at the Government House, a note was delivered at the station house stating that Stevens had authorized *de facto* recognition of the Provisional Government; and it was *after this that the Queen decided to abdicate.*

After studying Blount's report, President Cleveland said in a message to Congress, "Thus it appears that Hawaii was taken possession of by the United States forces without the consent or wish of the Government of the Islands, or of anybody else as far as is shown, except by the United States Minister [Stevens]." He added that at the time of recognition, the Provisional Government of Hawaii "was neither a government *de facto* nor *de jure.*"

He also noted that at the time of the proclamation of the Provisional Government the Queen had at her disposal all the military forces of the kingdom, including "possession of the barracks, of the police station, and at her command at least five hundred fully armed men . . . while the Committee for Safety, by actual search, had discovered that there were few arms not in possession of the Government [the monarchy]. . . . The Queen could have dealt with the insurgents, but the United States had allied itself with her enemies. . . . She knew she could not withstand the power of the United States, but she believed she might safely trust to its justice."

As a result, Cleveland sent a new minister, Albert S. Willis, to Honolulu, and on November 13, 1893, Willis met with the Queen at Iolani Palace. The reports on this event by Willis and by the Queen herself are somewhat in conflict, and since they have a bearing on the ultimate disposition of the Hawaiian Revolution by President Cleveland, both reports should be mentioned. According to Willis' account, he told the deposed Queen that he had been instructed by the President to ask her how she would dispose of the insurgents if she were restored to the throne.

The question he asked was, "Should you be restored to the throne, would you grant full amnesty to those who have been instrumental in the overthrow of your Government?" He said she "hesitated a moment," then "slowly and calmly answered, 'There are certain laws of my Government by which I shall abide. My decision would be, as the law directs, that such persons should be beheaded and their property confiscated to the Government.' "

Willis reported that he said, "repeating very distinctly" the words, "It is your feeling that these people should be beheaded and the property confiscated to the Government?" She replied, "It is."

Queen Liliuokalani, in a book written several years later entitled *Hawaii's Story by Hawaii's Queen*, reported this incident somewhat differently. She wrote, "I gave him [Willis] a document . . . agreeing that in view of [President Cleveland's]wishes, the individuals setting up and supporting the Provisional Government should have full amnesty in their persons and property . . . It was most unfortunate that the American Minister [Willis] should have so misrepresented me . . . or that I should have been so overburdened by the many aspects of the painful situation as to be ignorant or unconscious of the importance of the precise words read in my presence."

Whatever the "precise words" and her replies may have been, the incident cooled Cleveland's ardor as to the restoration of Liliuokalani to her throne, and he dismissed the matter, refusing to consider either restoration of the Queen or annexation of Hawaii. The new Provisional Government therefore had to rely upon its own resources in establishing a legal regime in Hawaii, and to await a better political climate in Washington before seeking annexation.

Although the delegation headed by Thurston had expressed a desire for a "full and complete union" with the United States, there was still some difference of opinion in Hawaii as to how complete the union ought to be. The sugar planters did not relish living under American laws prohibiting importing contract labor; nor did they want voting rights to apply to all citizens, including plantation workers. The Honolulu businessmen, such as the Cookes, Castles, and others who formed the Big Five, regarded these as minor impediments which could be smoothed over by some sort of legal semantics. The important thing was to have American troops handy in case the supporters of the Queen tried to restore her to the throne.

This effort came earlier than had been expected. Six months after Judge Dole assumed the presidency of the Republic in 1894, a plot to restore the Queen to power was unearthed. There were still a number of members of the Queen's Cabinet who had not given up hope of reestablishing the monarchy, including Sam Parker and Robert Wilcox, who were not only part-Hawaiian but anti-*haole*. Wilcox had been the leader in a movement in 1887 to oust King Kalakaua because of his partiality toward the *haoles* and place Liliuokalani on the throne; later he became leader of the Hawaiian Home Rule Party, a thorn in the side of the revolutionists.

The Republic of Hawaii had been proclaimed on July 4, 1894, succeeding the Provisional Government, with Judge Dole as the perennial head of state. Queen Liliuokalani had lost no time in her move to regain the throne, beginning with the appeal to the American government to "undo" the wrong she said had been done her. However, after Willis' report of her reaction to President Cleveland's request for amnesty for the insurgents, in which he quoted her as saying she would have them "beheaded," he apparently washed his hands of the affair. He told her envoy, Paul Neumann, that the matter was in the hands of Congress which "by its action and omission to act" had indicated the United States would not interfere in Hawaiian affairs.

The Queen then decided to do her own intervening. Arms and ammunition were brought in secretly from San Francisco and landed at night on the beach near Koko Head. Information about the plot had leaked out, however, and a squad of Honolulu police intercepted the small band of insurrectionists in Waikiki, where they were seized with their guns. The following day the Republic was placed under martial law and scores of suspects picked up and put in jail. The Queen was taken into "house custody" at Iolani Palace where she remained for eight days and then declared her allegiance to the new Republic of Hawaii, asking clemency for those who tried to restore her to the throne. Several had already been sentenced to death, and the Queen was fined $5,000, but these sentences were later commuted and the fine withdrawn. By the end of the year all were released and the Kingdom of Hawaii had passed forever into the dark archives of history, much of it written or censored by *kamaaina haoles,* the Hawaiian expression for "white old-timers."

In March of 1897 William McKinley, a Republican, took office as President of the United States and the climate was deemed appropriate for another try at annexation. By coincidence a shipload of Japanese sent to Hawaii as contract field workers was refused landing in Honolulu harbor and Japan protested, threatening to send gunboats if necessary. This was sufficient to bring cries of "yellow peril" from the *haoles* in Honolulu. The possibility of an "incident" in which a foreign power other than the United States might encroach upon Hawaii was quickly brought to the attention of President McKinley. In a message to Congress on December 6, 1897, he said,

> Hawaii has shown her ability to enter into a conventional union with the United States of America, thus realizing a purpose held by the Hawaiian people and proclaimed by successive Hawaiian Governments through seventy years of their virtual dependence upon the benevolent protection of the United States. Under such circumstances, annexation is not a change; it is a consummation.[4]

There was a certain amount of elasticity in the wording of the statement with respect to the facts of history. The Hawaiian kings prior to Kalakaua had not "proclaimed" their dependence on the protection of the United States; and certainly the people of Hawaii had no such purpose. But no one at the time was in a position to challenge McKinley's words, and the "consummation" took place the following year. On June 15, 1898, a joint resolution was introduced in the House and passed by a vote of 209 to 91; and on July 6 the Senate adopted the same resolution, 42 to 21. The following day McKinley signed the bill, known as the Newlands Resolution. Subsequently an "Organic Act" was passed by Congress, spelling out the "constitution" under which Hawaii would exist for the next sixty years.

Perhaps the most succinct summary of the whole matter was a comment in a letter written by Cleveland to Richard Olney, his former Secretary of State. "Hawaii is ours," he said, "but as I look back upon the first steps in this miserable business and as I contemplate the means used to complete the outrage, I am ashamed of the whole affair."[5]

One important point in the action of Congress was given little attention at the time. The only instance prior to the Newlands Resolution in which the United States had annexed a Territory by a joint resolution of Congress was in the case of Texas, which later became a State. A half century after Annexation proponents of statehood for Hawaii raised the point that this form of action by Congress constituted by precedent a commitment to statehood for Hawaii, as it did for Texas. At the time the Newlands Resolution was adopted, however, there was no consuming desire on the part of the new rulers of Hawaii—the baronial missionary-planter group—to introduce full electoral rights under statehood to their simple Hawaiian constituents. The Hawaiian people were angry and resentful at the takeover, but not sufficiently informed about the processes of democracy to do much about it.

A visiting professor from Stanford, lecturing at the University of Hawaii, wrote in 1926, "To think of Hawaii in an economic sense is to think of sugar. That industry is ruled by a financial oligarchy around which is built the business and social structure of the Islands." He might have added "political structure" as well. Ray Stannard Baker, a visiting newspaperman, put it more simply: "Sugar is King."

This domination of Hawaii economically and politically by the missionary-planter oligarchy did not come easily, however. Hawaiians and part-Hawaiians were still the largest single ethnic group at the turn of the century, and while they may not have possessed the sense of strategy, scheming, and intrigue that characterized the former members of the Citizens Committee for Safety, led by Lorrin Thurston, they had something else which either was not understood or was ignored by the new rulers of Hawaii: a deep and lasting hurt, a kind of racial sensitivity peculiar to the Polynesians. They expressed this in the polling places, to the intense surprise of the *haoles* who engineered the revolution and takeover by the United States. The first signs of an electoral upset occurred in the special election held shortly after passage of the Organic Act to fill the required Territorial offices. They followed this upset by sweeping the general election immediately afterward.

Annexation had posed two problems for the new regime. First, the democratic process of voting under American law was based on citizenship, not on property or income; and all Hawaiians were citizens. Second, under the Organic Act contract labor was illegal. A field worker was free to quit and go to the city, or go home, as he pleased. The latter law went into effect immediately, nullifying existing contracts, but its full effect was not felt

3

Rulers of Paradise

at the time because there was no shortage of field workers.

But the right of universal male suffrage did have an immediate result, as the Big Five junta soon discovered. Under the so-called Bayonet Constitution imposed in 1887 upon King Kalakaua by the same group that overthrew the Queen—Thurston, Smith, Castle, Dole, and the others—foreign-born residents of Hawaii were permitted to vote, but there were definite restrictions on certain other categories. Those who had less than $3,000 worth of land or less than $600 a year income were *not* allowed to vote. This latter group included most of the Hawaiians and part-Hawaiians who had collected little visible wealth from the easy communal life of Hawaii under the rule of chiefs and kings. However, the extension of voting rights to all American citizens changed the situation; if the Hawaiians and part-Hawaiians voted as a bloc, they could control the elections.

With this thought evidently in mind, some of the Queen's followers—led by part-Hawaiian Robert Wilcox who had headed the movement to put Liliuokalani on the throne in place of Kalakaua and later was a leader in the counter-revolutionary effort to restore the Queen to her throne in 1895—met in the drill shed behind the barracks on Punchbowl Street and formed a Home Rule Party. The slogan *"Nana i ka ili!"* ("Look to the skin!") was adopted as a political weapon. For the first time since the white foreigners arrived in Hawaii, racism became a factor in Island politics. The Hawaiians had paid little attention to the color of a man's skin prior to the revolution, but they were now being told to "look to the skin" and vote for the dark-skinned Hawaiian and against the white-skinned *haole*. In the special election to fill the unexpired term in the 56th Congress, Wilcox was swept into office by the predominantly Hawaiian vote as the first Delegate-to-Congress from Hawaii. The Home Rule Party repeated the performance in the regular election in the fall of 1900, and also won overwhelming majorities in both houses of the territorial Legislature. Clearly something had gone wrong.

The *Pacific Commercial Advertiser*, which Lorrin Thurston purchased in 1898, came out vehemently against this trend, warning that simple-minded Hawaiians were no match for wily Orientals, and once the latter achieved voting status by the purely biological process of being born in Hawaii, the rule of the Hawaiians would be short-lived. The solution was to let the *haoles* run the political show. Thurston himself wrote editorials attacking Wilcox and accusing him of being "un-American." He even suggested that Negroes should be brought in from the Southern States because they were experienced plantation workers and would be "good Republicans."

Meanwhile the Home Rulers ran riot in the territorial Legislature. The new Governor—the inevitable Judge Dole, appointed by President McKinley—was a Republican and was harassed and obstructed in every imaginable way.

Under the Organic Act the Governor had unusual powers. He could veto fiscal legislation and was not subject to impeachment, and the Organic Act also required that sessions of the legislature be held in the English language. In spite of this, the Home Rulers spoke Hawaiian exclusively in the legislature. They held up reading the Governor's first message to the House and Senate for a week and passed laws that made a shambles of the legislative process—all in Hawaiian, so that the few Republican and even fewer Democrats, who were chiefly *haoles,* seldom knew what they were voting for or against. One law passed by both houses, and later vetoed by Governor Dole, would have legalized *kahunas*—the Hawaiian version of witch doctors—as licensed physicians.

The men who plotted and successfully carried out the Revolution of 1893 and the Annexation of 1898 were not to be thwarted indefinitely, however. It was obvious that if a substantial number of Hawaiians and part-Hawaiians were to be won over to the Republican side, someone of Hawaiian blood must do it; and the soft underbelly of the Home Rule Party was Prince Jonah Kuhio Kalanianaole, son of the High Chief of Kauai. He was the younger brother of Prince David Kawananakoa, adopted son of Dowager Queen Emma, the widow of Kamehameha IV. Later both became *hanai,* or adopted sons, of Queen Kapiolani, wife of Kalakaua. Kuhio—also known as "Prince Cupid"—a young man who liked good living, was a loyal follower of Queen Liliuokalani and a member of the Home Rule Party.

According to a well-authenticated report, Harry Baldwin,

senior member of the powerful Baldwin family on Maui and one of the more adroit members of the Big Five, met Kuhio one evening at the Pacific Club. This was the inner sanctum of the *kamaaina haoles* and a place to which only the most royal of royal Hawaiians were invited. Kuhio enjoyed brandy, good cigars, and women, and appeared to be a natural target for the persuasive tactics of Harry Baldwin. The two were reported to have talked far into the night, and Kuhio emerged as the Republican candidate for Delegate-to-Congress in the elections of 1902. The battle cry *"Nana i ka ili!"* which had drawn Hawaiians to the Wilcox banner now worked the other way because Kuhio was more Hawaiian than Wilcox.

Meanwhile other arrangements for securing a grip on the electorate were going on at the plantation polling places. Pencils used to mark the ballot were suspended on strings fastened to a loop of bamboo directly above the list of Republican candidates. The strings were visible from outside the booth, so that any deviation from the Republican plumb line which would indicate a vote for someone other than a Republican could be noted by the *lunas,* or overseers, who were also election inspectors. The result was almost solid Republican voting.

Such devices as these, together with the popularity of "Prince Cupid" among the Hawaiians, easily defeated Wilcox in 1902, and for the next twenty years—until Kuhio died in 1922 —the position of Delegate to Congress was safely in Republican hands. By the same process and voting momentum, the Republicans also elected majorities in the territorial Legislature. The political affiliation of the Governor, appointed by the President, shifted with political tides on the Mainland, but this—as will appear—was no problem for the Big Five, particularly with their own man in Washington. During the period from 1902 to 1920 the control of this oligarchical form of economic-political rule was slowly but surely fastened on the Territory, its industry, its business, its life-blood as a society. In certain respects it brought a form of prosperity that the Hawaiians under the monarchial rule of Hawaiian kings and queens never could have achieved. Sugar exports increased steadily; tourism grew; and pineapples entered the economic life of the Islands. The advantages for the

Hawaiian people themselves were less discernible, however. Under the old monarchial system there were only two classes: the *alii*, or chiefs, and their subjects. The chiefs ruled with an iron hand; they were ruthless and sometimes cruel. But the Hawaiians were satisfied with this way of life; they had plenty of fish and *poi*, tropical food made of mashed roots of the *taro* plant. This was a land that provided joys of living without much labor. But, of course, they were not "progressing" in the American sense of the word. After the *haoles* took over, with less than seven percent of the total population of about 110,000, the Hawaiians began to "progress" in spite of themselves. They moved away from their fishing villages into urban areas—chiefly Honolulu—and lived in closely packed houses in the slums of Palama and Kakaako, if such a word as "slum" may be used in the context of a "tropical paradise." They also contracted the usual diseases of the slums, such as tuberculosis and syphilis.

While the number of pure-blooded Hawaiians—that is, people of only Hawaiian ancestry—decreased from an estimated 300,000 or more at the time of Kamehameha I (1775–1800) to less than 40,000 at the time of annexation, and was down to 25,000 by 1920, the proportion of Hawaiians living in Honolulu rose steadily. They did not like plantation labor. Few were skilled workmen. Most of them sought minor political jobs in the city or worked on the waterfront. Many lived a hand-to-mouth existence in shacks made of packing boxes and discarded pieces of lumber. At the same time the death rate of Hawaiians, largely because of tuberculosis and other imported diseases, increased until the rate in Honolulu was twice that of Hawaiians living outside the city.

In spite of these disadvantages, the Hawaiians continued to migrate into Honolulu, most of them working in Government jobs or as stevedores. The argument that the Islands were "better off" with the great technical advances in the production of sugar bringing both economic and social advantages for Hawaii as an industrial community, might have been true for the Big Five, but it could hardly be applied to the Hawaiians.

Prince Kuhio was aware of the decimation of his people, and in the latter years of his life he must have wondered rather bitterly whether his decision to switch from the Home Rule Party to the Republicans had worked out to the advantage of anyone except the Big Five and the *kamaaina haole* families. In the move to draw Kuhio into their fold the burgeoning oligarchy obviously had cleared away much of the political debris that followed the takeover by Americans in the 1890s. They had strengthened Republican domination by removing the threat of the Home Rule Party. Although their systematic development of the sugar industry obviously was studded with self-interest, the improvement could not be described as the result of wanton greed or ambition. They were "empire builders" in the true sense of the expression as it has been applied elsewhere in America. They were creating a prosperous and well-managed Hawaii. In assessing what occurred some fifty years later, when the descendants of the men who dethroned the Queen were themselves under attack in the "second revolution," this basic element of early economic and political paternalism should not be overlooked. The men who carved the Territory of Hawaii out of a mid-Pacific island kingdom were men of considerable vision, even if that vision in some respects was myopic; and therefore the ways in which they worked to make that vision a reality bear an essential relation to the ultimate changes in the structure they created.

Kuhio's usefulness in eliminating the threat posed by Wilcox and the Home Rulers did not extend to other political matters. When major decisions were made, he was ignored. He complained to his old friend, Colonel Curtis P. Iaukea, a former Minister in King Kalakaua's Cabinet who served as Kuhio's secretary without pay because he regarded the Prince as his "real King." Kuhio told Iaukea he had not been consulted about the selection of George R. Carter, an officer and director of C. Brewer & Co., one of the Big Five, as the recommended appointee as Governor to succeed Judge Dole.

For Kuhio it was a period of gradual disillusionment. He had hoped to build the Republican Party into a political instrument for the Hawaiians but he reckoned without the shrewd and at times ruthless political mastery of the men who had guided the revolution. Colonel Iaukea urged Kuhio to assert himself and recover political power for the Hawaiian people. After all, he had bailed the *haoles* out of a bad mess when Robert Wilcox and his Home Rulers threatened to take over the benefits of the revolution for the Hawaiian people. But it was obvious that the *haoles* had no real confidence in Kuhio, or in the Hawaiians as a self-governing electorate. Lorrin Thurston's estimate was accepted; they were the "ignorant majority." After Carter's term as governor they put in Judge Walter F. Frear, a *haole* who had served as Chief Justice of the Territorial Supreme Court. He had married into the Dillingham family and thus was closely linked with the sugar planters and the Oahu Railway & Land Company (owned by Dillingham), as well as being solidly entrenched with the *kamaaina* missionary families.

The manner in which many of these old families developed prestige and power is well worth some study. The Dillinghams offer an excellent example. The original member of that family in Hawaii, Benjamin F. Dillingham, was a stranded seaman who managed to break his leg riding a horse and was recovering at the Seaman's Hospital when his ship left Honolulu. He met a young lady, Emma Louise Smith, a member of a missionary family, who came to read to ailing sailors at the hospital. Friendship appears to have ripened into love, and that was the beginning of the Dillingham dynasty. Ben Dillingham married into the Smith family, and with the help of the missionary Castle and Campbell families he managed to acquire sizeable tracts of land. This was in the 1870s; and when Kalakaua became King in 1874, Dillingham got the concession to build a narrow-gauge railroad around Oahu. He also formed the B. F. Dillingham Construction Company. His son, Walter F. Dillingham, inherited not only his father's property but a considerable amount of his talent and enterprise, becoming the most powerful independent industrialist in the Islands. The Dillingham name began to spread over railroads, construction companies, dredging companies, terminals for land and sea transport, and today it extends to the Mainland and to such foreign lands as Spain and Australia.

Charles R. Bishop was another example. He sailed into Honolulu on a clipper ship in 1846, decided to stay and look things over, and became Collector of Customs for Kamehameha III. He also became the husband of Princess Bernice Pauahi

Paki, a granddaughter of Kamehameha I; and with influence in high places he and Sam Damon's father founded the Bank of Bishop Company which dominated banking in Hawaii until the days of the Republic, when the Bank of Hawaii was formed.

There were others. An Irish carpenter, Christopher Lewers, arrived in Hawaii from Dublin in the 1850s looking for a missing brother, and with Charles M. Cooke, of the missionary Cooke family, he founded the largest building supply firm in the Islands, Lewers & Cooke, Ltd. Joseph Ballard Atherton, a book-keeper working for Castle & Cooke, married Amos Starr Cooke's daughter and became a member of both family and firm. Seventy years later his grandson, Frank Atherton, was president of the Big Five agency.

During these formative years of the Territory, the basic structure of the domination by the sugar planters was taking shape, although Kuhio was among the last to recognize that it was entirely a *haole* structure. Even laws for county governments contained the elements of a closed society in which feudal rule over the Islands was to be monolithic. In a letter to Kuhio, written on January 19, 1904, Governor Carter advised the delegate that he should withdraw a bill for establishing the City and County of Honolulu if "any vital changes were made." The "vital changes" included an objection to a three-year residence clause for holding office, raised by a member of the House Insular Affairs Committee who said it was "un-American." To the Big Five, removing that limitation would expose Hawaii to the possibility of an "intruder" from the Mainland coming to the Islands to hold office. Carter also insisted that there be no educational qualification in a proposed immigration law since "this would cut off the sugar industry from this source of labor and seriously cripple them." However, he added, "I do not think anyone here would seriously object if Hawaii were *excluded* from the effects of such a law. . . ." In other words, Hawaii might be exempt from literacy qualifications that would apply on the mainland, thus insuring that illiterate Japanese laborers recruited for the plantations would be virtually bonded to Hawaii, barred from continuing on to California in search of better living conditions.

On July 12, 1909, Kuhio wrote Governor Frear to protest

the cutting of trees on six hundred acres of land in the Puna "jungle" on Hawaii which had been set aside as homesteading land. He pointed out that in ten years after the land had been settled by Hawaiians there still were no government roads, and the deforestation of the lands would virtually ruin the area for the homesteaders. Judge Frear seemed to regard the problems of the Hawaiian homesteaders with indifference and wrote Kuhio that the removal of the trees was "merely wood-cutting." The Prince wrote back even more vehemently, "I cannot agree that it would be better to have the wood cut off," adding that even if cutting down trees should prove desirable for future use of the land, "Why not let the citizen homesteader have the advantage of the timber, rather than some corporation?"

Kuhio never really fought strenuously to maintain his stated objective of "Hawaii for the Hawaiians," however. He remained tied to Big Five apron strings until finally his closest adherent, Colonel Iaukea, broke with him for allowing Governor Frear to dominate his actions. Kuhio even accepted the appointment of a genial gentleman named George McClellan, who reported regularly to the Big Five and drew part of his salary from the Honolulu Chamber of Commerce, as his secretary in Washington. This bit of questionable largesse on the part of the Chamber was actually welcomed by Kuhio, who seemed unable to grasp the mechanics of Big Five control. He wrote to E. D. Tenney, President of the Chamber, thanking him for the favor! McClellan later served as the Chamber's representative in Washington.

When Woodrow Wilson was elected President in 1912, it was a foregone conclusion that a Democrat would be appointed governor; but this again proved to be no problem for the rising political power of the oligarchy. Kuhio himself had wanted the governorship, and Colonel Iaukea returned temporarily to the fold to support him. To the surprise of no one, however, except perhaps Kuhio, a "responsible Democrat"—Lucius E. Pinkham, who had headed the Honolulu Board of Health and had once been a labor recruiter in the Philippines for the Hawaiian Sugar Planters Association—received the nod, and the Big Five continued to control both the legislative and the executive branches.

Kuhio's continual harping on the "rights of the Hawaiian people" finally became so obnoxious to the Big Five that they decided to unload him. In 1914 they ran Charlie Rice of Kauai against the Prince in the Republican primary. Rice was one of the most powerful politicians in the Islands, a member of a prominent sugar planter family and in many ways independent, but he could not buck the Hawaiian vote. Even the Democratic candidate, L. L. ("Link") McCandless, a nonconformist *haole* who operated a prosperous well-digging business, took the trouble to support Kuhio against Rice, urging his Hawaiian followers to cross party lines and vote for the Prince in the primary. As a result, Rice was badly defeated by the Hawaiian vote, a somewhat pointless victory for Kuhio since he simply remained in the service of the Big Five. He repaid McCandless for his support by accusing the rugged well-digger of being "anti-Hawaiian" when they ran against each other in the general election. McCandless had been notoriously independent of the *haole* influence and a vigorous supporter of land rights for Hawaiians, but the Hawaiians took Kuhio at his word and McCandless was swamped by the Hawaiian vote in the race for delegate.

It was on the "land for Hawaiians" issue that Kuhio made his final and what he considered his "greatest contribution" to the Hawaiian people—the so-called Hawaiian Homes Act of 1920. The bill, officially known as the Hawaii Rehabilitation Act, was finally passed in 1921 and was hailed by the Big Five and the Prince alike as a "triumph of justice for the Hawaiians"—a bit of irony that did not surface until several years after Kuhio's death in 1922.

Although this legislation had little effect one way or another on restoring the lands to the Hawaiian people, it was an act of such political perfidy that one has to go back to the record of Indian Affairs in the United States Department of the Interior —the arm of government which was also responsible for Hawaiian affairs—to find a parallel performance. It did have a belated effect on the growing bitterness of the Hawaiians, however, which burst forth some fifty years later in the second revolution and for this reason some account of the law's enactment is necessary.

The Hawaii Rehabilitation Act provided that citizens of at least half-Hawaiian ancestry might apply for homestead rights under a ninety-nine-year leasing arrangement for a dollar a year; approximately 185,000 acres of land were set aside under the Act for this purpose. Even after its obvious defects were known, the legislation might have passed for a well-intentioned but poorly planned effort to restore to the Hawaiian people land that had been taken away from them in the first place.

Actually it was neither. It was designed to kill homesteading of sugar lands, and it was well planned and superbly executed by the planters themselves. They sent John Wise, a part-Hawaiian member of the territorial Senate to Washington as head of a commission to help Kuhio plead his case, and he presented what *The Advertiser* described as "a most moving speech on behalf of the Hawaiians." Appearing before the House Committee on Territories, he painted a picture of the "dying Hawaiians" that stirred the Committee to immediate action, although it required two years finally to get the bill through Congress.

What the sugar planters wanted most was the elimination of a section of the Organic Act that provided that upon expiration of a lease, valuable sugar land could be withdrawn from lease lands and opened to homesteaders if twenty-five applicants should request this. For ten years the planters had tried to get this provision out of the Organic Act and had been blocked by Congressmen who wanted to protect homesteading rights. Hidden within the Hawaiian Homes Act was a clause that said "necessary revenues for accomplishment of the purposes" of the Act would be obtained by "authorizing the lease by sale at public auction of highly cultivated public lands of the Terri-

4

Signs of Discontent

tory for a term not to exceed 15 years, and any such lease
. . . shall not contain the withdrawal clause." Thus the lands of
the sugar planters would remain safely under lease without exposure to homesteading rights of the Hawaiian people.

Between 1917 and 1921 there were more than 200,000
acres of government lands upon which leases were about to
expire; these included 26,000 acres of prime sugar lands. When
this was brought to the attention of Prince Kuhio by a member
of the House Committee who wanted to know why some of these
rich sugar lands should not be reserved for the Hawaiian people,
Kuhio replied that Hawaiians "don't know how to cultivate
sugar cane." He added that the plantation system was "essential
for the support of the homesteading," which was like saying a
wolf is essential to killing sheep.

Another section of the Hawaiian Homes Act of equal benefit to the planters concerned the limit under the Organic Act
of a thousand acres of sugar land that could be leased by any one
plantation, putting the sugar planters to the trouble of setting
up multiple companies to evade this provision of the law. Kuhio
readily agreed to eliminate this inconvenience by inserting a
clause in the new law removing this restriction.

These changes were all approved by the new Governor,
Charles J. McCarthy, a Democrat appointed by Woodrow Wilson, who later became head of the Honolulu Chamber of Commerce. The Hawaii Rehabilitation Act swept jauntily through
Congress to the tune of much ukulele playing and hula dancing
at Hawaiian parties held in Washington hotels for Senators and
Congressmen who had supported the bill. It was not until the
Homes Commission put the law into practice a couple of years
later that the flaws began to appear. Some of the defects had
been exposed earlier, however, in a letter which Albert Horner,
a sugar expert of the Hawaiian Sugar Planters Association,
wrote Senator Miles Poindexter, of Washington, on November
8, 1920, when the bill was before the Senate Committee on
Territories, describing the land set aside under the Rehabilitation Act as "third-grade agricultural lands and second-grade
grazing lands." Some of the tracts were so bad, he said, that "not
even a goat could subsist on them."

For example, one of the areas on Kauai set aside for home-steading was described as "a windswept point" where there was no fresh water. Another tract of 1,200 acres on the same island had been released previously for homesteading in a project promoted by John Wise, the territorial Senator who made such a moving plea in Congress for the rehabilitation of Hawaiians through the Homes Act. Horner noted that this tract, also al-located for homesteading under the Hawaii Rehabilitation Act, had "already proved a dismal failure" and added, "Strange as it may seem, the promoter of this present project [Wise] is the same person who was director of the former fiasco."[6]

There were many similar examples. At Nanakuli, on west-ern Oahu, not only was the land set aside for homesteading "rough, rocky and dry," but the only available water came from nearby Waianae Plantation. Years later the weekly *Hawaii Senti-nel* reported on October 7, 1937, that homesteaders in Waianae Valley were giving up their lands because most of the available water had been diverted to "sugar lands controlled by American Factors [which owned Waianae Plantation] forcing homestead-ers to abandon their lands." The *Sentinel* accused Governor Lawrence M. Judd of conniving with American Factors to recover the homestead lands, citing a lease filed with the In-terior Department for the land, adding that "after eight years of dawdling" the territorial Attorney General, Harry Hewitt, had finally confirmed the need for the land by American Factors, stating that "every gallon of water is of vital import to the planta-tion."

A similar situation existed at Waimanalo, on windward Oahu, where land set aside for homesteading was described as "second class and could only be used if water were provided." Waimanalo Plantation, whose canefields covered much of the area, owned the water. Gradually the homesteaders left, turning their lands over to the plantation, which converted all its lands into a homesite development project, now studded with luxuri-ous homes.

There were innumerable cases of this sort disclosed in the years following passage of the Rehabilitation Act, in which land allocated for homesteading proved useless for that purpose. In one case, a former territorial Land Commissioner described a 25,000-acre tract set aside from the Raymond Ranch on Maui as being "not in any sense agricultural land. . . . It is totally covered with lava, and unwatered." Of the 185,000 acres set aside for homesteading by Hawaiians in 1921, only 18,991 acres, or 10.2 percent, was still being farmed by the original homesteaders in 1963. Approximately 40,000 acres proved worthless and the remaining acreage had been leased to plantations and ranches.

In a Michigan State University doctoral thesis, "A study in ideological transplantation," Dr. Allen A. Spitz wrote that the passage and subsequent failure of the Hawaii Rehabilitation Act were "major victories for Hawaii's political and economic elite." He pointed out that the sugar planters were "able to exempt sugar lands from homesteading, gain the political allegiance of the Hawaiians, and in the process kill any future homesteading in Hawaii."

Dr. Laurence Fuchs, in a sociological study published in 1961, put it more directly: "The bill was more of a triumph for the planters than for Kuhio, but he probably never realized it." Fortunately for Prince Kuhio he died before the more dismal aspects of the Hawaii Rehabilitation Act became apparent to the Hawaiians who were to be rehabilitated. It is doubtful, however, if the Hawaiians ever quite realized how much of a hoax had been practiced on them. As a people, they always had been notoriously careless about possession of land, as in the swift transfer of lands distributed in the Great Mahele of 1849 from Hawaiians to *haole* plantation owners. In less than fifteen years after the Mahele, three-fourths of the land distributed to the *alii* had passed into the hands of *haoles*.

Kuhio's last years in office, prior to his death, were spent in a belated effort to restore dignity and prestige to his people. He supported his sister-in-law, Princess Abigail Kawananakoa, who had married Prince David, in gaining for her the appointment as Republican National Committeewoman from Hawaii. He also assisted her in the formation of *Hale o Na Alii* (House of Chiefs), a society devoted to restoring the prestige of Hawaiians of royal blood; but this was mostly window dressing that added nothing to the political power of the Hawaiian people. About all that could be said of "Prince Cupid," last of the royal line of Hawaiian kings, was that as Delegate he had presided over the almost total decimation of his race. When he died, there were only about 23,000 pure-blood Hawaiians left in the Islands, compared with approximately 300,000 at the time of Kamehameha I.

During the period of Kuhio's tenure as Delegate—1902 to 1922—the "time of troubles" had begun to set in for the Big Five, although they were generally unaware of the problems to come. The troubles started when the plantation workers began to organize and stir up strikes. There were few discords within the Big Five itself. One of the dissenters was Wallace R. Farrington, a late arrival in the *kamaaina haole* camp who had become editor of the *Pacific Commercial Advertiser* in 1895, before it was sold to Lorrin Thurston. Farrington later acquired control of the *Honolulu Star-Bulletin* (which was formed in 1911 by a merger of *The Star* and the *Evening Bulletin*), and when he suggested moderation and more humane conditions on the plantations, Thurston accused him of "inciting the Hawaiians" and called him a "troublemaker."

When the Big Five tried to shelve Kuhio, Farrington again dissented, supporting the Prince for Delegate as the legitimate heir to what was left of Hawaiian royalty, and therefore a logical leader of the Territory's political interests, as long as he did not oppose King Sugar. Farrington's protests were mild, however, and had little effect beyond providing an early focus for the swelling tide of resentment that was building up among the Hawaiians, part-Hawaiians, and Portuguese, still the largest aggregate group of voters in the Islands, although they did not vote as a group.

At heart Farrington was a conservative Republican, born and reared in the frigid political climate of Maine; his most visible form of liberalism was supporting land reforms for the benefit of Hawaiians and advocating greater educational opportunities for non-*haoles*. Neither of these positions seemed to impinge directly upon the more civilized objectives of the Big Five, although some of the plantation owners did not like the idea of educating canefield laborers since it tended to arouse a desire for bettering their working conditions. Farrington never doubted, however, that sugar was king.

This phrase was not merely a catchword; it was a fact of life. Even the early effort to develop the pineapple industry, which started abortively in the time of Kalakaua when the first scrawny pineapples were exported to the Mainland, was subject to the decision of the Hawaiian Sugar Planters Association as to whether introduction of a "second industry" might adversely affect sugar growers.

In 1892—a year before the revolution—a small cannery was built by Captain John Kidwell in Honolulu to process pineapple grown in a nearby canyon, where the red volcanic dirt seemed particularly suitable. Red "Cayenne" pineapples had been introduced from the West Indies by Captain Kidwell, who experimented extensively with them; but it was not until the delightful flavor of "pure Hawaiian pineapple juice" attracted thousands at the Panama Pacific International Exposition in San Francisco in 1915 that the Hawaiian pineapple began to loom large in the plans of the Big Five. For fifteen years after that—until the early 1930s—the new industrial enterprise was in a precarious state. Finally James Dole, founder of the modern Hawaiian industry, was eased out by the Big Five, which took over the growing and canning of pineapple as a sort of prince to King Sugar.

Tourism, Hawaii's third industry, went through a somewhat similar process. The desire for tourists was minimal while the oligarchy was entrenching itself economically and politically in the early years of the Territory. Any substantial influx of *malihini haoles* (white newcomers) was unwelcome since they might dilute the power of the *kamaaina haoles.* After World War I, however, tourism was discovered to be an excellent way of improving Hawaii's balance of payments, particularly when the price of sugar went down. Tourist money was cash, and it came into the Islands to stay, with no exports needed to balance the flow. The Hawaii Tourist Bureau soon became an important activity of the Big Five. In 1925 the Royal Hawaiian Hotel was built, a complex of gaudy coral-colored turrets that eclipsed the old Seaside Hotel with its one-story yellow cottages and was in striking contrast to the sedate Moana Hotel.

Downtown Honolulu began to take on the appearance of a city. For years the Alexander Young Hotel had been the most imposing building, but new monuments to progress began to appear. Theo. H. Davies erected a block-long building on Merchant Street, and others followed. The term "Merchant Street" became a synonym for "big business" in Hawaii.

Dirt streets were paved beyond the tight complex of the business area, which had covered only about twenty blocks between Alakea and Nuuanu Streets and from the waterfront to Beretania. Bus lines replaced the old open trolleys, similar to San Francisco's cable cars. The Big Five began to construct larger offices and stores, new buildings with pink and green roofs along Merchant and Bishop Streets; new coral-colored Government buildings surrounded the old Court House (the original Government House); and in the upper terraces of Pacific Heights, Tantalus, and Manoa Valley there were many palatial new homes. Nuuanu Valley, the old royal road of the former monarchs of Hawaii, began to change as the descendants of the missionary families erased the last physical vestiges of the royal Hawaiian dynasty.

Within the space of less than a half century Honolulu passed through a major facelifting process. Landmarks along the waterfront, such as the old Lucas Mill, were cleared away to make room for pineapple canneries. Iwilei, once the red-light district of Honolulu, became industrialized in more mechanized ways. Bistros along the wharves were replaced by warehouses. The brawling little port town of the early nineteenth century, visited by English, Russian, and American sailing ships, was now a center of trans-Pacific commerce, with the Oceanic Steamship and Matson liners plying regularly through Honolulu, as well as Toyo Kissen Kaisha (later N. Y. K.) and Pacific Mail and Dollar liners making Honolulu a regular port-of-call between San Francisco and the Orient. Most of this growth was in the quarter of a century since Hawaii had become a Territory.

But even while the Big Five kept tight control over the burgeoning economic and industrial development and political situation, all was not tranquil in paradise. One problem in particular had increased rather than diminished—the need for supplying cheap plantation labor. As noted earlier, the contract labor supply had stopped when Hawaii became part of the United States. It was no longer legal to enforce a labor contract. This had worried plantation managers before Annexation, but it was not until the years leading up to the 1920s that it became a serious problem.

The two latest ethnic groups to arrive in Hawaii—the Japanese and Filipinos—became the most troublesome. Chinese and Portuguese field workers simply moved off the plantations when conditions became intolerable, to look for better jobs in the towns and cities such as Honolulu, Hilo on Hawaii, Wailuku and Lahaina on Maui, and Lihue on Kauai. But most of the Japanese and Filipinos remained on the plantations, and as the years passed they began to ask for more pay and better working conditions—a typically American custom that disconcerted plantation managers who thought the Japanese were "unassimilable."

However, the Japanese and Filipino way of going about it differed—as will be seen in the next chapter—from customary American labor practices, at least at first. This brings up a point not too well understood by many whose knowledge of racial problems in Hawaii is derived either from jingoistic writings on the subject or from the self-serving assessments of the sugar planters. That is the supposed "unassimilability" of the Japanese.

Two factors affected the growth of unrest among Japanese plantation workers in Hawaii. The first was the decision of many contract laborers to remain in the Islands. Most, if not all, had arrived with the intention of returning to their homeland as soon as they had worked out their contract and saved up some money. The transition of Hawaii from a Republic, where contract labor was permitted, to an American Territory where bonded labor was illegal and workers were free to leave whenever they wished changed the situation, but in a way that might not have been expected. Many were so deeply in debt to the plantation-owned stores that they could not leave; others found their roots had become firmly planted in Hawaii with families and children born in the Islands and educated in the territorial public schools.

The second factor was less obvious but more decisive. The children born in Hawaii of Japanese parents were growing to voting age and were being educated in the public school system —a point to be discussed later—which was of enormous significance. They were becoming "Americanized" in spite of the doubts of members of the Big Five and certain sociologists that they could ever "assimilate" American culture or traditions. The case of Dan Inouye, whose rise to political leadership and election to the United States Senate forms the nexus of this account of Hawaii's "second revolution," illustrates this point. He came up through the living habits and customs of a typically Japanese family. It is worth noting that the arrival of his paternal grandfather, Asakichi Inouye, in the Islands in 1899 was under precisely the conditions described above—as a contract laborer, later freed by American laws. Asakichi Inouye's decision to remain in Hawaii with his family was based on the reasons outlined. He was unable to pay his debts to the plantation store, or to work off an obligation his father had contracted in Japan; and his son, Hyotaro Inouye, and later his grandson were educated in public schools of Honolulu—all typical of Japanese families that came to Hawaii in the latter years of the nineteenth century and the first years of the Territory and remained to live in the Islands.

The transition from Oriental customs and traditions to an American way of life has often been regarded as an impossibility. Kipling's view that "East is East, and West is West, and never the twain shall meet" is cited to support this conclusion, which is usually accepted at face value. Yet this conclusion is palpably invalid in Hawaii's case.

The real duality in Hawaii was not between the East and West, but between the old and the new. Japanese who came to Hawaii in the early years brought their own religions—Shintoist folk religion and Buddhism—which in their eyes were as good as the Christian morality exported from New England to Hawaii by Congregational missionaries. They retained old customs and traditions and were regarded as a race apart, living by themselves, attending their own shrines, suspiciously secretive—in a word, "unassimilable."

This was not true of the new generation of Japanese origin,

born and educated in Hawaii. Their situation actually was not much different from that of American-born sons of Italian, German, Polish, or Swedish descent who grew up in New York, Hoboken, Scranton, or Minneapolis. Dan Inouye expressed this in a brief foreword in his book, *Journey to Washington:*

> My life, as I see it, is not really so very different from all the millions of others that have contributed to the American melting pot. My forebears came from the Orient and it is true that their facial characteristics set them apart from Americans whose roots are in the Western world. But their problems of assimilation were exactly the same: to find work, to maintain a pride in their heritage while adapting to the culture of a strange new land, and slowly, step by painful step, to work their way up the social and economic ladder toward independence and full acceptance by their fellow-countrymen.[7]

The opposite viewpoint—and for many years the prevailing one among *kamaaina haoles* in Hawaii—was loosely characterized by Western sociologists as "unassimilability" of the Asiatic in America. William (Doc) Hill, a political power on the island of Hawaii, put it in these terse words: "A Jap is a Jap. After a thousand years he won't be Americanized."

Part II / 1921-1940
The Melting Pot

Doc Hill's assessment of the nonassimilable character of the Japanese who came to Hawaii in the last decade of the nineteenth century and the first years of this century was, unfortunately, the common view held by most *haoles* and to some extent by the older generation of Japanese themselves. Yet this question—whether the Oriental and Western racial cultures could ever mix politically and socially—was one that would haunt Hawaii for nearly a half century. It became one of the most significant issues in the fight for statehood that began during the years just before World War II, and in the second revolution that followed the war.

The issue had been latent in the thinking of the missionary-sugar planter group since the coup that dethroned Queen Liliuokalani, but the question of unassimilability of the Japanese did not reach its peak until the early 1920s when labor unrest and the Japanese-language school question began to disturb the tranquility of the Big Five. While it is not necessary for the purposes of this book to plunge deeply into the ethnological and sociological questions involved, it is important to understand some of the basic reasoning—and perhaps the fallacies—which lay behind this customary assessment of Hawaii's complex racial mix as being due merely to the unassimilability of Orientals.

The first Japanese to arrive in Hawaii were contract field workers, permitted to leave Japan because of the widespread famine that beset that country in the 1880s. Initially only males were allowed to emigrate; but the second wave a decade later brought women and often children, as in the case of Moyo Inouye, the wife of Asakichi Inouye, and their son, Hyotaro—

5

The Pot Begins to Boil

Dan Inouye's father—who accompanied Asakichi to the Islands in 1899. For the next ten years there was a steady influx of field workers from Japan, although the contract labor system was abandoned since it was legally unenforceable once Hawaii became an American territory. These earlier contracts bound the workers to virtual serfdom during the last years of the monarchy and the period of the Republic, but in 1907 a "gentlemen's agreement" between Japan and the United States established rules restricting the flow of immigrant labor and to some extent this agreement also protected the workers.

By the end of World War I there was a new and significant element added to the problem of the increasing numbers of Japanese. This was the fact that sons and daughters of the early arrivals—the *nisei*—had reached voting age and could participate in the political scene. Their fathers and grandfathers had come to Hawaii with no intention of remaining; but as noted, many had stayed and established families. They had brought such traditions as filial respect of sons for their parents and adherence to the authority of the head of a family, and a respect for their homeland. They had learned the sacred virtues of self-restraint and ancestor-worship from Shinto and Buddhist priests, many of whom came to Hawaii to establish shrines in which Japanese away from their homeland could worship.

All this—the worship in non-Christian faiths, loyalty to Japan, respect for old people—tended to separate the older generation from the new, who were growing up in Hawaii and learning American traditions and customs. It is true that the younger Japanese, born in Hawaii, retained many of these ethnic characteristics, but they were not totally committed to the old ways, as their fathers and grandfathers had been. They were growing up in a Western culture, playing barefoot baseball and football with Hawaiians, Chinese, Portuguese, Koreans, and even *haoles.* This led to a schism within the Japanese community itself between the older generation and the younger—the *issei* and the *nisei.* The former were perturbed at the conduct of their children, often referring to them as *furyoshonin,* the Japanese equivalent of a "pool hall bum." The younger generation, now Americans, found themselves in the middle of a tug-of-war between the customs and traditions of their parents, which they respected but did not always practice, and the new manner of living in Hawaii, the only homeland they had known.

This internal conflict, or lack of traditional relationship in a family, was not well understood by the *haoles,* and in fact the sugar planters had no real desire to understand it. The problem of keeping the Japanese "in their place" with respect to such things as wages and living conditions on the plantations would only be complicated by regarding the Japanese field workers as anything but unassimilable.

In the period before Annexation some of the plantations operated under conditions reminiscent of the coal mines of Kentucky and West Virginia, or the cotton plantations in the South before the Civil War. Overseers, or *lunas,* often used whips to keep canefield workers from slowing down, and many reports of outsiders who visited plantations in Hawaii hinted that desertion or suicide were the only alternatives to the harsh treatment of field laborers under the penal clauses of their contracts.

There have been many misconceptions as to living and working conditions on the plantations of Hawaii, some due to overemphasis on the brutalization of field labor prior to Annexation and others seeking to minimize this aspect of plantation life, particularly in sociological studies indirectly subsidized by the oligarchy. The transition from the pre-Annexation years— before and after the revolution—to conditions that prevailed under American law was understandably slow. In order to evaluate these changes in the context of the labor strife of the 1920s when an organized labor movement began to emerge, several elements in the history of plantation development should be considered.

From the first years of sugar growing in Hawaii, beginning with the first plantation and sugar mill established at Koloa, on the Island of Kauai in 1835, the most pressing problem was field labor. Earlier mills were not part of the sugar industry; for example, a Chinese named Won Wong Chun ground cane into syrup to make rum which he sold to ships as early as 1802, but it was not for production of sugar in bulk, and labor was not a problem. When the industry first expanded in the second quarter of the nineteenth century the field work force consisted of Hawaiians, but plantation life did not appeal to them and the planters were forced to look to other lands for field workers. The missionaries described the Hawaiians as "indolent and lazy" because they preferred tending *taro* patches in the cool hours of the morning or evening, and fishing or swimming and other pleasurable pursuits during the day. After the Great Mahele, which enabled the *haoles* to take over the sugar lands, plantation life dominated Hawaii and the search for sources of field labor outside Hawaii began to sound the death knell of the Hawaiian people.

In 1850 a "Masters and Servants Act" was passed, patterned after American laws governing treatment of seamen. This created a condition on the plantations that resembled peonage. Contract field workers were often flogged by the *lunas*, and one missionary—the Reverend Elias Bond, known as "Father Bond" to Hawaiians—wrote that "the plantations are carrying the people back to barbarism."

The legend of the *luna* on plantations, which ranged all the way from the "father image" to Simon Legree, has undoubtedly been overdone in both directions—that is, there were cases of ruthless brutality as well as paternal concern for the welfare of workers. But in a realistic sense, conditions were harsh and bordering at times on the inhumane simply because there was no reason for them to be otherwise. The planters were descendants of missionaries—not missionaries themselves—and they accepted the influx of alien workers as practically as they would have accepted a new breed of mules, to be worked to the limit but not to death, because they were needed. In effect, they adopted the diverse ethnic influx—Chinese, Portuguese, and finally Japanese and Filipino field workers—as necessary elements of an industry that provided financial rewards, and they were willing to keep them as long as they "kept their place." The argument of unassimilability was merely a convenient device to that end, an ethnic myth with no more substance than the early "melting pot" theory developed for the benefit of tourists. When Hawaii passed into the jurisdiction of American law, con-

tract labor had to be abandoned, but new devices were introduced. One of these was the company store familiar to the coal
mining country. Under this system, the workers remained in
constant debt, which was equivalent to bondage. They also devised a system of "working out pay" which was the same as
indenture. A visitor to Kohala plantation on Hawaii reported
that "the deeper they [the field workers] got in debt to the
plantation store, the better their employers were satisfied."

Oddly enough, this system was cited by an investigator of
the U.S. Department of Labor, in its annual report in 1915, as
an aspect of "humane treatment" of plantation workers. The
report said,

> The plantation interests form a benevolent industrial oligarchy.
> The relations existing between the plantation manager and his
> laborers are semi-feudal. Laborers and their families on the sugar
> plantations, for the most part living in isolated village communi-
> ties, are accustomed to regard the plantation manager as an
> earthly providence whose paternal business is to supply them with
> certain utilities with or without their advice and consent. Other
> industries are unable . . . or unwilling to do as much for their
> laborers in the way of medical, nursing, and hospital treatment,
> water supply, camp and house sanitation, amusements and the
> like.[8]

Whether or not this was said seriously or with tongue in
cheek, it described accurately the situation as it existed; and the
generally favorable tone of these reports may be attributed to
the fact that the government experts sent down to Hawaii were
always treated with a form of hospitality for which Hawaii was
notorious. They were guests of plantation managers, enter-
tained in royal fashion at homes of old *haole* families, and what
they saw was largely what the sugar planters wanted them to see.
Their reactions, reflected in sociological studies by visiting
professors and official reports of government investigators from
the Labor Department, did not always present a factual picture
of what life on the plantations was actually like, and for many
reasons this was unfortunate for the planters as well as their
critics.

Conditions on plantations in Hawaii were neither as bad as painted by more biased critics, nor as good as presented in surveys by the visiting sociologists and investigators, some of whom were literally brainwashed by the planters. While wages and living conditions, particularly prior to Annexation, were of an unusually low order, they were no worse than in many similar plantations elsewhere in the world and the virtual peonage of the field workers was not much different from treatment accorded natives in South America, for example, by their own wealthy landowners.

The fundamental point at issue is whether it was preferable to leave Hawaii as an "island paradise" similar to Tahiti or develop it as a viable economic and commercial asset. Located as it was at the "crossroads of the Pacific" it would have been virtually impossible for Hawaii to have remained an independent island community, pleasant and beautiful but economically useless. Its only possible fate was to be taken over by one of the great powers of the Pacific.

If the latter development were to occur, a certain kind of ruthlessness was essential. There was no other way to achieve economic progress. The question is how ruthless did it have to be, and was it necessary to destroy the Hawaiian people in the process? This question will be raised again as the story of Hawaii's transition is unfolded. The point to be made here is that the process of empire building in its early stages required a form of feudal control, regardless of whether it was morally justified.

The extent and manner of this feudal control of field labor was the most sensitive aspect of the case for the sugar planters, and one that has been subject to little objective analysis. As an example, a number of Japanese laborers who had contributed to local Japanese "banks" that were little more than informal credit unions, demanded upon the abrogation of labor contracts following Annexation in 1900 that their deposits be returned to them. The "banks" operating under regulation of the plantation management, refused to pay. As one plantation manager explained, "If the money were paid each laborer, he would be free to come and go as he pleased and the plantation managers would not know whether they had one man or several hundred to depend on at any time."

Even the Japanese consul frequently supported the planters in these disputes, and the combination of low wages, regulation of their funds, and lack of any effective means of redress left the Japanese field workers in a state of virtual servitude, and ultimately drove them into the hands of so-called labor agitators. At Olowalu and Lahaina plantations on Maui the plantation managers on one occasion refused to pay the workers at the end of the month, fearing they would all quit; and although a court ruled that the workers' rights had been violated, and 2,300 workers walked off the fields in protest, the *Hawaiian Gazette*, a *haole* newspaper, described the walkout as "the work of agitators" who were trying "to show the employees that they [the Japanese] were as good as anybody else."

This attitude, disclosing the basic racism of the white overlords, unfortunately prevailed from the time of Annexation until the 1930s when professional labor organizers began to form unions on sufficiently broad and militant bases to enforce their demands. During that period the sugar planters exercised almost unrestricted control over the plantation labor force, using the courts and legislature, and the powers of a controlled press, to exercise what amounted to feudal rule over the Islands.

The planters were due for a rude awakening after the first few years following Annexation, however. They had been lulled into a sense of security by such opiates as a U.S. Labor Department report (in 1906) that assimilation of Japanese workers—or "even their descendants"—as Americans would be "impossible" because there was no common ground of racial customs between the white man and the Japanese.

The first inkling the sugar planters seemed to have had that the Japanese field workers were learning something of American customs, if not assimilating the culture, was in 1909 when a Higher Wages Association was formed by Japanese plantation workers on Oahu, and they declared a strike. There had been a few riots earlier under the Republic, and a minor uprising at the Waipahu Plantation three years before the 1909 outbreak. The *Pacific Commercial Advertiser* had described the strikers as an "obstreperous and unruly lot" and suggested that they all be fired as "an obect lesson to little brown men on all plantations." The first strike was quickly quelled, as was the 1909 walkout in which

strikebreakers were brought in at a pay rate of $1.50 a day—fifty
cents above the going wage. Two leaders of the strike—
Yasutaro Soga, editor of the *Nippu Jiji*, a Japanese language
newspaper, and Fred Makino, a drugstore proprietor who was
later to become publisher of the *Hawaii Hochi*, the largest of the
Japanese-English newspapers in Hawaii—were jailed and fined
for "inciting to riot." Even Charles J. McCarthy, who took office
as governor seven years later, found this treatment hard to
stomach, describing it before a Senate subcommittee hearing on
Hawaii's labor problems in 1921 as "steamroller" tactics.

The simmering unrest on the plantations came to a boil
during the first years of the decade from 1920 to 1930. The
Japanese plantation workers began to adopt the tactics of the
American labor movement, with some minor variations. Back in
1908 a committee of field workers on one of the plantations on
Oahu, after politely expressing in a letter to the plantation management their "fondest and most cherished hope" that they
might "continue to help the development and progress of your
plantation" had then stated that "it has become our painful
burden to hereby respectfully present to you our request for
reasonable increase of wages." The polite request was, of
course, ignored.

By 1920 this attitude of Oriental courtesy no longer prevailed. The Japanese worker, like his American counterpart, had
become somewhat hardened by refusals, and more tough-
minded. A newly formed Federation of Japanese Labor in 1919
advised the planters the Japanese would walk off the fields unless there was an increase in wages and better living conditions.
The pay rate then was about $30 a month, plus bonuses. The
planters refused to bargain, and on January 24, 1920, all plantations on Oahu were struck.

The *Advertiser*, still owned by Lorrin Thurston, assessed the
situation with customary simplicity. "By its action," the newspaper said editorially, "the Japanese Labor Federation has forced
the issue on a question that has been looming larger and larger.
. . . Is Hawaii to be an American territory, or is it to be an
Oriental province?" It added: "What we now face is an attempt
on the part of an alien race to cripple our principal industry and

gain dominance of the American Territory of Hawaii."

The threat of the Empire of Japan taking over the Territory of Hawaii through the agency of striking plantation laborers who wanted more than a dollar a day in wages was probably not visible to anyone except the sugar planters and their mouthpiece, the *Advertiser*; but this became a theme song that was played for the next twenty years. The theme was temporarily abandoned in 1924 when the Filipinos, who were also in a striking mood, began to show signs of organized discontent, since no one—not even the Hawaiian Sugar Planters Association— was able to discern signs of a threat to Hawaii from the Philippines Commonwealth, with its Governor General appointed by the President of the United States. The note of peril to Hawaii's status as an American territory was raised again, however, when military involvement in the Pacific reached its crisis in the late 1930s.

Filipino labor imported during the second decade of this century to work in the canefields became an important and rather unusual part of Hawaii's racial pattern. There were no Filipinos on the plantations in 1902, but thirty years later—in 1932—they comprised two-thirds of the plantation workers. A few followed the Chinese pattern of leaving the canefields for better work in Honolulu, but unlike the Chinese most did not seem to be adapted to anything but unskilled work, either on the docks or in the fields. Many Filipinos participated in a longshoremen's walkout in 1917, and on the strength of this a fiery Filipino lawyer, Pablo Manlapit, organized a Filipino Federation of Labor.

During the Japanese plantation strike of 1920 the planters for the first time introduced what became their most effective strikebreaking weapon—the stirring up of racial hostility between the two Asiatic groups, the Japanese and Filipinos. The Filipinos first supported the Japanese, then switched as a result of quarrels between leaders, and there was talk of bribery and payoffs. The *Advertiser* was quick to step into this situation, charging a plot among Buddhist priests and Japanese language school teachers to control the plantations through "Asiatic paganism."

The attack on the strikers with an assortment of religious, racial, and political arguments served to increase the division between the Japanese and Filipinos and stifled any effort to settle the dispute. Even religious leaders within the *haole* community criticized the planters for seemingly promoting unending warfare between the Japanese and Filipinos which they said was threatening the economic life of the Territory. The Reverend Albert Palmer, pastor of the prestigious *haole*-supported Central Union Church, tried to settle the dispute amicably, suggesting in a sermon that the strikers return to work and the Hawaiian Sugar Planters Association agree to collective bargaining. He said in his sermon,

> One of the most disheartening things I know of in Hawaii is the oft-repeated formula: "That may all be very well on the Mainland, but you couldn't have it here, conditions are different." . . . Isn't it about time we wake up to the fact that we are part of America?[9]

He suggested they try to settle the strike "the American way."

The suggestion that an organized labor movement among plantation workers might be more American than Oriental, and not an Asiatic plot to take over the Islands, fell on deaf ears. The sugar planters were determined to bring the simmering issue to a showdown. The real problem obviously was not "Americanism *vs.* Orientalism"; it was whether or not plantation field workers had the right to organize and strike.

By July the plight of the strikers had become desperate. They were losing the support of Japanese businessmen in Honolulu, whose contributions had dried up when the *haole* business community threatened economic reprisals. The mood of the strikers changed from determination to one of frustration. Squabbles broke out among Japanese and Filipino strike leaders, and between strikers and strikebreakers. Riots occurred in plantation villages, and several people were stabbed. After six months the Japanese Federation surrendered meekly with "no concessions whatever"—in the words of John Waterhouse, the sugar planter spokesman—on the part of the planters. After the strike was broken and the strikers had returned to the fields, the planters voluntarily increased wages moderately. Thus by a combination of force and paternalism the oligarchy had established a formula for settling labor troubles; they had broken the strike and notified the workers that they could achieve some measure of progress only through the largesse of the sugar planters themselves, the extent to be determined by the planters' own evaluation of workers' requirements. The end of the strike confirmed the principle that the American method of settling labor disputes through the formation of unions and collective bargaining would not be tolerated in Hawaii.

However, the Big Five were smart enough to realize that the Japanese plantation strike and its termination would not permanently close the doors to further trouble. There was only one certain method of preventing plantation strikes and that was to get a more abundant supply of cheap field labor. In spite of warnings they had issued about the "yellow peril" and the takeover of Hawaiian industry by Orientals, the Hawaiian Sugar Planters Association turned to the one sure source of supply, if they could get them into the country: the Chinese, who of course were also Oriental.

The same people who had argued that the Japanese were "inherently Oriental" and, therefore, a threat to Americanism in the Territory, now framed a plan designed to abrogate provisions of the Chinese Exclusion Act as far as Hawaii was concerned by declaring a "labor emergency" in the Territory.

This necessitated an appeal to Washington, and in early April of 1921 Governor McCarthy, who would soon be replaced by Wallace R. Farrington, a Republican and owner of the *Honolulu Star-Bulletin*, called a meeting of newspapermen, businessmen, and political leaders. These included Lorrin Thurston of the *Advertiser*; Walter Dillingham, the most powerful industrialist in Hawaii although not a member of the Big Five; Albert Horner, formerly head of the HSPA, representing the pineapple growers; E. Faxon Bishop, one of the Big Five, representing the sugar planters; Prince Kuhio, the Delegate to Congress, and the two leaders in the territorial Legislature, Charles F. Chillingworth, president of the Senate, and Henry L. Holstein, speaker of the House.

Whether Governor McCarthy, who was soon to leave his job

to become head of the Honolulu Chamber of Commerce, took this action as a measure of public-spirited concern for the good of the Territory or for private interests can hardly be determined at this late date; but the makeup of the group was a clear-cut portrait of Hawaii's Big Five political and economic profile. The purpose of the meeting was to present the Territory's "labor emergency" to the proper people in Washington. Notably absent at the initial meeting was George W. Wright, head of Hawaii's Central Labor Council and the official representative of organized labor in the Territory, which included small trade unions.

Later Wright reported in *The Labor Review of Hawaii*, a weekly newspaper published by the Central Labor Council, that he had been called upon by several members of the Governor's committee, including Dillingham, Horner, and Bishop, who promised to recognize the smaller unions affiliated with the American Federation of Labor if the Council would support the effort to import Chinese coolies to Hawaii. When he refused, the members of the committee reportedly told him that they would "never agree to collective bargaining of any sort in the Territory."

The plan devised by the Governor's committee was to send a special commission to Washington to ask for abrogation of the Chinese Exclusion Act with respect to Hawaii by declaring a "labor emergency" in the Islands. The flaw in the plan was failure to take into account the two forces most opposed to salvaging the Hawaiian sugar planters: the American Federation of Labor and the beet and cane sugar interests on the Mainland. Wright went to Washington to argue against the measure from the labor viewpoint, and enough Congressmen were opposed to bringing more Asians into the country on any grounds to insure a majority vote against the proposal. When it came to a vote in the House in 1923, it was defeated. The commission, composed of Dillingham, Chillingworth, and Horner, had dallied in Washington for several months but failed to crack the façade of indifference to Hawaii's plight and returned empty handed.

Less than two years after the commission returned without breaching the barrier of exclusion of Chinese coolie labor from American territory, the sugar planters had another strike on their hands. The Filipino field workers, who had been brought into the Islands after the Japanese strike in 1909 as a hedge against future troubles, had formed their own Labor Federation just before the Japanese strike of 1920; and by 1924 they were ready to challenge the planters.

With the experience of the 1920 strike behind them, the sugar planters were well prepared. They had been importing Filipinos to Hawaii since the first years after Annexation, but it was not until the defeat of the Chinese coolie bill that they turned more actively to bringing in sufficient labor from the Philippines to offset any discontent among the existing plantation work force. They also brought in an investigator from the Philippines, Cayetano Ligot, to assure a favorable report to General Leonard Wood, then Governor of the Philippines, as to working conditions on the plantations. Ligot reported the Filipinos themselves were to blame, accusing their leaders of stirring up unrest.

Manlapit, the aggressive little Filipino lawyer who had led the strike, was sent to prison on a charge of bribery, and Jack Butler, secretary of the HSPA, bragged in a report to Governor Farrington that he had established a system of surveillance and knew where every "labor agitator" was at all times. These included Fred Makino, publisher of the *Hawaii Hochi* who had been sent to jail in 1909 for "inciting to riot," and George Wright, the trade union head who had now become editor of the English section of the *Hochi*, the most liberal newspaper in Hawaii.

The real issue was decided on the plantations, however, and here the immigrant field workers learned their lesson. The most decisive battle was fought at Hanapepe, on Kauai, where a score of people, chiefly strikers, were killed. The riot was triggered by a comparatively unimportant incident. There was bitter feeling between the Ilocanos, from the northern provinces of the Philippines, and the Visayans from the south. Two young Ilocanos, both nonstrikers, rode on bicycles into Hanapepe to buy shoes, passing the camp of the strikers on the way. Several strikers stepped into the road and ordered the two young men into the camp.

This was September 9, 1924. When seizure of the two men

was reported to Deputy Sheriff William Crowell he went to the strikers' camp and demanded release of the two prisoners. The strikers, mostly Visayans, refused, and Crowell sent for Captain Oneha of the Hanapepe police to serve a warrant to obtain the two prisoners. As they were led out of the camp, several strikers followed, shouting insults at both the Ilocanos and the police. Oneha later gave Honolulu newspaper reporters a vivid description of what happened.

> As the strikers began to close in on us, some of us spread our arms wide and told them to go back. We had about a dozen rifles, five shotguns and some pistols in the posse. As we backed away trying to turn back the enraged strikers fired a volley at us. One Filipino slipped up behind me and tried to stab me just as Crowell was cut down by a cane knife.[10]

Then the battle started. Strikers claimed the police fired first, and the police denied this. When it was over, four policemen lay dead and thirteen strikers were dead and three others died later from shotgun wounds. The National Guard was called out, two machine-gun squads were sent to Kauai, and Jack Butler, secretary of the HSPA, flew to Kauai in a Navy seaplane. When order had been restored by the arrest of every known Filipino strike leader on Kauai, Commissioner Ligot announced officially that strikers caused the riot, and the leaders from Manlapit down to the field organizers were sharply censured by the Governor.

The "bloody battle of Hanapepe" was not the only riot that occurred in the 1924 strike, but it set the tone for public reaction. On Hawaii and Maui there had been fighting and shooting prior to the Hanapepe affair, a Filipino striker was shot near Lihue a few days after the Hanapepe battle and at Kapaa shots were exchanged between police and strikers; but Hanapepe, because of the number killed, became a symbol of the futility of resistance by strikers. It was a clear-cut demonstration of what would happen to any dissident workers who resorted to violence —and violence was the only weapon the Filipinos really possessed.

From this point until the professional labor organizers moved in during the 1930s it was plain that pleas for higher wages and better living conditions would be handled by strict paternalism, with the use of strikebreakers backed by police and the National Guard if necessary. Complaints of the Filipinos were spurned by Commissioner Ligot, who had been sent to Hawaii presumably to see that the Filipinos got a fair deal; and the leaders such as Manlapit and his lieutenants were systematically eliminated through bribery or imprisonment.

Attorney General John A. Matthewman, legal spokesman for the Territory, added to the bitterness of the Filipinos by issuing a decision that the imported Filipino field workers were "neither citizens nor aliens" since they came from a commonwealth currently governed by the United States but were not born on American territory. Therefore he decided they were "subjects" while living in the Territory, a rather unusual term in a democratic society. This combination of factors involving civil rights—or lack of them—not only broke the Filipino labor movement in Hawaii, but it broke the spirit of the Filipinos. They were literally a people without a country and therefore without rights.

Of all the racial groups in Hawaii, the Filipinos were least understood by the sugar planters. Perhaps the political seeds planted among them in 1924 grew into Hawaii's strangest admixture to its political pot forty years later when the Filipino voting bloc became the most intangible and yet the most sought-after "racial" group in the Islands in the decade that followed statehood. Their population figures form a queer pattern of growth. Up to the time of Annexation there were few Filipinos in Hawaii. By 1910 there.were only 2,361; but by 1930 their numbers had increased to 63,052. There was a sharp drop when the Philippines won independence and then the figure jumped back to 68,000 in the year of statehood.

Of even greater interest is the fact that the later surge of Filipino immigrants to Hawaii tended to become naturalized citizens of the United States. They also brought families, something that had not been customary when they were imported as field workers. As late as 1930 the proportion of males to females was more unbalanced than in any other ethnic group, with approximately 60,000 males and slightly over 3,000 women. They also tended to return to plantation work after a try at the cities of Honolulu and Hilo, and by 1930 they constituted 70 percent of the work forces in the canefield and pineapple plantations.

They were far less assimilable than the Japanese, with little interest in the American educational system and less in the habits and customs. While they followed the Chinese practice of leaving the plantations for work in the big cities, they seldom went into business as the Chinese did and usually returned to the plantations, which were the only places they could find regular employment.

Later, when the second wave of Filipinos came to Hawaii following World War II they appeared to be of a different type, more professionally advanced and more ambitious; and it was in this context that they became an important political factor in the years that followed statehood—a phenomenon that will be discussed later in relation to that period.

It may be helpful to point out, by way of balancing the account, that the manner in which the sugar planters regarded and treated the racial groups that became their sources of field labor was not necessarily motivated by naked greed. They believed the closed system they had created in Hawaii, economically and politically, was the best way to guide the Islands and that they were best fitted to do the guiding. It is doubtful if they ever thought of their rule as a form of feudalism and certainly not as totalitarianism—which it was. But as second and third generation descendants of missionaries and traders who came to the Islands a century earlier, they had won control of the place and they intended to keep it.

In certain ways their methods were similar to those of the freebooters of America's economic development in the last half of the nineteenth century—the Vanderbilts, Harrimans, Goulds, and the rest. As Frederick Martin, a spokesman for the so-called robber barons candidly put it,

> It matters not one iota what political party is in power or what President holds the reins of office. We are not politicians or public thinkers; we are rich; we own America; we got it, God knows how, but we intend to keep it if we can by throwing all the tremendous

weight of our support, our influence, our money, our political
connections, our purchased Senators, our hungry Congressmen,
and our public-speaking demagogues into the scale against any
legislation, any political reform, any Presidential candidate who
threatens the integrity of our estate.[11]

The word "estate" may be the key to this style of thinking.
The missionary and merchant families who built the original
fiefdom in Hawaii were not ruthless men, nor as arrogantly
committed to seeking power as those who carved an empire out
of the American frontier; but their descendants were determined men who were committed to hold and rule what they had
won. The fact that this required scheming and maneuvering did
not disturb them. Nor did they feel it necessary to worry about
the characteristics or customs of the field laborers—Portuguese,
Chinese, Japanese, or Filipinos—who worked for them. The fact
that they did not at first possess the clear-cut power to exercise
control also made their situation different from that of early
American robber barons. They had overthrown Queen
Liluokalani by strategy and political maneuvering, not by
strength. They were more cunning and more determined than
the simple *kanakas.* As Lorrin Thurston said of Blount's report:
"As a Southerner he is thoroughly familiar with the difficulties
attendant upon a government with an ignorant majority in the
electorate."

Most of the planters on the outer Islands—the Rices, Wilcoxes, and Robinsons on Kauai, the Baldwins on Maui, the Ship-
mans on Hawaii—were descendants of missionaries who had
been sincerely devoted to saving souls. They must have inherited some of the instinctive desire of their forebears to assume
paternalistic protectign of the natives and to instruct them in
Christian ways of living. The one Christian virtue these descendants of missionaries and traders apparently did not possess was
a sense of humility and understanding. This brings out a point
made by Professor Andrew Lind of the University of Hawaii,
who wrote a number of sociological studies of the varied racial
components of Hawaii. He characterized the sugar planters as
possessing a sense of "equalitarianism" rather than racial *equal-*

ity. They realized their field workers were alien people, and they learned to live with them, which gave rise to the fiction current among tourist visitors to Hawaii that there was no racial problem as such.

The fact is the sugar planter oligarchy was confronted with something far more complex than Southerners in the United States ever faced. This was the *multiracial* problem in Hawaii, which probably has no parallel on the face of the earth. The planters had to deal with Portuguese, Chinese, Japanese, Filipinos, and in all fairness to the oligarchy, they dealt with this situation with an absence of visible superiority. But it was there. Racial equalitarianism was imbedded in Hawaii, and the proof of this was in the rise of the "second-class citizen" following World War II, once the inability of the Big Five to dominate the political and economic structure of Hawaii had been demonstrated.

This distinction between equality and equalitarianism will become more apparent as the story of Hawaii's second revolution develops; but it will be worthwhile to note at this point that the *kamaaina haoles,* in their attitude toward field workers of alien ethnic origin—particularly Orientals—and to the Hawaiians themselves, left no doubt as to who was the ruler and who was ruled. This principle had been set forth by the earlier monarchs of Hawaii in the Masters and Servants Act of 1850, and it was woven into the warp and woof of Big Five control of the Islands, even after Hawaii became a Territory.

The difference between racial *tolerance* and *acceptance* was never more amply demonstrated than in the events that followed the outbreak of the war in the Pacific when Big Five control passed—temporarily, as they thought—into the hands of the military establishment. The details of that shift in power will be taken up in their proper place, but the indications were already apparent two decades earlier. The racial problems which spokesmen for the Hawaii Tourist Bureau insisted had never existed in the "melting pot of the Pacific" were stewed not by the many racial groups that came to Hawaii, but by the *kamaaina haoles* themselves.

This brings up a point that has been to some extent touched

on earlier. There have been, and probably will continue to be, diverse viewpoints as to the justification of the methods employed by the small group of foreigners—chiefly Americans—who came to Hawaii during the nineteenth century and created out of this "paradise for the indolent" a powerful economic and commercial community, a political entity capable of sustaining the United States' economic and diplomatic interests in the Pacific. The question was raised earlier as to whether Hawaii could have survived in the intensely competitive conflict among nations, populated as it was by a kindly and tolerant people, unafflicted with the virus of aggression that permeates our Western civilization today.

The answer seems obviously to be negative. Some great power would have seized Hawaii, so why not the United States? Furthermore, if any other of the powers then casting covetous eyes on Hawaii—notably England, Russia, and Japan—had beaten America to it, would not the result in terms of colonial despotism have been worse? The answer to that is, of course, problematical. Hawaii today, in its strategic location in the middle of the Pacific Ocean, appears to have survived the feudal control established by the descendants of missionaries, sea captains, and traders who fomented and carried out the Revolution of 1893. The "second revolution" of the 1950s has taken place, and Hawaii is more firmly democratic as a state than it was as a monarchy, republic, or territory.

But one may ask a simple question: Was it absolutely necessary to decimate a race of kindly, tolerant people in the process? Is this subtle form of genocide the price civilization must pay for progress? Do we have to destroy indigenous peoples to pave the way for the advancement of civilization? If this is so, then perhaps the world would do better with less civilization and more humanity.

Prince Kuhio died in 1922, but this posed no immediate problem for the political strategists of the Big Five-GOP coalition. For twenty years Kuhio had acted only as a figurehead, and a wobbly one at that. They decided to get a candidate upon whom they could depend without having to worry about too much sympathy for the Hawaiians, so they selected John Wise, the part-Hawaiian territorial Senator who had assisted so ably in the Hawaiian Homes campaign in Congress.

Their choice of Wise exposed an unexpected vulnerability which the oligarchy either did not recognize or did not consider worth worrying over. This was underestimation of the increasing resentment of the Hawaiians themselves toward the growing power of the oligarchy. Wise was known as a pro-*haole*, and when the Democrats picked Billy Jarrett, also a part-Hawaiian, to run against Wise, Jarrett—who was anti-*haole*—won handily. This did not upset the Big Five too much, since the governorship was assured with Warren Harding in the White House, and they controlled the Legislature. But two years later, when they substituted Phil Rice, a *kamaaina haole* of impeccable missionary lineage, he was beaten more decisively than Wise—again by Billy Jarrett. Quite evidently something was wrong with the Big Five-GOP strategy.

Royal Mead, the Big Five political expert, toured the Islands, demanding explanations. On Hawaii a part-Hawaiian party worker told him, "You don't expect a hand-picked *haole* like Rice to win votes against a *kanaka* like Billy Jarrett, do you? A fellow everybody likes?"

The loss of the delegateship for two terms was not a serious blow to the Republicans, with men like Harding and Coolidge in the White House and the Republicans in control of Congress;

6

The Dividing Line

but it exposed a weakness in the oligarchy's political planning. The territorial Senate and House had gone solidly Republican: all fifteen seats in the Senate and twenty-nine of thirty in the house; but the winners were either Hawaiian or Portuguese, or very popular *haoles* in their districts. Yet they lost the delegateship. The party worker on Hawaii had given Mead the right answer: Hawaiians had voted for Kuhio in the past because he was of royal blood; but they were not likely to vote for a *haole* like Rice, a full-fledged member of the sugar planter group, against a popular Hawaiian like Jarrett. Had the Big Five experts examined these results more carefully, they would have detected the basic flaw in their political strategy.

As one writer noted,

> In Hawaii it was not so much income or occupation that determined one's friends, voting affiliations, or prospects for power and prestige. In the forty years that followed Annexation, the peoples of Hawaii thought of themselves not primarily as doctors, lawyers, druggists, or field hands—or even as Americans—but as *haoles*, Hawaiians, Portuguese, Chinese, Japanese and Filipinos.[12]

This was a subtle difference, and it was not clearly recognized by the *haoles* themselves. But it helps to understand what was happening to the "melting pot of the Pacific" during the years before and after World War II.

The area in which this difference was most significant and most firmly defined was in the field of education, since it had economic and social overtones as well as racial importance. The evolution of education in Hawaii will be dealt with more specifically in the context of the second revolution, but it may be helpful to relate it here to the conditions under which Dan Inouye grew up in Honolulu and particularly to the way he was educated. This was an important factor in the part he played in the creation of a new Hawaii.

When Dan Inouye was born, in 1924, Queen Emma Street was a crooked road, twisting up from the downtown area into the Punchbowl section. It was a dividing line between two residential areas, one that spread to the south, or "Waikiki" end of the city, and the other that lay to the north, or "Ewa"—the terms used for directions in Honolulu. Dan Inouye was from the Ewa side, where small frame houses clustered along little lanes that branched off from the main streets—Vineyard, Kukui, School. On the south side of Queen Emma Street, beyond the Pacific Club, which was the social shrine of *kamaaina haoles*, were palatial homes of missionary families and those associated with the Big Five. Children of the latter families for the most part attended Punahou Academy, while those from the ghettos and the slums, which spread northward through Palama to Kalihi, went to public schools such as McKinley High School.

This was a difference that was ingrained in Honolulu society and would affect Hawaii deeply in years to come, although the physical dividing line has been erased. Queen Emma Street is now a wide, paved thoroughfare, crossed by a freeway sunk below the level of the old streets, which cuts through the Japanese ghetto, and many of the frame houses have been bulldozed out of existence. But even before the advent of the freeway, many families had moved out to Moiliili, where there was a slightly improved ghetto known as McCully tract. Years ago the Waikiki trolley branched off from King Street at Pawaa Junction and ran across a causeway through the Chinese duck ponds, a region of swampy pools, until it reached solid ground again at Cassidy's Siding and continued along Kalakaua Avenue to the Waikiki Beach area.

All this was changed in the late 1920s. The Ala Wai canal was dredged through the swamp, draining the pools, and Kapiolani Boulevard created a wide traffic artery through the new land that had been filled in by dredging the canal and now offered solid soil for low-cost housing developments. Houses and stores were built on the raised ground for Japanese, Chinese, Portuguese, and part-Hawaiian families who once lived across from the Pacific Club in the slums of Queen Emma street and Palama. In his autobiographical story, *Journey to Washington*, Senator Inouye has a particularly crisp comment on the location of the Pacific Club, almost directly across the street from the house where he was born:

There are places like it all over the world, the private retreats of men of proper station. But it is a neat little irony that this particular bastion of Hawaii's planters and great merchants and their ladies, which rigidly barred all Orientals, should have been set down in the very heart of the Japanese slum.[13]

This was more than merely ironic. It was a clear-cut line of demarcation in the fabric of Hawaii's society, and it affected educational as well as economic developments, which in turn affected historical changes in the political system. There was outward harmony in the "Paradise of the Pacific" but little basic racial mixture except where it was consistent with the objectives of the *kamaaina haoles.* Some members of the old missionary families had married Hawaiians of royal blood, and there was even careful marital mixing with the more affluent and influential Chinese, but little miscellaneous crossbreeding except among the lower levels of the ethnic mix; and few non-*haoles* and almost no Orientals ever walked into the Pacific Club. The situation referred to by Senator Inouye as "a neat little irony" was at the very heart of an element of discord only lightly touched on in most Hawaiian historical reviews. This was the educational system.

In order to place this educational system in perspective, particularly as it related to the growth of a new social and political consciousness in Hawaii that finally emerged in the second revolution, it is necessary to outline the three basic forms of educational institutions that developed in the Islands. The type that drew the most attention, and yet was least important, was the foreign language school established by ethnic groups—the Japanese in particular, and to a lesser extent the Chinese and Koreans—as a means of training their children in the languages, customs, and traditions of their homelands.

The second type was the private school inherited from the days of the missionaries, who ardently advocated education with the important reservation that there be one kind of school for the savages, as the Hawaiians were called, and another for children of missionaries. These latter schools later became the private privilege of those who one day would be the rulers of Hawaii.

The third and by far the most important type, both educationally and historically, was the system of public school education. Again quoting from Dr. Fuchs's sociological study of Hawaii, these were the schools that would plant "the seeds of educational liberalism that would one day destroy Hawaii's oligarchy."

Foreign language schools were tolerated on the plantations because they provided field workers with a means of educating their children without exposing them to too many American institutions and democratic processes, such as labor troubles and elections. Private schools were part of the caste system that had developed in the monarchy and Republic and was carried over into the Territory. But the public school system was a different matter. Two plantation managers expressed it quite bluntly. Discussing the problem over drinks, one pounded his fist on the table and said, "Every penny we spend educating those kids beyond the sixth grade is wasted." The other disagreed.

"Public education beyond the fourth grade is not only wasted," he said. "It is a menace."

This hostility at first was based mainly on the interference of public schooling with the discipline of plantation field workers. Later it spread to other and more serious matters—the discipline of the electorate itself.

Japanese language schools were never a serious problem in the Territory except to the jingoist mentality of extreme racists, particularly during the years before World War II when baldish Buddhist priests sought to inculcate into the young Hawaiian-born students unswerving loyalty to Japan. Although there were as many as 175 such schools in Hawaii as late as 1930, after a federal law regulating them was declared unconstitutional, it was the public school system which really constituted the "menace" against which the sugar plantation managers had warned.

After Annexation, public schools were established as a natural result of Hawaii's having become part of the United States, but they were mainly for "second-class citizens." Children of *kamaaina haoles* continued to attend Punahou Academy, which had been founded for "instruction of the children of missionaries." As one writer expressed it, "Punahou was not merely a school; it was a way of life." Some of the lower ranking *haole* and part-Hawaiian families sent their children to sectarian schools—St. Louis College for Catholics, Iolani School, and St. Andrews Priory for Episcopalians. Many Hawaiians were able to attend Kamehameha Schools, founded in 1887 under the will of Princess Bernice Pauahi Bishop, granddaughter of Kamehameha I, who had married Charles R. Bishop, the itinerant sea captain, in 1869.

Education of the children of Japanese, Chinese, Portuguese, Koreans, Filipinos, most Hawaiians and part-Hawaiians and low-ranking *haoles* was left for the most part to the public schools, which did not have the enthusiastic support of the *kamaaina haoles,* some of whom thought it was an extravagance, while others, like the two plantation managers, considered it a menace. Fortunately for the democratic process, the passion for learning is not always subject to the dictates of economic interests. During the Republic a mainland educator, Henry S. Townsend, had been appointed general director of the public school system in Hawaii, and he brought in prominent educators like Dr. John Dewey of Columbia University and Dr. Francis Parker of the University of Chicago to lecture on the advantages of education as a bulwark of democracy. Townsend was fired for his "radical" ideas, but the public school system persisted and its flame grew, fanned by the desire for knowledge among Hawaiian-born Japanese, Chinese, and Portuguese.

It should not be assumed that an effective system of public schools was universally opposed by members of the sugar planter group. Many of them believed, theoretically at least, in progressive educational methods. Farrington, one of the *kamaaina* elite who usually spoke firmly for the Big Five control of the Islands, nevertheless was a strong exponent of better educational institutions, and as Governor he opposed efforts to reduce either the size or quality of Hawaii's school system. What constituted better education and the kinds of things that should be taught in public schools was a matter of judgment, of course, and any ideas that seemed too progressive for the comfort of the oligarchy were usually censored and where possible suppressed.

Few members of the *haole* elite were so lacking in social consciousness as to take the position of the plantation managers previously quoted, that public schools were a menace. But they were committed to a socioeconomic philosophy that what was good for King Sugar was good for Hawaii. They did not advocate stifling educational opportunity; but they felt these opportunities should be directed along lines of greatest advantage to Hawaii, such as sugar technology, which coincidentally was of advantage also to the sugar planters. When the College (later University) of Hawaii was founded in 1907, one of the primary requirements in the curricula was sound training in agricultural studies by which students would be equipped for work with the Sugar Planters Experiment Station, and on the plantation.

There were many who believed on general principle that education was a necessary adjunct of economic progress. Harry Baldwin, for example, was a firm supporter of a good public school system even on Maui, the one island of the Hawaiian group which most resembled a medieval fiefdom. As early as 1913, in discussing with a group of Maui plantation managers the need for bringing in highly trained educators from the Mainland, he is reported to have said that if Maui were to become "a first-rate American community" it must have above all else adequate public school educational facilities.

There is little doubt, however, that the public school system in Hawaii, with its roots sunk deeply into a land ruled by feudal overlords, actually developed in its broader and more democratic aspects in spite of the oligarchy, not because of it. Containing a mixture of races slowly being schooled in American ways, it continued to grow and to resist the self-serving educational theories of the Big Five social philosophers. The fact that it survived with little government support and ultimately became one of the vital factors in overturning the oligarchy is a tribute to the men of vision who served it—the educators and teachers—who could foresee what Hawaii would be like without it.

Daniel Inouye grew up in the middle of this period of

change when new forces in the Islands were just beginning to appear—the advances in educational processes and the time of troubles for the Big Five. During the early years of his life he obviously knew little of what was happening politically and economically in an arena where he would later emerge as one of the central figures. As to the location of the Pacific Club, across the street from the boxlike house where he was born, he said, "If I ever thought of the Pacific Club at all, it was probably with passing regret that no native kids lived there; the immaculate lawns seemed a perfect place for a baseball game."

The events of his early life have been set forth in his own book on the subject. However, in order to place his personality and the environment in which he grew up in proper perspective, it is necessary to describe to some extent his background and the elements that impelled him to take part in the molding of a new Hawaii during the two decades that followed World War II.

He was born on Queen Emma Street on September 7, 1924, the fifth "first son" in five generations of the Inouye family. This could have been considered an omen, although there is no evidence that it was so regarded at the time. Five generations of male primogeniture in the Japanese tradition were more than a coincidence; it was usually believed to be a gift of heaven.

His great-grandfather, Wasaburo Inouye, had been a leading citizen in the tiny village of Yokoyama, which his forefathers had founded, on the southern island of Kyushu in Japan, until an accidental fire occurred which changed everything for the Inouyes. The emigration of Asakichi Inouye to Hawaii was no accident or fortuitous decision; it was a matter of honor.

The fire had broken out in the village in the fall of 1899, and it was traced to the Inouye house. The damage was estimated at about $400. Wasaburo Inouye had only two choices: he could leave town, have his name scratched off the list of those living in the village and escape with his entire family, who would then become "nonpersons," or he could pay the debt of honor. The sum was beyond his capacity to pay, limited as he was by earnings from small farming; and the only possible way of repaying the debt was to have his eldest son, Asakichi, go out into the world and earn it.

Asakichi accepted the obligation without question. A labor recruiter from a distant and beautiful land—Hawaii—had passed through town a few days earlier looking for men to work in the sugar fields of Hawaii and had painted a glowing picture of the rewards for such service. It was necessary to sign a five-year contract, and Asakichi hurried to the nearby city of Fukuoka where the recruiter was staying and signed up. In a few days he was on the ship *Peking Maru* with his wife, Moyo, and his four-year-old son, Hyotaro, sailing for Honolulu. He was placed in line there, examined for physical defects much the way Negroes were examined in the American slave markets of the South a half century earlier, and assigned to work on the McBryde Plantation on Kauai.

At the end of each month Asakichi collected what was left of his pay after deductions for purchases at the plantation-owned store. It usually amounted to about ten dollars, and he sent as much of this as he could spare—two or three dollars—to his father in Yokoyama to be applied to the $400 debt. At the end of five years only a small amount of the debt had been paid, and he agreed to work another five years at McBryde, although under American law he was no longer under bondage.

It soon became evident to young Hyotaro that he would be a full-grown man still working in the canefields by the time the debt was paid off; and so he asked permission of his father to go to Honolulu and attend school. At the age of sixteen he entered Mills School, a church-supported school known as Mid-Pacific Institute, which had been founded by the Reverend Francis W. Damon, a missionary with previous service in China, and liberal notions about the education of Orientals. Damon had established the school for young people of non-Caucasian and non-Hawaiian stock who could not afford the cost of an education. Each student was expected to pay part of the tuition and board, however, by working during off hours when he was not in classes.

Hyotaro worked his way through Mills School, serving as dormitory master for twenty dollars a month and earning money during the summers by working in canefields on nearby plantations. He joined the Methodist Church, much to the regret of his parents who were descended from a long line of Buddhists; and in 1923 he married Kame Iwanaga, an orphaned girl from the Island of Maui whose parents had also come over as immigrant contract workers, from Hiroshima Province in Japan. After they died she was sent to the Susannah Wesley Home for Girls in Honolulu, a Methodist orphanage.

She met young Hyotaro Inouye at a Methodist Church on River Street—the heart of the slums—in 1922 and they were married in September, 1923. A year later Dan Inouye was born.

In the same year—1924—another Hawaiian-born Japanese, Wilfred Tsukiyama, joined the Republican Party. This is noted because in a sense it focuses upon a factor not ordinarily understood by those unfamiliar with the growth of racial balance in Hawaii. Tsukiyama was the first American of Japanese descent to achieve an important position in Hawaiian politics. He went to McKinley High School, as did Inouye; he studied at the University of Hawaii and received his law degree from the University of Chicago Law School. He was Deputy City Attorney during the famed Massie Case in 1932 in Honolulu; and he later became the first Chief Justice of Hawaii's Supreme Court following the Territory's admission to statehood in 1959.

Nevertheless, his political career was diametrically opposite to Inouye's. He had moved rapidly up the ladder of political success until the tension between Japan and the United States began to develop in the late 1930s, erupting into World War II. Then, in 1940, Tsukiyama quietly withdrew from public life, resigning from the Selective Service Board in Honolulu to which he had been appointed after serving a four-year term as City Attorney of Honolulu, the first of his racial origin to attain that eminence.

Wilfred Tsukiyama may be said to have acted in the Japanese tradition. If this is true, then he also acted as an American. He was intelligent, capable, and honest; his early career—and the events of his later life—confirm the sincerity of his dedication to the country in which he was born. He withdrew from public life at the time because of the wartime pressure of public feeling against *nisei*—the same feelings that later caused Dan Inouye to enter the political field. In order to place this in a more objective perspective, it may be appropriate to quote again from the sociological study of Hawaii by Dr. Lawrence Fuchs:

> Tsukiyama was accused by a new generation of Japanese politicians of having sold out to the Caucasians. Why, they asked, did he resign from a Selective Service Board under *haole* pressure at the start of the War? Why hadn't he asserted Japanese interests over the years? To accuse Tsukiyama was, in a sense, absurd. His entire generation might well have been indicted. Tsukiyama, true to his Japanese heritage, had bowed to authority and tried honestly and vigorously to represent his people within Hawaii's authoritarian political system. If he lacked reforming zeal, so did his entire generation, with only a few exceptions.[14]

Dan Inouye, Spark Matsunaga, and Patsy Takemoto Mink— all now in the Congress—were among those exceptions. But the difference was in style, not motivation or integrity. The significance of this point, in a study of Hawaii's second revolution and achievement of statehood, is that the rise of democracy in Hawaii and the overturning of the Big Five *was not a racial phenomenon,* even though there had been racial overtones in Hawaii's economic, social, and political system since the overthrow of Queen Liliuokalani in the Revolution of 1893 and the subsequent Annexation in 1898. Racism in Hawaii, to the extent that it existed, was generated by the *kamaaina haoles* who could never forget their own color and prestigious position, not by other ethnic groups who were struggling to apply an American concept of democracy to what was basically an undemocratic system of government. The difference between Dan Inouye and Wilfred Tsukiyama, a generation apart, was one of method and personality, not of motive. Both were of the same ethnic origin and both were essentially Americans.

New patterns of voting were beginning to emerge in Hawaii, and the most visible signs of the troubles ahead for the Big Five were to be found in their efforts to control these upsurges within the electorate. However, these were not the only problems that confronted the Big Five during the decade that followed Kuhio's death. There were other portents, mostly in the economic field, that were not as obvious as the political events, but more indicative of what was happening.

One of these was a lawsuit begun shortly after World War I by heirs of the Isenberg Estate, which owned a controlling interest in H. Hackfeld & Co., Ltd. This was the sugar agency founded by Captain Hackfeld in 1849 and held largely by German interests. During the war it was seized by A. Mitchell Palmer, the U. S. Attorney General, as "alien property." Palmer then suggested to some members of the Big Five that they form a company to purchase these frozen assets. Several *kamaaina haole* families—the Cookes, Athertons, and Wilcoxes, all full-fledged members of the missionary-sugar planter oligarchy—formed American Factors, Ltd., with A. W. T. (Jack) Bottomley as its head, and bought the Hackfeld holdings from the United States Government for $7,000,000. The Hackfeld heirs sued to recover $12,000,000 from American Factors, claiming that the assets were peddled to the favored group in closed trading which made it impossible to get reasonable prices. Shares of Kekaha Plantation, for example, which paid forty to fifty percent annually on the face value of its capital in 1917 and 1918, were sold in a single lot at what was said to be a fraction of their actual worth in the open market.

The case dragged through the courts for years and was finally settled, but the disclosures exposed some of the financial

7

Straws in the Wind

machinations of the Big Five to public view. There were other cases: the so-called Waterhouse Trust affair, for example, in which funds held by the trust company were invested in the booming stock market—permissible under Hawaiian law—and were wiped out in the crash of 1929. None of these happenings were of monumental importance in themselves, but they served to bring to the attention of the average citizen the manner in which financial matters were handled by the descendants of some of the early missionaries and traders in Hawaii.

Two old financial institutions—the Bank of Bishop, founded during the monarchy by Charles R. Bishop and Samuel L. Damon, and the Bank of Hawaii, established under the Republic—controlled practically all financial dealings of importance in the Islands. They permitted small Chinese and Japanese banks to service their respective racial groups, but the big banks operated all the major business. They worked closely with the sugar agencies, with interlocking directorates, so that the banking business in Hawaii was for the most part controlled by the same men who were heads of the Big Five sugar factors. When trust companies were formed, they were formed by the banks—Bishop Trust and Hawaiian Trust, both organized at the turn of the century. Smaller banks and trust companies on the outer islands were gradually absorbed by the major institutions in Honolulu so that by the early 1920s the entire financial structure of the Islands was a tightly held combination, with officers and directors of banks and trust companies a cross section of officers and directors of the Big Five agencies.

In this manner they controlled all business. A manager of a plantation store who tried to set up his own store found that suppliers would not give him credit. Anyone presumptuous enough to try to establish a major business in Honolulu—such as a department store in competition with the Liberty House, or a hardware store in competition with E. O. Hall & Son, or a building materials firm in competition with Lewers & Cooke—discovered that shipments from the mainland were left on the docks in San Francisco, or lost in transit. Credit at the banks was withdrawn, and the banks also refused credit to retailers who bought from independent wholesalers. The Big Five control by

1930 was virtually a complete and seemingly unbreakable monopoly.

The pineapple industry was a case in point. The Hawaiian Pineapple Company was founded in 1901 by James D. Dole as an outgrowth of Captain John Kidwell's experiments with the red Cayenne pineapple. By 1910 about 5,000 acres were under cultivation; by 1920, almost 50,000 acres; and by 1930 nearly 65,000 acres were producing pineapple. The Big Five had given the burgeoning industry a chance to develop, and by 1930 they were ready to take it over.

The break came when Dole decided to accept bids from steamship companies to transport pineapple to the Mainland— a business the Matson Navigation Company, formed by the Big Five and controlled by Castle & Cooke, had always enjoyed without competitive bidding. The Isthmian Line offered rates lower than Matson, and when the price of pineapple broke during the depression, Dole decided to switch shippers. From the standpoint of Hawaiian Pines this obviously was a good decision. From the standpoint of Frank Atherton and Alexander Budge, who headed Castle & Cooke, it was bad. In 1932, with the bottom dropping out of the market and Dole seeking loans to bolster his company, he found the door closed at the banks in Honolulu and San Francisco. He was dumped, and Atherton Richards, a missionary descendant, former treasurer of Castle & Cooke and director of Ewa and Waialua Plantations, took over as general manager, although Dole was retained as a figurehead president because his name was synonymous with Hawaiian pineapple.

It might be readily assumed that the takeover of the Dole pineapple empire by the Big Five was an indication of solid strength; but as events proved, it was this type of thing that hastened their ultimate breakdown. The monolithic position of the oligarchy could be maintained only as long as it retained influence and control over the men who made the laws, and this influence was beginning to weaken with each new revelation or exposure.

Signs of political weakness had already become evident in the election of Democrat Billy Jarrett as delegate in 1922 and

1924. While Jarrett could not do much harm wandering around
Washington with little support of any sort from Hawaii, it was
obviously necessary to patch up this crack in the political structure of the Big Five-GOP coalition. This was accomplished in
1926 when a candidate of suitable Hawaiian antecedents—Victor K. Houston, a part-Hawaiian Commander in the U. S. Navy
stationed at Pearl Harbor—was brought into political service by
the GOP and beat Jarrett handily in the election that fall.

A second problem, eventually more troublesome to the
oligarchy than Jarrett, was the increasing importance of the
Japanese vote. They had offered no candidates in major races up
to 1928, but there was always the possibility that they might, and
with the large number of Hawaiian-born Japanese eligible to
vote, it was necessary for the Big Five to do something about it.

There were two obvious ways of meeting this potential
threat. One was to lure Japanese into the Republican fold by
taking them in as party workers and possibly putting up a few
Japanese for minor offices. Wilfred Tsukiyama was an example
of this when he became a Republican in 1924. He was young,
energetic, and politically ambitious and was appointed Deputy
District Attorney in Honolulu. The other way was to try to deny
as many *nisei* as possible the right to vote. This method was
crude, and as it turned out, largely ineffective. Senator James
Phelan of California had offered a bill in Congress, with Hawaii's
encouragement, seeking a constitutional amendment under
which children whose parents were ineligible to citizenship
would not themselves be eligible, even though they might be
born on American soil. This failed to arouse much enthusiasm
anywhere except in California and among the Big Five-GOP
coalition in Hawaii.

Another less obvious method of curtailing the *nisei* vote was
to tighten regulations for registration. *Nisei* were required to
prove their citizenship in complicated ways, even to the extent
of being asked to obtain affidavits of midwives who had attended
their birth. Since many of the midwives were either illiterate or
dead, this posed a problem, and many eligible Japanese did not
register.

The two lines of attack in some respects worked at cross-purposes. Bringing Hawaiian-born Japanese into the Republican Party tended to stimulate interest of the Japanese, who had not previously voted in very large numbers; but the effort to bar *nisei* from registering neutralized the efforts of these new party workers. However, the overall effect seemed to turn out successfully at first for the Republicans, no matter how poorly it was conceived. On the outer islands of Hawaii, Maui and Kauai, the Japanese vote went strongly Republican. Even in Honolulu there seemed to be beneficial results in the beginning.

By 1930, however, it was evident that stirring interest among the Hawaiian-born Japanese had increased their support for Link McCandless, the standard bearer of the Democratic Party, although not in substantial numbers. The sudden surge of *nisei* voting interest, however, aroused a calculating gleam in the eyes of Democratic planners such as Johnny Wilson, son of a one-time minister of the Queen and Mayor of Honolulu.

Wilson and McCandless were leaders of the Democratic Party in Honolulu, where its main strength lay. Wilson had worked for years to interest Japanese who were eligible to vote. Unfortunately the response had been lukewarm, particularly due to the continued advice from Japanese language newspapers—the *Nippu Jiji* in particular—to young Japanese to refrain from taking too strong a position in American politics, and thus contributing to the *haoles'* claim that the Japanese in Hawaii constituted a threat to America. In addition, the few prominent Japanese who did interest themselves in politics were drawn to the Republicans as historically the winner in the Territory. Any Japanese businessman who opposed the Big Five could readily be run out of business.

Wilson, a part-Hawaiian, saw in the rising interest of the Japanese voter a portent of the future, however. In Honolulu, where the Democrats traditionally elected the Mayor and a majority of the Board of Supervisors, the more astute liberals of the Japanese professional community—teachers, lawyers, ministers, and doctors—whose business was not threatened, began to urge *nisei* to join with the Democrats to achieve political identity in opposition to the dominant influence of the "czars of industry," as Fred Makino of the *Hochi* had described the Big Five.

The leading Japanese language newspaper in Hilo, the *Hawaii Asahi*, editorially urged the Japanese to switch from Republican to Democratic allegiance.

This sudden surfacing of *nisei* aroused the fears of the Big Five-Republican political thinkers. Jack Butler, still secretary of the HSPA, wrote Delegate Houston in Washington that the "insidious influence" of the Japanese language newspapers in Hawaii threatened to undermine Republican solidarity and thus was a "threat to Hawaii." Wilson, who had been returned as Mayor of Honolulu in 1932, took advantage of this growing fear on the part of GOP strategists and began to drive home to Japanese voters the idea that they could play a key role in wrestling territorial control from the Republicans. With the aid of a highly articulate former newspaperman, Willard K. Bassett, he delivered scathing speeches (written by Bassett) denouncing the Republicans as "political pygmies" and branding the Big Five as "tin-horn political planners" who "send deluded men of Hawaiian blood to do their talking for them." Wilson undoubtedly remembered the admonition of his father, who had been the Queen's Marshal during the revolution, that "Hawaiians must learn to look out for themselves because the *haoles* will not help them. They must choose their friends wisely." Another part-Hawaiian, Bill Richardson, whose father had been jailed during the counterrevolution in 1895 for supporting the Queen, and who was one of the organizers of Hawaii's second revolution, later told how Wilson had enjoined him: "Bill, you've got to work for the Hawaiians. Politics is the only way."

During the Roosevelt administration Wilson wrote James A. Farley, the President's political strategist, that the Japanese *nisei* in Hawaii would one day form the key to Democratic strength —an example of political prescience that was almost prophetic.

Nevertheless, as events proved, the Japanese did not vote as a bloc in the election of 1932. They helped to sweep McCandless—who was no lover of the Japanese—into office, but most of the Japanese in territorial elections voted for Republicans in spite of a Democratic landslide on the Mainland.

The election of 1932 was by no means the turning point politically for the Big Five-GOP control of the Territory. They

lost the delegateship to a Democrat, and Judge Joseph B. Poindexter, also a Democrat, was appointed governor—a bitter pill
for Wilson to swallow, since he had anticipated getting that job
himself, due to his close friendship with Farley. However, the
Republicans remained solidly in control of the territorial Senate
and House.

Another event occurred in 1932 prior to the election that
year, more racial than anything Hawaii had experienced since
the revolution, that overshadowed the political scene and
shaped Hawaii's destiny for the next two decades. This was the
Massie Case in which five so-called native youths were accused
by the wife of a young naval officer of having picked her up,
driven her to a lonely spot on the Ala Moana Road, and raped
her seven times.

The importance of this case has to a large extent been
overlooked by historians of Hawaii's second revolution and its
transition to statehood. The *kamaaina haoles* would prefer to
forget it; yet it is imbedded in the final disintegration of the rule
of the Big Five.

The Massie Case began in an atmosphere of purely local
interest. The young woman in the case, Thalia Massie, had attended a party of young naval officers and their wives at the Ala
Moana Inn, a fairly respectable roadhouse near the entrance to
the Waikiki Beach section of Honolulu, on September 12, 1931.
She was the wife of Lt. Thomas H. Massie, attached to the
submarine base at Pearl Harbor. She left the party sometime
before midnight and turned up at her home two hours later,
claiming that she had been picked up and assaulted by five native
boys. Later she said she was raped.

Five boys were arrested during the night and ultimately
brought to trial after Thalia Massie identified them. They were
tried on evidence so uncertain and flimsy that the jury refused
to bring in a verdict. This was known as the Ala Moana trial.
While the five young men—two Hawaiians, one Chinese-
Hawaiian, one Japanese-Hawaiian, and a Japanese *nisei*—were
awaiting a retrial, one of them—Joseph Kahahawai—was lured
into a car by Thalia Massie's mother, Mrs. Grace Fortescue, her
husband, and two sailors, and driven to a house in Manoa Val-

ley, where he was accidentally shot. He bled to death while his captors were trying to figure out what to do.

The case was local until the boy was killed. It then became of national interest. Mrs. Fortescue, young Massie, and the two sailors were tried for murder early in 1932. Clarence Darrow, the great criminal lawyer, came down to Honolulu to defend them in a case which drew national attention. All four were convicted of manslaughter and sentenced to ten years in prison. Under pressure from Southern Congressmen, Republican Governor Lawrence Judd commuted the sentence to one hour, spent in the Governor's chambers at Iolani Palace, and they were released. The verdict and aftermath created a racial explosion that threatened to tear Hawaii apart. The *haole* editor of the *Hawaii Hochi*, George Wright, wrote,

> More harm has been done the cause of Americanization by recent events than can be remedied in many years. . . . Republican leadership has been discredited and many of the most powerful people in public life stand branded as traitors in the eyes of the common people. . . . The voters are saying that Republican inefficiency made the Ala Moana case possible; that chicanery of officials bungled the first trial and sought to railroad certain suspects without sufficient evidence; that their cowardice prevented adequate defense of Hawaii's honor when it was attacked on the Mainland following the killing of Joseph Kahahawai; that acquiescence of these leaders in the reign of terror was climaxed by the surrender of the principle of self-government. . . .[15]

The Governor ordered an investigation of the entire case by the Pinkerton Detective Agency, and the conclusion reached in the report of the investigators—never publicly released—was that the entire affair was a miserable miscarriage of justice, that the five youths, one of whom was killed, could not have been involved in the assault—if there was one; and that Mrs. Massie had lied in her original accusation and in her testimony at the first trial. The four convicted defendants in the second trial hurried back to the Mainland and the case ultimately was dropped due to the lack of a prosecuting witness.

However, the effect on social and political tension in Hawaii, which had been smoldering for a quarter of a century, was to widen the gap between the ruling oligarchy and those whom they regarded as second-class citizens—particularly the Hawaiians and Portuguese. This further deepening of racial and social wounds was not immediate, since the rift between the various racial elements was not easy to define. It did not reflect itself specifically in social, political, or economic relations but was rather a combination of all three. The immediate result of the Massie affair was, in a sense, a boon to the Big Five because it was a factor in delaying for another twenty-five years Hawaii's admission to statehood. But in the long term it was a prelude to the second revolution.

The fact that the ruling Republican politicians in the Territory had been willing to toss five "native boys" into the sacrificial pit to appease the Navy, rather than insist on a genuine inquiry into the unsupported allegations of the Navy officer's wife, left a scar on the public conscience and also left the missionary-sugar planter faction exposed in all of its totalitarian nakedness. This started a swing of the working-class electorate in Honolulu toward the Democratic Party. The fact that there was no immediate shift of sufficient strength to change the balance of political power in the Territory was due chiefly to an inherent trait of the Democrats. Their own factions—part-Hawaiians, Portuguese, independent *haoles,* and to some extent a small group of politicians of Oriental extraction—immediately became embroiled in an internal dispute over who would control the newly achieved power, even before they achieved it.

This internal struggle, characteristic of Democrats once they have gained a triumph over their Republican adversaries, involved a personal contest between Johnny Wilson and Link McCandless for the governorship following the Roosevelt landslide of 1932. Wilson was a short, tough, courageous man who had become mayor after serving as City Engineer of Honolulu. A few years earlier, faced with a three-to-two Republican majority on the Board of Supervisors, Wilson had listened grimly to the insulting comments of the Republican leader of the Board, Ben Hollinger, reflecting on his integrity; and then he had banged his gavel on the bench, adjourned the meeting, stepped down and belted Hollinger in the jaw. Wilson was known as a shrewd politician, honest to the core; and he was experienced in the rough-and-tumble, no-holds-barred fighting in Hawaiian politics. He also had the support of most Hawaiian voters.

McCandless had made a fortune in the well-digging business. He was a bluff, power-hungry man who had the backing of some of the Hawaiian vote and most of the Portuguese. He had hoped to be able to resign as delegate and be appointed governor. Farley, on Wilson's advice, refused to risk a special election in Hawaii, and McCandless regarded this as personal treachery to himself. He broke with Wilson and this split the Democrats —Wilson heading up the Hawaiian, *nisei,* and independent *haole* group while McCandless had the backing of the Portuguese and an element of the *kamaaina haoles.* Even Charlie Rice of Kauai, descendant of missionaries and the most powerful politician among the *haoles,* supported him openly in the primary election against Wilson.

The result was a Democratic debacle in the general elections of 1934. Wilson accused McCandless of betraying the Hawaiians by going over to the Big Five-sugar planter oligarchy and McCandless accused Wilson of fomenting racial hostility by appealing to the Hawaiians to vote against him. McCandless, with the help of Charlie Rice, who had temporarily migrated to the Democratic side, won the nomination for delegate again, but in the general election he lost to Samuel Wilder King, a part-Hawaiian who had been selected to succeed Houston. King, like Houston, had been an officer in the Navy; he was popular among the Hawaiians and loyal to the Big Five on all key issues.

In this welter of dissension in Democratic ranks, a new force was emerging in Hawaii, and to some extent in the Democratic Party. This was the International Longshoremen's and Warehousemen's Union (ILWU) led by a shrewd union organizer from San Francisco, Jack Hall, who would dominate labor in Hawaii for the next quarter of a century.

Hall brought with him a new element—the so-called Communist menace, which was beginning to infiltrate not only the labor movement but the political structure of Hawaii. Through the leadership of Hall and several of his lieutenants who were accused of being card-carrying Communist Party members, labor became a target of attack that spread to the Democrats and became one of the principal issues in the future fight for statehood.

Hall was a big, strong-willed man who had been a seaman since he was seventeen. He arrived in Honolulu in 1935 with a reputation as a skilled labor organizer. The ILWU was then firmly under the control of Harry Bridges, who was embroiled in San Francisco's waterfront and shipping disputes, and Hall was a member of the Seamen's Union. He was suspended from that organization when his efforts to bring Hawaiian waterfront labor into the CIO-affiliated ILWU were disclosed, and he began immediately to organize longshoremen, truck drivers, hotel employees, and sugar and pineapple field workers. This effort had just about gotten off the ground when the sudden explosion of World War II in the Pacific, after the bombing of Pearl Harbor, interrupted his efforts.

Hall's methods of sowing the seeds of labor discontent in Hawaii were far more organized and sophisticated than the walkout of Japanese and Filipino plantation strikers in the early 1920s. He also expanded the challenge of labor into the political field. The blooming of these seeds into flowers—good or evil, depending on the viewpoint—marked the beginning of the decline of the Big Five. If they could not control labor, they could not control industry. The plucking of the flowers, at least politically, was accomplished, however, by a newcomer to politics, a man who at the time Hall arrived in Honolulu was a detective in the Honolulu police force. This was Jack Burns, who began to gather a group of political dissidents shortly after the war ended: Dan Inouye and the returning war veterans; independent *haoles* who were disgusted with futile bickerings within the Democratic Party; the discouraged "second-class citizens," including part-Hawaiians and Portuguese who were tired of being ignored by both Democrats and Republicans.

This was the group that ultimately displaced the oligarchy, led by Jack Burns, a spare, austere man they called "Old Stone Face." He came literally out of nowhere immediately after the war, drew around him a collection of alienated personalities who frequently could not get along with each other, and challenged the fifty-year rule of the Big Five.

The underlying element in all this, however, that provided the power of Hawaii's second revolution was not the revived Democratic Party or the leadership of Jack Burns, or even the political muscle of organized labor supplied by Hall and the ILWU. It was something more subtle and less easily defined, and far less spectacular than Hall or Burns. It was the public school system that the Big Five tried to disinherit; and it provided in its accomplishment a fascinating example of how nonviolent revolution can be achieved within the structure of a democratic society.

The year 1924 was significant to Hawaii, although its importance was not apparent at the time. It happened to be the year
Daniel Inouye was born, but that was a coincidence. It was also
the year McKinley High School moved from the old gray stone
building at the south end of Thomas Square to new and more
modern quarters on King Street; and it was also the year the first
English Standard School was launched, a new departure in the
educational system in the Territory. In both of these latter respects 1924 was a turning point in the history of Hawaii. That
year saw the start of a process that produced men such as Dan
Inouye, and in the end this process brought about the overturning of the Big Five.

It has been noted that the public school system in Hawaii
was the force that in reality undermined the rule of the Big
Five-sugar-planter complex and, as Dr. Fuchs predicted, "would
one day destroy Hawaii's oligarchy." In his study, *Hawaii Pono*,
he wrote, "The teachers of the 1920s and 1930s were the god-
parents of modern Hawaii."[16]

The shifting of McKinley High School to a new and better
location might have been regarded as a minor item of educational progress, but in point of fact it split off the Oriental
children socially, culturally, and racially from most of the *haoles*.
It accomplished this by the simple process of requiring written
and oral tests that would relate the various schools to the ability
of students to speak English. This system provided separate
educational facilities for Orientals who spoke "pidgin English"
and for those who came from English-speaking families but
could not afford to go to private schools.

To understand what was happening, and how it produced
the Dan Inouyes who a quarter of a century later joined Burns

8

"Tokyo High"

as creators of the new Hawaii, it is necessary to describe the English Standard School system, and its contribution to school segregation. When McKinley High was moved from its old building on Thomas Square, which it had occupied since 1910 when it replaced the original Honolulu High School, the first public secondary school in the Republic of Hawaii, its old building was taken over by Lincoln School, the first of the new English Standard Schools.

The purpose of the English Standard School system was to enable those students who could pass certain written and oral tests in English to attend schools where the linguistic habits of a foreign language spoken in their homes—or the more familiar "pidgin" spoken on the streets of Honolulu—would not be an impediment. Many *haoles* complained that their children came out of public schools talking more like Orientals than when they entered. Oren Long, who later became Governor of Hawaii and was then Deputy Superintendent of the Department of Education in Honolulu, believed the new system would help stimulate better use of English. Others, like Dr. A. L. Dean, president of the University of Hawaii, took the position that the new system was not even democratic.

Whatever it was, the influence of this system created what Dan Inouye later described as "subtle segregation." When he entered McKinley High School at the age of fourteen, all Hawaii's high schools theoretically were open to all students who lived in the Territory. But by the ingenious device of having oral as well as written tests, those who spoke English at home gravitated toward the English Standard School while those who had difficulty with phonetics wound up in McKinley High and other "nonstandard" schools.

The written tests were routine, but the oral tests were more complicated for Orientals. Such letters as "r" and "l" and the diphthong "th" are notoriously difficult for Chinese and Japanese to pronounce, whereas they presented no problem to those reared in English-speaking homes. Even part-Hawaiians like Bill Richardson who later became a leader in Jack Burns's crusade for a new Hawaii found it troublesome to convert the pidgin he spoke in the slums of Palama, where he grew up, into standard

English. He later told Burns his brother and sister had been
denied admission to Roosevelt High, an English Standard
School, even though their grandfather had been an aide to King
Kalakaua and their father was one of Queen Liliuokalani's supporters in the Revolution of 1893.

The result was a new duality in the public school system,
created along racial and social lines. That may not have been
the purpose of those who devised the system, but that was
what happened. For instance, the McKinley High School
football team in 1922, which won the Interscholastic League
championship that year, included a part-Hawaiian, Jimmy
Whittle, at one end, and a Japanese, Saichi Matsumoto, at
the other end. One tackle was "Duke" Thompson, a Hawaiian, and the other was "Ike" Ikuta, a Japanese. One guard
was Chinese—Fook Hing (Bear) Tong, and the center and
the other guard were *haoles*. The quarterback was a *haole*,
"Yabo" Taylor, and so was one halfback, Frank Dunn. The
other halfback was Bill (Dog) Wise, the son of Senator John
Wise, the part-Hawaiian candidate on the Republican ticket
who lost to Billy Jarrett in the race for delegateship that
year. The fullback was Henry Chang, a Chinese.

This was a mixture that should have satisfied the most
exacting standards of a racial melting pot. Yet ten years later,
after the English Standard School system had been in effect
for nearly a decade, there was not one *haole* on the McKinley
team. This probably did not have much significance to the
kamaaina haoles, whose sons and daughters went to Punahou,
yet it forecast a future trend.

The "radical" ideas, such as the teaching of American
history and emphasis on social and civic studies, which Henry
Townsend had introduced during the days of the Republic
when he founded the school system in Hawaii, had taken
root in the public schools. The educational philosophy of
John Dewey and Francis Parker, who had come from Columbia and the University of Chicago at Townsend's invitation to help establish a public school system in Hawaii
devoted to democratic ideals, was growing—not at Punahou,
or even at Roosevelt High and Lincoln School; but at McKin-

ley High School, which became known as "Tokyo High" in the 1930s.

Much of this was due to the persistent efforts of Miles E. Cary who came to Hawaii as an instructor in history in the early 1920s and remained as principal of McKinley High for a quarter of a century. He established what he called a core curriculum devoted primarily to studies in English and the social sciences, with less emphasis on chemistry, physics, and agricultural technology. He encouraged students to take part in democratic processes of school administration—programs which were described as radical ideas by members of the oligarchy but proved to be basic training for the second revolution in Hawaii.

Although many members of the *haole* elite continued to regard McKinley High School as "Tokyo High," and some of them hinted that it was probably a training ground for future Japanese spies who one day would explode the "time bomb" of Hawaii, an educator from the Frick Foundation, making a study of American educational systems, visited Hawaii in 1931 and reported that "outside the United States, the best institution surveyed educationally was McKinley High School in Honolulu."

The outcome of this *de facto* segregation in public schools was, in a way, a measure of the obtuseness of members of the oligarchy who had rejected Miles Cary's educational theories as too radical and wanted the public schools to devote more time to training students in agricultural pursuits. The result was that the children of Hawaii's second-class citizens—that is, those who were not of the *haole* elite—who one day would make up the great body of the electorate went to McKinley High School and other non-standard schools and studied under Miles Cary's core curriculum in which English literature and American social and economic institutions were stressed. Two decades later these same students would become a dynamic force, sweeping the old political and economic structure out of existence and bringing in statehood.

Members of the oligarchy were not merely lured into this trap; they actually walked into it as a result of their singular obsession with the belief that they were somehow ordained to be the ruling class in Hawaii, just as their missionary forebears assumed they were assigned by divine authority to bring Christian enlightenment to the Sandwich Islands.

The duality of school systems between missionary schools and private schools that had developed during the monarchy was now transferred to the public school system, and it had a somewhat reverse effect. The social consciousness that Miles Cary instilled in the students at McKinley High was not really needed in the private schools or even in English Standard Schools, where the future rulers of Hawaii and their subalterns were being educated. There was no point teaching democratic principles to young people who would not have to use them. They might even become a nuisance. But public school teachers from the Mainland, on the other hand, were inspired by the enthusiasm traditional American ideals aroused in the Oriental mind, to whom these concepts were new and exciting. The teachers were not particularly concerned with the distinctions that the *kamaaina haoles* drew between those who would be recipients of Hawaii's brand of democracy and those who were destined to rule the Islands. Thus, by a process of dividing the schools into one set for the children of *haoles* and another for Orientals and less-advantaged Hawaiians and Portuguese, the *haole* children were left out of an educational process that might have fitted them to cope with the problems of the future—one of which was the survival of the economic and cultural system on which they had been nurtured.

As Dr. Fuchs described it in his study of Hawaii's social and ethnic problems,

> Because Hawaii's public school students were predominantly dark-skinned and slant-eyed, the teachers concentrated more than usual on American history and government, free-enterprise, and the meaning of democracy. Hawaii's elementary and high school curricula were loaded with patriotism. The Gettysburg address, with its emphasis on government by the people, was popular during the 1920s . . . little *nisei* boys seriously recalled "our Pilgrim forefathers." . . . A teacher on Kauai, who did not dare say he believed labor unions would be good for Hawaii, enthusiastically and openly taught the Declaration of Indepen-

dence and the Bill of Rights. . . . America was individualistic, competitive, full of opportunity and reward. It was, in short, everything that their homes and Hawaii were not.[17]

Little of this educational philosophy appealed to the members of the oligarchy, but they were too busy consolidating their power and meeting other more realistic problems to do much about it at first. The significance of what was happening finally dawned upon them at the beginning of the 1930s. A belated effort was made in 1928 in the Legislature to reduce the number of students who could be retained in the public school system after they had passed the tenth grade by arbitrarily eliminating 20 percent of those eligible for advancement. Oddly enough this highly discriminatory provision stirred the *nisei* to greater effort. By 1935 the increase in enrollment of Japanese at McKinley High was 40 percent over the number enrolled in 1928.

By 1930 the oligarchy had begun to seek ways of redirecting educational opportunities for agricultural workers. Educators were brought in from small colleges to study the situation and devise a program which would produce more sugar technologists and fewer young people educated in American ideals of citizenship. Dr. Charles E. Prosser, head of a technical college in Minnesota, was retained by the Honolulu Chamber of Commerce to make an educational survey of the Territory, the avowed purpose of which was to "discourage theorists . . . and encourage students to prepare themselves for work on the plantations."

The *kamaaina haoles* were not solidly against improvement in education, and many approved of Miles Cary's efforts. Governor Farrington, both in his official capacity as governor and as publisher of the *Honolulu Star-Bulletin*, had urged increasing both junior and senior high schools. But Robert Hind, president of the HSPA, voiced the majority view of the oligarchy when he said the "mistaken idealism" of "visionary highbrows" should be brought to an end and the public school system should perform the function for which it was intended—that is, to create more efficient agricultural workers for Hawaii's plantations.

In 1931 Dr. Prosser's report finally was released, advocating stepping up the training of students for agricultural work and warning against the mistaken assumption that students would improve their economic conditions by going to school. It recommended expansion of vocational training and curtailment of purely academic studies, with limitation of funds for senior high schools and reduction in enrollment in public schools.

The report was roundly applauded by the voice of the Big Five—Lorrin Thurston's *Advertiser*—and was received with more tempered enthusiasm by the Farrington-controlled *Star-Bulletin*; but it was bitterly censured by the teaching profession and by such gadfly media as the *Hawaii Hochi*. George Wright in an editorial said the report set up "two educational systems—one for dark-skinned peasants and one for fair-skinned aristocrats." Benjamin Wist, head of the old territorial Normal School wrote in the *Hawaii Educational Review* that "schoolteachers [of Hawaii] definitely oppose sacrificing the objectives of good American citizenship to . . . questionable [educational] practice."

Although the Legislature, not quite the rubber-stamp body it was in the heyday of the oligarchy, continued to appropriate funds for schools in spite of Dr. Prosser's advice against this, a major part of the money went to the English Standard Schools. Senator Inouye, whose wife attended Roosevelt High, was able to testify to the difference: "They had the equipment and about all we had was the desire to use it." However, the students at the non-standard schools were more interested in learning about democracy than in laboratories and modernized buildings.

The winds of public opinion, blown up by the Massie Case, became whirlwinds after the release of the Prosser Report. The latter aroused a storm of indignation even among some of the local *haoles*, and gave birth to a new generation of independents who became the core of the political insurrection of the 1950s.

Many of the upper-middle-class *haoles* continued to send their sons and daughters to private schools, and the number of sectarian schools expanded, leaving McKinley High and other non-standard schools on the outer Islands to "second-class citizens," chiefly Orientals. Some of the wealthier Chinese even switched to private schools to avoid the "Oriental influence" of too many Japanese at McKinley High.

The result of all this was that by the end of the 1930s the line between English Standard and non-standard schools had been drawn; and although the Big Five did not realize it, the "battle of McKinley High" had been won. The victory was not along racial lines, although Japanese, Portuguese, and Hawaiians profited most—but along educational and political lines. The Oriental students, for example, were getting more Americanism than the *haole* elite and far more than many minority groups on the Mainland. They were getting ready to put their convictions to the test in the polling places.

In the case of Daniel Ken Inouye, his knowledge of democracy was acquired in a normal progression of the public school process. He had come straight out of the melting pot without really knowing it existed. When he turned fifteen and became a sophomore, he was recommended for the McKinley High School Citizenship Club. The future Senator from Hawaii showed up wearing an *aloha* shirt and blue denim pants—barefoot! One of the members of the Student Council which was to pass on his qualifications asked,

"Why don't you wear shoes?"

"I have only one pair," he said. "They have to last."

He also had only one white shirt, which he wore to church on Sundays, so he had worn the colored sport shirt. They asked who his friends were, and he told them.

"Delinquents!" one of the Council members snapped.

Young Inouye knew by this time that he was not going to be accepted. He yelled back, "Why? Because they don't wear shoes? Because they're poor? I thought this was an honor society—but if you're looking for guys that wear shoes and white shirts, you don't want me, and I for sure don't want you!"

He walked out. As he said years later, "It wasn't race prejudice. That had nothing to do with it, because most of them were as Japanese as I was. It was a kind of reverse bigotry. It was not my Japanese ancestry that the panel attacked, but my refusal to hide it."

Two years later, as a senior, he went through a somewhat similar but more edifying experience. He was nominated to be chairman of the homeroom student body organization. He had grown up on the streets and sandlots of Honolulu where most elective offices were decided with a baseball bat, and his *nisei* schoolmates with the white shirts and shoes decided to put him through a parliamentary wringer. He was peppered with motions, motions to table, requests for rulings, and so on.

"Somehow I stumbled through the meeting," he said later. As he left the room, dazed and angry with himself for having been lured into the trap, his homeroom instructor tapped him on the shoulder and handed him a copy of *Roberts Rules of Order*.

It was the first time he realized that there was such a book. He sat up most of the night reading it and by the next meeting he could quote most of it verbatim. He opened the meeting with a suggestion that the senior class hold a Red Cross drive. One of his white-shirted constituents asked him to put it in the form of a motion. Inouye glared at him. The chairman, he explained icily, was not permitted under parliamentary rules to make a motion. There was a good deal of skirmishing, but the young chairman quoted *Roberts Rules of Order* by rule and rote until the white-shirted opposition finally gave up. It was his first political triumph.

Inouye's first real lesson in politics, however, came in a rather odd way from Miles Cary, the principal. He had been inspired by some minor achievements to write an essay on "How It Feels to be a *Nisei*," based on his experiences the day Japanese warplanes attacked Pearl Harbor. He had been a member of the volunteer Red Cross and had spent the day of the bombing in charge of a litter squad carrying wounded civilians to first-aid stations set up at strategic points around the city. It was only later that the growing hostility against everyone with Japanese features struck him forcibly and stirred the anger and resentment that would later drive him into the political field.

The essay had won a prize, and when the annual presentation of awards was made, Inouye appeared as usual in dungarees and a sport shirt. "I had intended to come barefoot," he said later, "but at the last moment I decided I would make at least that one concession to the proprieties."

After the ceremonies, during which he accepted his prize

among an assemblage of white-shirted students, chiefly *nisei,*
wearing pressed coats and pants to match, and neatly tied neck-
ties, he stood in the hallway holding his medal. He felt a hand
on his shoulder and looked up at Miles Cary.

"Do you have a minute, Dan?"

The boy nodded and said, "Yes, sir."

"You own a suit, don't you?"

"Yes, sir."

"Why didn't you wear it?"

He looked at his blue denim pants. "This is what I wear
every day."

"But this isn't every day, Dan."

Cary, a middle-sized, calm man with a broad forehead
and deep-set, inquiring eyes, looked at the young *nisei* just
about to be graduated from the educational system that Cary,
in a great measure, had created. Twenty years before Daniel
Inouye had become a senior at McKinley High, Cary had
been a history instructor at the old McKinley High on
Thomas Square. He was a teacher with a profound impact on
his students; he gave history personality and depth, even in
the high-school courses. His determined and persistent demand that the schools of Hawaii be devoted to inculcating an
understanding of America's background and growth through
the efforts of those whose forefathers had come from lands
where democratic processes were nonexistent, was in a large
measure responsible for the emergence of the Dan Inouyes
of Hawaii.

He finally led the rebellious young *nisei* student away
from the crowd.

> I can certainly understand how you'd feel angry and maybe a little
> bit vindictive toward some of the kids who've put you through the
> wringer here. But don't carry it too far, Dan. In a few years, by
> the time this war is over, your people will have as much oppor-
> tunity as any white man in these Islands, in the army, in business,
> in politics. It's bound to happen, it's already been too long hap-
> pening. And all I want to tell you is that I'd like it if you were ready
> for these opportunities. . . . Don't spoil things for yourself by
> being a hardhead. Do you understand?[18]

Daniel Inouye's recollection of this was put into words some years later, after World War II and after he knew that what Cary predicted would happen *had happened.* His remarks may have been colored to some extent by this knowledge. Nevertheless, the prediction was borne out. The changes that were in the making when Cary spoke to him that day had taken place. There appears little doubt in retrospect that the educational process Cary had put into practice at McKinley High School, and which had an effect upon the entire public school system of the Islands, became the most important single influence on the emergence two decades later of an electorate devoted to building a new Hawaii by nonviolent means.

In the case of Inouye it imbedded in his mind one of the essential characteristics of political leadership. This is revealed in an interesting anecdote reported in *Hawaii Pono* by Dr. Fuchs:

> The heavy-set *nisei* stirred in his hospital bed as he thought of the past. He recalled his father's thwarted ambitions for an education and respectability, and specific episodes, such as the brutality of the police in the 1924 strike at Hanapepe, and he wondered what it all meant. Sakae Takahashi turned on his side and looked into the face of the one-armed war hero in the next bed, Daniel K. Inouye. Takahashi wanted to share with his friend from Hawaii his thoughts of his ambitions for himself and other *nisei* from the Islands.
>
> The two men—Takahashi, a wounded veteran of the 100th Battalion, and Inouye, of the 442nd Regiment, whose body was still filled with lead—talked until they were exhausted. . . . The war veterans should study hard, enter politics, and right the wrongs that had been done the Japanese community of Hawaii. Inouye, who one day would become the first United States Representative from the State of Hawaii, agreed to Takahashi's argument, but without passion. . . . There would, he predicted, be a new Hawaii after the war, a democratic Hawaii, and he was determined to help bring it about.[19]

The phrase "without passion" is of considerable significance. It draws attention to one of the important differences— perhaps the most important—between the second revolution in

Hawaii and similar revolutionary movements on the Mainland United States. The emergence of the new Hawaii was accomplished under the leadership of thoughtful men, like Jack Burns and Dan Inouye and many others, with a minimum of loose rhetoric and an absence of violence. In this respect, Miles Cary's insistence on public schools as the way to progress proved more fundamental in the long run than Mayor Johnny Wilson's advice to Bill Richardson that "politics is the way."

Part III / 1941-1955

Revolt in Paradise

There is an old Hawaiian proverb, *"Aole make ka waa i ka ale owoho, aia no i ka ale oloko o ka waa,"* which means, "A canoe is not swamped by the outside wave, but by the inside wave." This refers to a rush of water that often billows beneath the surface of an outrigger canoe when it is riding below the crest of a giant comber off Waikiki, and with an unexpected nudge may twist the canoe sideways so that it will broach on the wave and be swamped. The expression was often used in a political sense, however; troubles in a society do not usually arise from an attack from outsiders, but from those within the society itself.

In the case of Hawaii—and more particularly in the case of Daniel Inouye—the nudge was World War II. To the *kamaaina haoles* it seemed almost providential. They had been riding the crest of an uneven wave for a decade, and their canoe was leaking badly when, on the morning of December 7, 1941, Japanese warplanes swept across the Koolau range and dived down upon the American fleet at Pearl Harbor, bombing it almost out of existence. Within twenty-four hours the Territory was under military rule and all the annoying problems of democracy that had been rearing their ugly heads were swept away for the time being. Lieutenant General Walter C. Short, commandant of the Hawaiian Department, U. S. Army, relieved the oligarchy of the responsibility for running the Territory by taking over that chore himself. He "assumed the position of Military Governor of Hawaii"—an act that was later declared unconstitutional by the Supreme Court—and took charge of the government. Governor Poindexter, who had been appointed by President Roosevelt during the squabble between Mayor Johnny Wilson and Delegate Link McCandless in the mid-1930s, immediately declared martial law, which was constitutional.

9

The Inside Wave

For the next three years—until October 24, 1944—the Territory remained under military rule. For the first few weeks this was to be expected; but even after the crisis had passed it continued. The press was censored and virtually licensed. All Japanese-language newspapers were closed down except the *Nippu Jiji* and the *Hawaii Hochi*, which were permitted to publish under strict supervision by the Army's G-2 Section at Fort Shafter. Both were required to change their names, the *Hochi* becoming the *Hawaii Herald* and the *Nippu Jiji* the *Hawaii Times*. The pay of all workers—including plantation laborers—was frozen, legal holidays were suspended, and no overtime pay was allowed. Absenteeism became a crime, punishable by a jail sentence.

All these orders were quite satisfactory to the members of the oligarchy. In fact, three weeks after General Short "assumed" the position of Military Governor, the Honolulu Chamber of Commerce sent a telegram to President Roosevelt protesting efforts of some civilian groups to end military government and allow Governor Poindexter to resume legal control of civil affairs. Benjamin Thoron, Director of Territorial Affairs in the Interior Department in Washington, remarked to Garner Anthony, a Honolulu attorney, that he was "somewhat disturbed by the telegram . . . which gave the impression that a large group of American businessmen had so far departed from normal American thinking as to prefer military control of all activities of civilian life [to] the normal processes of American Government."

One of the reasons the Big Five supported military rule was that their representatives were quite comfortably ensconced in nooks within the inner councils of the military establishment. Lorrin P. Thurston, son of the former owner of *Advertiser* who helped foment the Revolution of 1893, became "public relations advisor" to General Short; and Walter Dillingham, the powerful industrialist, was assigned as head of "production control"—in charge of wage freezing, food rationing, and so on. Dillingham was quoted by Anthony, who made quite a study of military government in Hawaii, as having referred to protests against the arbitrary rule of the Army as "hooey" that "nobody cares a damn about."

The principal target of military control and censorship was, of course, the Japanese community, without much regard as to whether they were *issei* (noncitizens) or *nisei* (citizens). There were rumors of Japanese spies throughout the Territory and anyone with an Oriental cast to his countenance was automatically suspect. Many *haoles,* particularly those living in expensive homes in Manoa Valley and on Pacific Heights and Tantalus or along Diamond Head who employed Japanese domestics, asked for protection against suspected servants. Although there was not a single verified report of sabotage in Hawaii by Japanese during the War, the feeling prevailed that many Japanese were agents of Japan planted in Hawaii to report military movements and disrupt civil life. Undoubtedly there were a number of Japanese espionage agents in Hawaii, most of whom were probably known to American counterespionage agencies; but the widespread reports that the Islands were honeycombed with spies and that the *nisei* were potential traitors have been proved to be utterly without foundation.

The real value of military rule, so far as members of the oligarchy were concerned, was that their own weakened authority was now replaced by the discipline of martial law, relieving them of that burden; and this, as events proved, was also their Trojan horse. The Big Five would have done well to have studied Machiavelli, who wrote many centuries before that "when princes have thought more of their ease than of arms, they have lost their estates." Military government was a simple solution for their immediate problems, but in the long run it was their undoing.

Dan Inouye awakened early, as he usually did on Sunday, to prepare for church on the morning of December 7. He had automatically turned on the radio on a shelf over his bed when he suddenly realized that a rather frenzied voice was coming over the ether waves. "This is no test! This is the real McCoy! Pearl Harbor is being bombed by the Japanese! I repeat: this is not a test or a maneuver! Japanese war planes are attacking Oahu!"

Inouye stood frozen by the words. He looked around and

his father was standing in the doorway, listening to the radio. His expression also was frozen with—as Inouye described it—"that special horror instantly sensed by Americans of Japanese descent." Although Hyotaro Inouye was born in Japan, he had come to regard himself as American.

The voice of the announcer—Webley Edwards of Station KGU—went on with increasingly shrill intensity. "This is the real thing! Pearl Harbor has been hit and we now have to report that Hickam Field and Schofield Barracks have been bombed, too. . . . We can see the Japanese planes. . . ."

Inouye and his father went outside. He was then seventeen and in his senior year at McKinley High School. He was also a member of the volunteer Red Cross. He realized instantly that there was work to be done. On the streets above McCully tract there were puffs of smoke spurting from shell holes where antiaircraft fire from Fort Ruger, only a couple of miles away, had fallen on the city. He could see the planes with red dots on their wings soaring upward into the blue, sunny sky. To the north above Pearl Harbor there were clouds of black smoke, with planes zooming out of the clouds and soaring off to the east over the sharp, bony ridges of the Koolau mountains which lay behind the city.

He hurried back into the house and heard the phone ringing. It was from the Red Cross first-aid station at Lunalilo school, where he was an instructor.

"How soon can you get here, Dan?" the caller asked.

"I'm on my way," he said. He rode his bicycle to the school-house and for the next twenty-four hours he worked almost without sleep, guiding hurt and scared people to the aid station, dragging maimed men, women, and children from their burning homes. It seemed impossible that so much damage had been done in so short a time. Much of it had been caused by antiaircraft shells fired at the planes without time fuses so that they exploded when they hit the ground. Craters were blasted in the streets and small frame houses blown apart. Further up on Wilhelmina Rise jets of smoke spurted up; and once young Inouye looked up at the sky and yelled, "You dirty Japs!"

The first day was a nightmare, but it absorbed his thoughts

and he had little time to realize the horror that was growing within him. He performed functions he had been trained to do: going into torn buildings to look for people; carrying those who could not walk to first-aid stations; helping doctors who were treating their wounds. Once, as he watched, he saw a small house explode from a stray shell, and "the tokens of a lifetime —dishes, clothing, a child's bed—strewn pathetically on the street."

Lunalilo School, where Dan Inouye had passed through the first six grades of grammar school, was itself struck by an errant antiaircraft shell, and the equipment and supplies of the first-aid station had to be carried out to the street. A nearby building caught fire and the tenants staggered out, faces and clothes smeared with blood. The rescuers tried to reach others trapped inside, but flames drove them back and as he wrote later, "There was nothing anyone could do about it. . . . By the time the firemen brought the flames under control there was nothing left alive in that burned-out hulk."

During the first day he worked in a daze, carrying dead bodies in corrugated boxes to an impromptu morgue, guiding old men and women and those who had lost track of their families to places where they were likely to find them. It was only after the initial excitement had passed that young Inouye began to realize the change that had been wrought in his own life. He was no longer a free young *nisei*—an American—in a free country. He would be called "a dirty Jap" just as he had yelled these words to the vanishing warplanes of Japan. His father had sensed this instantly, with experience born of years on the plantation on Kauai, and later in Honolulu; but the son had never actually experienced a feeling of being "outside" his community. At McKinley High he was one Japanese among many; but from this day forth there would be a new distinction. His Oriental face would mark him. He would be "a Jap."

Later he wrote,

> Remembering those traumatic days, the great turning point of my life, I can see how my need to become totally involved in the war effort sprang from that invidious sense of guilt, the invisible cross

lashed to the back of every *nisei* at the instant when the first plane bearing that rising sun appeared in the sky over Pearl Harbor.[20]

In actual fact, as he was able to realize years later, no rational man would have applied this stigma; and no factual evidence ever sustained the blame and the hatred that was heaped upon the *nisei* in Hawaii. But all men are not rational, and it was there. It required a generation to efface it.

The logic of the segregation of *nisei* in concentration camps could never really be understood by Americans of Japanese blood; and in point of fact, it was not advocated by most of the *haole* community in Hawaii. Except for extremists or alarmists, most responsible members of the *haole* elite defended the rights of *nisei* as citizens. Harold Rice, a nephew of Harry Baldwin of Maui and chairman of the Farm Security Board in Hawaii, was reported to have complained to Judge Ingram Stainback, legal counselor to General Short, that he had been refused permission by the Department of Agriculture to make farm loans to *nisei* who were citizens and were entitled to them.

The noisy clamor of the more hysterical segments of the *haole* community drowned out these saner voices, however, and for three years—until military rule ended—Japanese in Hawaii lived in constant fear of repression and relocation or deportation to the Mainland. John Balch, an officer of the Hawaii Telephone Company and a member of the *haole* elite, produced a pamphlet, privately circulated, entitled, "Shall the Japanese Be Allowed to Dominate Hawaii?" It suggested that 100,000 Japanese in Hawaii, including aliens and citizens alike, be sent to "farm states" on the Mainland since this would "secure" Hawaii against *"political* and *economic* domination of Hawaii within the next decade" (my italics)—a proposal that had little to do with military security, and actually would have decimated the plantation labor force.

The fact that only 1,500 Japanese were interned in Hawaii during the war as contrasted with more than 100,000 similarly interned in California was evidence that the system of "security" against political and economic power that might be achieved by the Japanese was far less stringent in the Islands than on the

Mainland. Nevertheless, the internment of that number—only about a third of whom were *nisei*—would be difficult to justify under any democratic code of justice, since there were no legal proceedings involved and one of every three was an American citizen.

Dan Inouye later summed it up in these words: "I think most Americans now agree that this was a dreary chapter in our history. But I believe it to be equally important that they understand that greed, as much as war hysteria, made possible this momentary triumph of the vigilante mentality."

The underlying spirit of resignation and acceptance that marked the conduct of the *nisei* in Hawaii during the war years was due to that inherent sense of *on*, or traditional respect the Japanese had for the land which was now their home. Loyalty to America was an obligation, a matter of honor. It was more than what is loosely described in Western psychology as "saving face." The sneak attack of Japanese warplanes on Pearl Harbor was in a sense the personal shame of each Japanese *nisei*, and even of the *issei* who had come to regard Hawaii as their home. They felt the need to atone for it personally. To the younger generation this feeling was coupled with a burning desire to prove that they were "Americans." They accepted any sort of work in the war effort, no matter how degrading. This included ditch-digging, stringing barbed wire on the beaches, even collecting garbage. It also generated internal dissension in Japanese families; the older Japanese, clinging to traditional custom, continued to believe the Emperor must be right, while the younger generation insisted on throwing out of their houses all relics or tokens of their ancient culture. In some cases Japanese funeral rites were abandoned as anti-American. More than a score of language schools were closed. Buddhist temples were shut down and religious groups dissolved.

Many of the Japanese *nisei* who had become involved in politics quietly withdrew. George Watase, who had served on the Kauai Board of Supervisors for nearly a decade, refused to run as a candidate for reelection. The case of Wilfred Tsukiyama, who resigned from the Honolulu Draft Board, has already been noted. As one Japanese politician observed, "A

108: REVOLT IN PARADISE

kettle that is already boiling should not boil over."

The most intensive reaction, however, was among the younger *nisei,* who sought to join the armed forces. At first every Japanese name was removed from National Guard enrollment and lists of eligible draftees. This was relaxed, however, by the War Department in June of 1942, when the 100th Battalion was activated, composed of *nisei* Guardsmen and draftees. In September of 1943, more than a year later, the 100th landed on the coast of North Africa in the first phase of the invasion of Italy and later joined the 442nd Regiment in a dozen bitter engagements of the Italian campaign.

Early in 1943 President Roosevelt authorized acceptance of 4,000 *nisei* volunteers, partly from Hawaii, to form the 442nd Regimental Combat Team, consisting of the 442nd Infantry Regiment, the 552nd Field Artillery Battalion and the 232nd Combat Engineer Company.

For Dan Inouye and other young *nisei* in Hawaii this was the chance they had been waiting for. He had passed entrance examinations for enrollment in the University of Hawaii as a premedical student; and he had also passed the age of eighteen. The President had said, in authorizing activation of the 442nd RCT: "The proposal of the War Department to organize a combat team of loyal American citizens of Japanese descent has my full approval. No loyal citizen of the United States should be denied the democratic right to exercise the responsibilities of his citizenship, regardless of ancestry. Americanism is a matter of the mind and heart; Americanism is not, and never was, a matter of race or ancestry."

These words struck deeply into the minds and the hopes of the young *nisei.* As Inouye later described it, "It was as though someone had let us out of some dark place." The original activation order authorized only 1,500 *nisei* from Hawaii but this was increased to 2,500 due to the flood of enlistment applications.

Inouye was one of the first to volunteer, and as the list of those accepted was read off, each man whose name was read ran for the truck that was to carry them to Schofield Barracks and into the Army. When the list was completed, The name "Inouye" had not been read.

He looked desperately at the faces of his family, who had gathered to bid him good-bye. Then with his ukulele still slung over his shoulder, dragging his rucksack, he ran for the truck. The *haole* captain who had read off the names listened while Dan explained that they had missed his name. The captain shook his head.

"Sorry, son. If your name wasn't read, it isn't there. . . ."

For days Inouye called at the draft board office. There was no new information. His name simply had not been selected. He returned to his premedical classes at the University utterly disheartened. Then he decided what he was going to do. He went down to the draft board office.

"I'm going to sit here," he told the man at the desk, "until I find out why I was rejected—and if there is any chance that I can get in."

The man riffled through some files and finally found the folder marked, "Inouye, Daniel Ken." There was some discussion in the rear of the office, and finally Inouye was called into an inner office where a man sat at a desk looking at the file.

"We've located your records," he said, "and there seems to be no mystery about the decision." He explained that it was on two grounds: Inouye was a member of the volunteer Red Cross and a premedical student at the University of Hawaii. Both were essential services, currently and potentially. Did that clear it up? Inouye said it did, except for two things.

"If you'll call the aid station and the University in about an hour, they will tell you in both places that I've given my notice to quit by the end of the week."

He went to the Red Cross office and resigned. Then he went to the University and told the Dean of Men he would be leaving the following Friday. Then he went back to his classes to await a call. He was in the zoology class when it came.

"Daniel Ken Inouye?"

It was a woman's voice.

"Yes."

"You're to report at the Nuuanu YMCA at 8 A.M. Saturday for transportation to Schofield Barracks."

"Yes—*ma'am!*"

His father drove him to the Nuuanu "Y" Saturday morning, where he boarded a truck and joined the 442nd RCT at Schofield that day.

His mother, who—as he later described her—"was a very understanding woman" talked with him that morning before he left home. "You will do the right things," she said, looking steadily at him. "I know that the old ways—the ways of your father and me—will not be so important to you. You may marry. . . ." She hesitated, and then said, "It would make me happy if you married from among our own people, a Japanese girl. Still, this may not happen, and that is not so important today to younger people. So I will tell you again how kind the Hawaiian people were to me when I was young and needed help."

Recalling his mother's words, Senator Inouye, sitting in his office in the Old Senate Office Building in Washington many years later, smiled reminiscently. The office was numbered—not uncoincidentally—Room 442. "Few people really understand the Hawaiians as a people," he said. "My mother was an orphan, and as a little girl she was taken in by a Hawaiian family on Maui. She was a Japanese girl, but to the Hawaiians there is no such thing as racial distinction. There is not even a word for 'race' in the Hawaiian language. A Hawaiian is a *kanaka* and all others are *haoles.* It is only by usage that the word *haole* has been applied to the white man. To the Hawaiians it simply meant 'stranger.'

"The Hawaiians are an unusual people. They actually bear no malice, which may explain their inability to cope with the 'strangers' who came to instruct them in Christian ethics. My mother lived as one of them—the *keiki o ka aina* as the children are called. Although she was slant-eyed, like all Japanese, they saw no difference betweeen her and the other children. That is why I understood so well why she wanted me to marry a Hawaiian girl, if I could not find it in my heart to marry a Japanese girl."

This nonracial attitude of the Hawaiians is essential to an understanding of the role they played in the events that followed the seizure of their Islands by the *haoles,* dethroning Queen Liliuokalani and gradually gaining control of the mid-Pacific tropical paradise. They were, as Senator Inouye described them, a people "without malice" although they were not without resentment, a trait of character that undoubtedly developed more positively after their exposure to the forms of Christian charity dealt out by the descendants of the missionaries.

Young Inouye not only had a deep understanding of the Hawaiian people as a result of his mother's experiences as a young girl raised by a Hawaiian family, but he had grown up in the streets of Honolulu, apart from the *haole* elite who inhabited Manoa Valley and Pacific Heights. He had played barefoot football and baseball with boys of many ethnic origins and the word "racial" was actually meaningless to him except as it applied to the *haoles* until the outbreak of World War II.

After his mother talked with him, his father—last of the Inouye name who had been born in Japan—also spoke to him as they drove downtown.

"You will be far from home in strange places, and among people much different from those you have known here," he said. "Men's weaknesses sometimes get the best of them. Only remember, do not get into water too deep for you to get out. Do you know what *on* means in Japanese?"

Daniel Inouye nodded. It was the sense of honor which, as he explained in his book, "requires that when one is aided by another he acquires a debt that is never cancelled, and must be repaid without reservation."

His father continued, "The Inouye family has a great *on* for America. America has been good to us. And now—and I would never have chosen it this way—you must try to return the goodness of this country. You are my first son and very precious to your mother and me, but you must do what must be done." As the Army truck pulled up to load the recruits, and young Inouye prepared to climb aboard, his father said in a low voice, "Do not bring dishonor upon our name."

A week later he was in San Francisco and by mid-April he was in the throes of training at Camp Shelby. It was during the period of training that the 442nd became a cohesive fighting force and adopted the slogan for which they later became famous—"Go for broke!"—an expression that in the Islands was equivalent to "Shoot the works!" A year later the Regiment

landed in Italy and began the long march up the Italian penin-
sula. The 442nd, together with the 100th Battalion which later
joined it, became the most highly decorated organization in the
United States Army, with ten unit citations, nearly 4,000 individual decorations including forty-seven Distinguished Service
medals, a Congressional Medal of Honor and enough Purple
Hearts to clothe a Roman emperor. Both the Regiment and the
100th Battalion furnished more than half of Hawaii's contribution to American fighting forces and more than four-fifths of the
battle casualties of men from Hawaii.

After battling northward along the Italian coast the 442nd
was detailed to rescue a "lost battalion" from the 141st Infantry
Regiment, a Texas unit which was completely surrounded by
Germans in southern France. They hacked their way in and
brought the men out.

Less than two weeks before the war in Europe ended, Daniel Inouye—now a First Lieutenant—was assigned to lead his
platoon in an attack on a high ridge of Mount Nibbione to cut
off retreat of the enemy into the Po Valley. The ridge was heavily
defended by the Germans. He had borrowed a camouflaged
field jacket from the First Sergeant, Dan Aoki, who would later
become one of the leaders of Hawaii's second revolution. On
the way up the slope he was hit in the side with a bullet, but
managed to get close enough to heave a hand grenade into a
German machine gun nest. It was one of three, and seemed to
have been put out of action. The other two were still firing.

He waved to those behind him to attack the others and
staggered up the hill, throwing two more grenades. Behind him
he could hear the cry of the 442nd—"Go for broke"—as they
charged up the mountain. A figure suddenly stood up in the
bunker ahead, waist high, pointing a grenade rifle from a distance of about ten yards. Inouye pulled the pin in his last grenade and drew his arm back to throw, when the man in the
bunker fired. He felt his right arm torn away. The grenade
clenched in his right fist was ticking off seconds and due to
explode.

He turned and yelled to the men behind him: "Get back!"
Then he reached over with his left hand and twisted the grenade

from his right fist, breaking it free from the rigid muscles of an all-but-dismembered right arm. He threw it with his left hand and it exploded in the face of the German who was reloading his grenade gun.

That was about all Inouye remembered clearly, except that one of the men in the bunker ahead must have squeezed a trigger as the grenade exploded, and the bullet hit him in the right leg. He lay on the ground, hardly conscious and making an effort to press down on the pulsing artery in the stump of his right arm, which was almost severed. First Sergeant Aoki had come back down the hill as they ripped off the field jacket and the wounded man managed to mumble that he was sorry about the jacket.

They hauled Inouye back to the field hospital, and that was the end of his combat service. It was April 21, 1945. Two days later the Germans surrendered in North Italy and nine days later the war in Europe ended.

It was spring of 1946 and the war was over. Two men strolled along the wide flat beach that spread out below the boardwalk at Atlantic City. Shops glittered with new styles of bathing suits and beach wear. The Steel Pier, jutting out into the gray Atlantic, was beginning to bustle with the noise of shooting galleries and the other tawdry bric-a-brac as evidences of the eternal carnival-like atmosphere of America's gaudiest resort city.

One was heavy-set and thick-chested; the other was thin almost to the point of looking emaciated. An empty sleeve flapped where his arm should have been. The two, Sakae Takahashi, the schoolteacher from Hanapepe, Kauai, who had become a Captain in the 100th Battalion, and Daniel Inouye, the boy who grew up in the streets of Honolulu and became a First Lieutenant in the 442nd RCT, had met for the first time at a rehabilitation hospital converted from the Traymore, one of the old resort hotels that line the beach at Atlantic City. Both had grown to manhood under similar circumstances; and they were both *nisei* in Hawaii when Japanese warplanes bombed Pearl Harbor.

Sakae turned to his friend and said, "What kind of Americans are we, Dan?"

The smaller man looked at him, and said, "What are you getting at?"

"I mean, what are we, really? I want to know why I don't *feel* as good as all the others. Why were all those *nisei* in California locked up? Most of all I want to know why there has to be a limit to our hopes."

Dan thought this over, and shook his head. "Who says there's a limit?"

"Suppose you wanted to join the Pacific Club. Can you?"

"Go for Broke!"

"Big deal," Dan snorted.

"Suppose you wanted to be Governor of Hawaii?"

Inouye nodded thoughtfully. "We ought to have that right," he said.

"We ought to have every single right that every single other American has," the older man said vehemently. "We shed a lot of blood in the war. What was that all about? Was it all wasted?" He turned to face Dan Inouye. "I'm not looking to put the blame on anyone. I don't even really care about all that stuff that happened. What I'm interested in is tomorrow. I want my kids to have an even break. I demand it!"

In the days that followed Inouye thought seriously about what Sakae had said. There was something inherently different about the status of Americans of Japanese descent in Hawaii, compared with other racial groups. Their houses were small frame buildings, crowded into small spaces in the ghettos. They seemed to accept these conditions. They held low-class jobs or owned small shops. There were a few exceptions, of course, such as doctors, and now and then a lawyer like Wilfred Tsukiyama, or a teacher, as Sakae Takahashi had been before the war. But there were not many.

As Inouye wrote later in his book, *Journey to Washington*:

> What Sakae was saying, and what I came to believe with all my heart and soul, was that the time had come for us to step forward. We had fought for that right with all the furious patriotism in our bodies and now we didn't want to go back to the plantations. Times were changing. The old patterns were breaking down. We wanted to take our full place in society, to make the greatest contribution of which we were capable, not for Japanese-Americans, but for Hawaii.[21]

It was during the last stages of his convalescence that Inouye decided he would study law with the aid of his pension and a GI scholarship, and then enter the political field. The sentiments he had expressed to Sakae Takahashi during their discussion on the beach and in the hospital were not those ordinarily attributed to Japanese-Americans by people who warned of the "yellow peril." They were not based on a desire to dominate Hawaii as John Balch suggested in his pamphlet. They were simply the expression of a new point of view, a change in the traditional attitude of Japanese, a slight modification of the ancient virtues of self-restraint ingrained in Japanese character from time immemorial. Daniel Inouye might not have accepted this view fully at the time, but his own thinking had been revised and the traits of his forefathers were being assessed in terms of a new era and a new world. Politeness and courtesy were not wrong; but they were not the only virtues and they were not the most effective in a place such as Hawaii, undergoing the transition from war to peace. The silent submission of *nisei* to the indignities they had suffered during the war demonstrated this.

When Inouye finally returned to Honolulu the thoughts implanted in his mind by Sakae Takahashi, together with the seeds planted by Miles Cary at McKinley High School, were taking root. They had become the ground of a firm and purposeful determination to help build a new Hawaii in which *nisei* could take part.

During the twenty months spent in rehabilitation centers he made up his mind. He was going to go back home to Hawaii, finish his education as a lawyer—not as a doctor, because he had only one arm—and in the words of the motto of the 442nd, "Go for broke!"

An incident occurred on the way home to Hawaii that burned in Inouye's mind like a branding iron, and perhaps reinforced his decision. He had gone into a barbershop in Oakland, across from San Francisco, and the man at the door asked, "Are you Chinese?"

"I'm an American," Inouye replied. He was in Army uniform.

"Are you Chinese?" the man repeated.

"I think you want to know where my father was born," Inouye said evenly. "My father was born in Japan. I'm an American."

"You're a Jap, and we don't cut Jap hair," the man said.

Inouye stood for a moment looking at him. He wore silver captain's bars on his shoulders, four rows of ribbons on the left side of his chest, a Presidential citation on the right side, a Distinguished Service Cross and the combat infantry badge. He also had an empty right sleeve where his arm should have been. But the barber "didn't cut Jap hair."

Inouye said, "I'm sorry for you, and the likes of you," and walked out.

In 1942, a few months after the War in the Pacific broke out, President Roosevelt at the urging of Harold Ickes, the Interior Secretary, replaced Governor Poindexter of Hawaii with Judge Ingram Stainback, who had been serving as legal advisor to General Short. He had been Attorney General of Hawaii under Governor Lucius Pinkham during the Wilson administration, and later served for twenty years as a Federal Judge in Hawaii. With the Army running the civil government, Stainback's job was of little importance, but his appointment was highly displeasing to the regular old-line Democrats. For the fourth time in four selections of a governor by a Democratic President, the post had been given to a man so closely allied to the Big Five as to be virtually one of them. The most displeased of all was seventy-year-old Johnny Wilson, the Mayor of Honolulu, who still harbored hopes of sitting one day in Iolani Palace. He had also hoped to rebuild the Democratic Party in the Territory so it could take control of the Legislature after the forty-year rule of the Big Five-GOP coalition.

Stainback remained in the Governor's chair for nearly a decade, until President Truman shifted the post to Oren Long, the former director of the public school system. During that time Stainback established a record of appointing more Republicans than Democrats to fill major political positions in the Territory. He named ten Big Five-GOP selections to fill thirteen top jobs in the territorial Government. Neither Pinkham, McCarthy, nor Poindexter—none of them notoriously hostile to the Big Five—could match that accomplishment.

Shortly after the end of the war, with military rule lifted from Hawaii, the most important shift in political power during the next two decades began to take place. It consisted of two basic elements: the rising influence of labor under Jack Hall, the leader of the Longshoremen's Union, and the emergence of an "independent" Democratic faction led by Jack Burns, the former Honolulu police detective who had turned to politics.

Burns began to draw dissident Democrats—among them Daniel Inouye—into the political force that ultimately carried out the second revolution in Hawaii. For the decade after the war Burns fought Hall for control of the Democrats; and mixed with this was another phenomenon that had begun to surface throughout the country—the emergence of the "Communist menace," a threat of conspiratorial peril—real or fancied—that affected both labor and political organizations.

Stainback had become incensed when he discovered that Hall, whom he had appointed to the Honolulu Police Commission in 1945, was listed as a suspected Communist. Hall, incidentally, became quite acceptable to industrial leaders in the Islands in later years, after he had engineered a couple of strikes; and when he died on January 4, 1971, he was eulogized as "the man who brought labor and management together" in Hawaii. But at the time of his exposure as a suspected Communist, he was anathema to the Big Five and *ipso facto* a target of Stainback's wrath. Also, in those years he was less mellow, and more of a fighter: a tough, shrewd organizer who spurned the overtures of the Big Five who sought to beguile him into submission, as they so often had done with their opposition in the economic and political struggles in Hawaii.

When the U. S. Army's secret list of other Democrats presumably tainted with communism—either Party members or sympathizers—was disclosed to Stainback in 1947, he became enraged and launched a veritable *auto-da-fe* to weed out the culprits from Democratic rolls. He asked the party committees to screen their lists of candidates for any who might be suspected of Communist inclinations and he also took aim at the school system, pointing the finger particularly at Professor John Reinecke, then teaching at Farrington High School. He was a scholarly, bespectacled educator whose wife was a Hawaiian-born Japanese. Reinecke was accused of pro-Communist sentiments and had to leave the school system. Some confessed Communist Party members began to come out from behind the woodwork, accusing their former cellmates of Red sympathies or connections as they sought to recant their own views and admit the error of their ways.

The ILWU, under Jack Hall's skillful leadership, used this opportunity to move into the Democratic Party, weakened by charges and countercharges among its members, and confused by Communist infiltration. In spite of the fact that for fifteen years the Democrats had controlled the White House in Washington, they had never gained control of the Legislature in Hawaii and the Governor was in every case more closely allied to the Big Five than to rank-and-file Democrats. Jack Hall took advantage of this discord and attempted to take over the party. At the territorial Democratic convention in May, 1948, the ILWU had the largest single bloc of delegates and elected several of their members—some of them reported to be Communists—to key committee chairmanships. The old guard was badly outnumbered in the voting and lost control of the party machinery, although none of the contests had much to do with the Communist issue. The unexpected development at the convention was the emergence of a new political presence—Jack Burns and his independents. While the old guard was fighting Hall, Burns was maneuvering his own group, and those who were allied with him, into several important committees, and in the final shakedown, Burns had as much power in the convention as Hall and more than the old guard. As Hall later told a *Star-Bulletin* reporter, "We made an error in 1948 when we tied ourselves to the Democrats. Some of our worst enemies have been Democrats."

Burns was the man chiefly responsible for that "error." There were both similarities and differences in these two men who would have such a profound effect on political changes in Hawaii in the years that followed. Hall was burly, given to wearing shabby clothes and driving an old, dilapidated car. Burns was more conservative in appearance, thin and austere. Hall was a man of absolute integrity; when he said something, he meant it. Burns was equally sincere, but more cautious and thoughtful. Hall was ruthless in his objectives, which were to advance the interests of labor unions. Burns was equally tough, but dedicated to people rather than organizations. Both men came from the "lower side of the tracks" but by different routes. Hall was a seaman at seventeen; Burns, born in Montana, was the son of an Army sergeant-major who was transferred to Hawaii and left his family when young Jack Burns was ten. He grew up in Kalihi, a lower-middle-class section of Honolulu near Fort Shafter, with his mother and three brothers. He joined the Honolulu police force in 1934 and became a detective.

It was through his police work that he came to know many of the *nisei* and to understand their problems. They had been virtually driven out of the mainstream of Honolulu's economic and social life by the odium attached to their Japanese ancestry. There was also a report, sufficiently authenticated to mention, that part of Burns's deep interest in the problems of the *nisei* concerned certain incidents following the bombing of Pearl Harbor on the night of December 7, 1941. He had been officer on duty at the Police Station in Honolulu and members of the Volunteer Patrol reported to him. One former member of this volunteer group on windward Oahu recalls orders issued by Burns to round up all Japanese, whether aliens or citizens, and if necessary put them in jail for the night.

Burns's later concern with the injustices that grew out of the first vigilante performances of police and military authorities may have been caused by the recollection of this early episode. He was a man with great sympathy for the underdog and later was regarded as the one person in authority the *nisei* could turn to when flagrant injustices were committed under military rule. He was known to have persuaded Roy Vitousek, Republican leader in the territorial Legislature, to block a bill that would have prohibited anyone of Japanese blood, whether alien or citizen, from holding government office in Hawaii.

Burns knew Vitousek well before the war and was a member of a group led by Vitousek, who was disturbed by the Big-Five domination of the Republicans and sought to form a liberal coalition. Burns refused to join, telling Vitousek, "I've always been a Democrat, and if the political situation in Hawaii can be straightened out, I'm going to do what I can through the Democratic organization."

While his publicly avowed reason for entering the political arena was "to be of service to the community," he later said privately, "If the control of society in Hawaii had been as firmly in the hands of the Democrats as it was on the other side, I think I would have joined the Republicans." He was an ardent Catholic and had attended St. Louis College, a sectarian high school in Honolulu, and worked at odd jobs such as night switchboard operator at the *Star-Bulletin* and as a soda jerk to defray the cost of his schooling.

As a result, Burns learned early in life what it meant to be a *haole,* yet not of the *haole* elite. This undoubtedly colored his interest in the *nisei* and sympathy for the underdog in his later political activities. Andrew Lind, in *Hawaii's Japanese,* quotes Burns as saying of the wartime record of the *nisei,* "Investigation has disclosed no evidence of plans for a concerted group action among persons of Japanese ancestry against the United States," although he admitted receiving reports from younger Japanese of attitudes of the older generation *(issei)* that were "inimical to the United States."

Clarence Ching, one of the newer Chinese tycoons and a strong supporter of Burns, described him as "a political statesman rather than a politician." This coincided to some extent with Burns's own appraisal of his political ambitions. He liked to work for principles rather than electoral success. Both Burns and Hall preferred to play the role of the man behind the scenes rather than front man, but they differed as to methods. Hall was bluff, forthright, a forceful leader of men; Burns was uncommunicative and somewhat cold, a planner and strategist rather than an activist. Together, in spite of their differences in methods and personal characteristics, they were more influential than any other men of their time in forging a new Hawaii.

When Jack Hall died, Burns, then Governor, called him "a fighter for the rights of the common man" and added that Hawaii was "indebted to Jack Hall for the full flowering of democracy in the Islands." As for the democracy, the events will take care of that point; but as "a fighter for the rights of the common man," Burns had the broadest perspective. Hall was primarily a fighter for the rights of labor.

In the last year of the War in the Pacific Burns became chairman of the Democratic County Committee on Oahu, and it was in this capacity in the 1948 Convention at McKinley High School that he first challenged Hall and the old-line Democrats for leadership of the Party. Hall felt the ILWU was a natural power base for the Democrats, but Burns was convinced that democracy came from the political grass roots—from "all the people," not just organized labor. Above all, Burns—far more than Hall—hated power complexes.

In 1960 Hall endorsed Richard Nixon against Jack Kennedy in the presidential election because, he said, "Kennedy will try to dictate to labor." When he was asked whether labor was trying to dictate to Kennedy, he smiled and said, "We have influence." Burns despised that influence.

His collision with Hall and the ILWU in the battle of the 1948 Convention for control of the Democratic Party in Hawaii was on the question of how much influence labor should have. From 1948, when he maneuvered his new independent Democratic faction into control of the Convention, he began to create the political pattern of a new Hawaii. It was done with the help of the ethnic and economic groups that had been second-class citizens in Hawaii. These were primarily the *nisei* and to a lesser extent the Hawaiians and *malihini haoles*—the latter newcomers to the Islands who were for the most part ignored by the *kamaaina haoles*.

As head of the Police Vice Squad during the war, Burns often talked with the outcasts and socially undesirable—prostitutes, thugs, and thieves who began to abound in Honolulu with the influx of defense workers from the Mainland. He became liaison officer between the police and the Morale Group, an unofficial body devoted to maintaining civilian morale during the war. He was both tough and elastic and his independence often created conflicts with his superiors in the Police Department. He was as shrewd as Hall, but more restrained and sometimes aloof to the point of being regarded later as a political dictator. He combined sympathy for the downtrodden and disadvantaged, such as the Japanese community in Hawaii, with a desire to right some of their wrongs—which may explain why he disliked power complexes such as the Big Five. He instinctively turned toward people and away from those who regarded achievement of power in politics as the main goal of political activity.

Burns's frequent sorties into the areas where the outcasts of Honolulu lived—the socially disinherited underdogs—often drew censure from his superiors in the Police Department, who felt it distorted his viewpoint and made him less effective in his work as liaison with the Morale Group. Burns took exactly the opposite view, and this finally led him to leave the police force for the political field.

It also brought him many friends among the *nisei,* particularly returning war veterans who had served in the 442nd RCT and the 100th Battalion, who had come home to find Hawaii much the same as when they left. They had given arms and legs to fight the war and received little in return. Doc Hill's axiom was still accepted by many *haoles:* a "Jap was a Jap, and even after a thousand years he would not be Americanized." It was Burns's recognition of the justice of this resentment that enabled him to understand the *nisei;* and it was in this manner that he came to know Daniel Inouye.

The one-armed hero of the 442nd, now a Captain, returned to Hawaii in 1947, and with financial aid furnished by the "GI Bill of Rights" he reentered the University of Hawaii to complete his studies, this time as a prelegal student instead of premedical.

The words of Sakae Takahashi rang vividly in his mind; he decided to get into politics. So one day he picked up the telephone and called Jack Burns. "I knew him, but not well enough to do that," he said later. Burns was a candidate for delegate more or less by accident. Judge Heen was expected to run, but he did not want to risk his political prestige against the Republican incumbent, Joe Farrington, who was trying for his fifth term. As an eleventh-hour choice, Burns had filed his papers.

As Burns said later, no one with any political sense would expect to defeat Farrington, "but it would be worse to give up the fight without even trying, so I put my name in the bucket."

Inouye wrote in his book, *Journey to Washington*, "Jack Burns' political hallmark was absolute honesty." In addition, he had proved himself a friend of the *nisei* during the war.

Inouye asked Burns, "Do you think you can win?"

"Hell, no!" Burns replied. "But that won't keep me from trying."

Many veterans of the 442nd who returned from the war and wanted what Sakae Takahashi had described as "an even break" had decided their best chances lay with the Democrats, who were not already rooted in power as the Republicans were. "We had a chip on our shoulder," one *nisei* veteran said. "We were damned if we'd join the Republicans!"

A public opinion survey early in 1948 had indicated a definite trend toward the Democrats. The two largest ethnic groups —Hawaiians and *nisei*—were beginning to leave the GOP ranks. Even the Chinese, usually conservative and solidly Republican, showed a preference for Democratic candidates in preprimary tests. Oddly enough the poll also showed, true to the ambiguities of Hawaii's polyglot politics, that Joe Farrington, who had succeeded his father, Wallace R. Farrington, as publisher of the *Star-Bulletin*, was the most popular choice for delegate, and Samuel Wilder King, the part-Hawaiian ex-Governor, was next. Both were Republicans. Even if Burns were nominated—and he was the only Democrat to file—he stood little chance of winning.

"If you did win, you'd give everything you had, wouldn't you?" Inouye's question was somewhat rhetorical, but Burns answered.

"I think I'd be a good delegate," Burns replied slowly, as if he intended to give thought to each remark. "I have strong feelings about Hawaii and its people. I think I know its problems. And I think I can express to Congress our great desire for statehood."

This seemed to be good enough for the young war veteran.

"Do you need any help?" he asked.

Burns laughed. "No one ever needed it more."

As a result of this telephone conversation, Inouye and several other members of the 442nd Veterans Club, formed as a social organization, became active workers for the candidacy of

Jack Burns for Delegate to Congress. Although they knew Burns only slightly, they knew a great deal about him from other *nisei*. He had gone to college only one year—at the University of Hawaii—but he was well-read. He was familiar with Aristotle and Plato as well as Thomas Aquinas; and he knew the writings of Thomas Jefferson and Thomas Paine. Burns was also definitely an independent—"his own man," as Inouye described it. He had been drawn into politics by his own decision, and not by any faction such as the old guard, which included Judge Heen, Delbert Metzger, Mayor Johnny Wilson, and Chief Justice James L. Coke. Nor was he indebted in any way to Jack Hall and the ILWU, as he demonstrated in the Democratic Convention of 1948 and for the decade that followed.

More important by far to Inouye and his fellow-*nisei* veterans, who had returned from the war still disillusioned about the status of young people of Japanese ancestry in Hawaii—even those who had fought in the war—Burns understood the problems of the *nisei* and was their friend.

However, not all members of the 442nd Veterans Club were Democrats; most favored Joe Farrington, a liberal Republican, for delegate. Dan Aoki, the First Sergeant in Inouye's Company "E" who had lent him the camouflaged field jacket the day his arm was shot off, was president of the Club. He was a heavyset, bull-shouldered man, with positive views on not getting the veterans' club mixed up in politics. He told Inouye quite frankly that he was opposed to any political activity in the Club. Aoki had been born on Maui, the son of a Japanese minister, and had grown up in the domain of the Baldwins. There was for all practical purposes only one party on Maui, the Republican Party. Young Inouye tried to explain to him that after nearly a half-century of Republican rule, they had still done little for non-*haoles* and perhaps the Islands needed a change. Aoki shook his head. No politics in the 442nd Veterans Club.

The veterans' club had raised a substantial sum for establishing club quarters, and a club birthday party was arranged to which Delegate Farrington was invited as a guest of honor. Inouye was a member of the Board of Directors, and he seized on this point. If the club was nonpolitical, why ask a politician to speak as guest of honor? If Farrington was to be invited, why not his Democratic opponent, Jack Burns?

Aoki finally agreed, and both were invited, each given three minutes to speak, with no political overtones. This actually turned out to be a breakthrough for Burns. Aoki was impressed by his quiet manner and joined the Democratic independents. There were others: Matsuo Takabuki, son of a plantation worker at Waialua who graduated from Waialua High School and studied law at the University of Chicago; Mitsuyuki Kido, a product of Miles Cary's educational theories at McKinley High; Mike Tokunaga, a draftee with bitter resentment of the treatment accorded *nisei* during the war who had joined Burns to help bring about a political change, although he did not seek office. There were many others who joined for similar reasons: Chuck Mau, a Chinese lawyer; Tom Gill, a Hawaiian-born *haole* who resented domination by the Big Five; Jack Kawano, a former lieutenant of Jack Hall in the ILWU who later accused Hall of being a Communist. Gill and Kawano were independent Democrats but not personally allied with Burns. Many others joined the movement, not as members of Burns's faction but because the movement the former police captain had initiated seemed to be the only way to break up the old-line leadership and consolidate the Democrats into a viable political force that could wrest control of Hawaii's political structure from the Big Five-GOP coalition.

Many of those who joined Burns at the time became part of an intraparty opposition to Burns in later years, or at least were not Burns followers. These included Vincent Esposito, the son of Joseph Esposito, a sharp-witted lawyer from New York who had bucked the oligarchy; and Frank Fasi, a one-time Marine from the Mainland who was articulate, independent, and energetic, and later became Mayor of Honolulu.

Burns filed for the Democratic nomination for the delegateship after the Democratic Convention of 1948, largely because no regular Democrat was willing to run. The Democratic old guard—Heen, Metzger, and Coke—had become entangled in a contest with Jack Hall, at the Convention and Burns and the "independents" slipped into the breach, taking over nominal control of the Party. The Democrats were no stronger as a party than they had ever been, however, and Burns was snowed under by Farrington in the general election. For the eleventh time since Billy Jarrett won against Phil Rice in 1924 the Democrats had lost, and nine of these defeats occurred at a time when the Democrats were sweeping the Mainland elections.

There was an undercurrent of change, however. The election of 1948 was not a triumph of the old Big Five-GOP coalition. The Republicans who won were more liberal than the old guard, and this was the beginning of the end of Big Five domination of Island politics. Just as the Polynesian rulers of Hawaii Nei were pushed out by the Revolution of 1893, in the inevitable process of change, the members of the *kamaaina haole* group were being displaced by a new generation of voters, and by changing economic forces that came from within Hawaii as well as with invaders from the Mainland.

The Democratic Convention of 1948 was in a sense the turning point in the change that led Hawaii to statehood. The change did not actually take place until a half-dozen years later, but the elements that brought about the change had stewed in the melting pot for a quarter of a century, beginning with the events of the early 1920s—the passage of the Hawaii Rehabilitation Act, which was a fraud upon the Hawaiian people, and the plantation strikes of 1920 and 1924.

In order to place these events in perspective, it is necessary to ask several questions: What were the essential forces that brought about this change—were they racial, economic or political, or perhaps a combination of these factors; and to what extent can the events in Hawaii, where a rising tide of "second-class citizens" brought about the downfall of a feudal regime that had lasted for a half-century and seemed well-nigh impregnable, be compared with similar changes in political leadership being wrought on the Mainland? And perhaps most important of all, from the standpoint of this comparison, how were these results achieved in Hawaii without resort to public demonstrations and violence?

All these factors have been dealt with to some extent, but in the context of what occurred following the gaining of control of the Democratic Party by the independents led by Jack Burns, it seems desirable to review them briefly. There were three primary elements that brought about the transition: first and perhaps foremost, the economy of the Islands was slowly outstripping the demand for its two basic products—sugar and pineapples; second, the labor movement was breaking through the barriers of feudal control; and third, the public school system had created a conscious citizenry that could no longer be contained within the racial and economic limits imposed by the Big Five.

Two of the three elements mentioned in the previous chapter were essentially political, and both were the result of major errors of judgment on the part of the Big Five in their effort to perpetuate the rule of the oligarchy over Hawaii. Both miscalculations, incidentally, occurred at the very beginning of that rule.

These were the failure of the sugar planters to understand and evaluate properly the racial characteristics of the imported Japanese field workers who would become the major source of supply of plantation labor; and the equally significant failure of the oligarchy to assess the role the public educational system would play in a feudal system such as they were creating in Hawaii. The second error, to some extent, grew out of the first.

One separate factor that could not be foreseen at the time, however, but which permitted these two related misjudgments to coalesce into a single monumental blunder, was the unexpected outbreak of World War II, which triggered the second revolution.

In order to evaluate these mistakes as they pertain to the creation of a new Hawaii and statehood for the Islands, it is necessary to retrace our steps momentarily over ground already covered. As previously noted, the Japanese contract laborers arrived in Hawaii beginning in the year 1882, and by the end of the century they had also brought their women, including wives and "picture brides" who were allowed to emigrate from Japan to Hawaii with the expectation of marrying men they had not met before. In substance, they were importing entire families, transplanting homes, living conditions, and ethnic customs of Japan to the new land. This is an aspect of importation of Japa-

11

The
"Second-Class Citizen"

nese canefield workers that was given little if any attention by the sugar planters. The planters made no effort to understand the cultural background of the people who would be their chief labor source. The Japanese were essentially Confucian in ethical and social standards; that is, they had lived for centuries in a stratified society in which there was little movement from one level to another. To a Japanese worker, the farm or factory where he worked was "home." The concept of a massive plantation strike, such as occurred in 1920, was alien to his way of thinking. It was like striking against his own home.

As noted earlier, the first Japanese contract field workers who arrived in Hawaii intended to return to Japan as soon as they had worked out their contract. But certain conditions intervened. They were not able to amass the sums of money the prospectuses had described; and they soon began to bring their women with them. At that point, Hawaii became their new home. By the end of the nineteenth century more than 30,000 Japanese plantation workers were more or less permanently established with their families in Hawaii, the largest single ethnic group except for the Hawaiians themselves.

Had there been any real effort to understand the habits and customs of these people, who for the next three decades would constitute the planters' principal source of field workers, the revolt of labor might have been avoided. But the planters regarded them as practically subhuman creatures, useful only for working the cane fields, and in some cases they were treated almost like domestic animals. This failure to attempt to bridge the cultural gap between the plantation operators and their basic work force, which was no longer transient but an established element of the population, contributed as much as any other factor to the discontent that erupted in the Japanese plantation strike of 1920. Beyond permitting the establishment of Shinto and Buddhist shrines and language schools, there was no effort whatever to understand or meet the human needs of the Orientals in their traditions and customs. In order to evaluate the significance of this, it is necessary to understand some of these customs and traditions.

A labor strike, in the American sense, would have been

unthinkable to the Japanese who first arrived in Hawaii in the latter years of the nineteenth century and the early part of the present century. A walkout was not regarded as a weapon to enforce demands, but rather as a reminder that they needed more pay. For example, in order to avoid serious interruptions in their work—which was also their livelihood, as well as the objective of management—most strikes were called in the early hours of the morning, between four and six o'clock. The incident on the plantation on Oahu in 1908 will be recalled, in which a polite letter was addressed to the management expressing "keen appreciation of your past kindness and favor" before stating that it was the "painful burden" of the workers to ask for more pay.

This incident alone should have stimulated the interest of a curious person as to what kind of people would take such unusually polite measures to obtain consideration of their need for better working conditions and higher wages; but to the sugar planters, apparently not concerned about anything beyond their economic self-interest, it was a matter of no importance. They simply ignored the request; and when the field workers walked off the job, they resorted to the customary American procedure of breaking the strike by bringing in strikebreakers.

This insensitivity to the thought processes of the Oriental mind was quite surprising to the Japanese. It was also obstructive to solutions of problems. Yet this attitude permeated almost every incident on the plantations where there was a confrontation between management and labor. The sugar planters preferred to accept the psychological theories advanced by Dr. Stanley Porteus of the University of Hawaii, who referred to the Japanese field workers as "unscrupulous and aggressive" or the summary assessment of Lorrin Thurston's *Pacific Commercial Advertiser* that the "little brown men" were "an unruly lot" and should be taught a lesson—for the offense of asking for more pay and better living conditions.

Had members of the oligarchy made even a rudimentary attempt to understand the Japanese field laborers, they would have discovered that centuries of working the land in Japan and their passive acceptance of conditions as they found them in

Hawaii might have created an ideal work force for the plantations. But the plantation managers preferred more direct methods: the use of whips by *lunas* to accelerate the work pace in the
fields during the earlier period, prior to Annexation; close control of their finances; and, in the later years, the quick and
sometimes bloody suppression of any signs of revolt, in case the
workers adopted the American habit of striking.

Many of these conditions changed during the years after the
1920 strike, which as previously noted ended in the defeat of the
Japanese strikers who—in the language of Lorrin Thurston—
had been "taught a lesson." But it required three decades for
the sugar planters to learn their own lesson, which was that they
would get much better results in their own self-interest by fair
treatment of their work force, rather than by continuing to treat
the Japanese as if they were creatures from another planet.

The Japanese learned their lesson fairly rapidly after the
events of 1908. They stopped writing polite letters and organized a labor union. It was a crude effort at first, but it was the
beginning of labor unrest that would plague the planters for the
next forty years. It was not until the end of the war that they
acquired sufficient understanding of Asians whom they had
casually dismissed as unassimilable to be able to deal with them
—and by that time it was too late. Actually, there was no basis
for the theory that Japanese were not as open to acculturation
as any other people of alien origin; yet this theory was stub-
bornly held by the oligarchy. Even the notorious brutality and
harshness of the plantation overseers in the early days of the
Republic, and to a lesser extent after Hawaii became a Territory,
would not of itself have brought on the wave of bitterness that
culminated in the plantation strikes of the early 1920s, although
it did provoke riots. The men who ruled Hawaii were not gifted
with excessive insight into sociological and ethnic problems,
however. They were for the most part members of *kamaaina haole*
families who were *descendants* of missionaries, not the missionaries themselves. The latter had come to Hawaii dedicated to
helping the "savages" by inculcating principles of Christian morality. The members of the oligarchy were second and third
generations of these families, sprinkled with a few traders and

merchant entrepreneurs; and they were dedicated solely to the business of building a rich and profitable insular empire in the Islands they had seized from the Hawaiians.

They also failed to recognize a second basic factor, the hunger of the Japanese for education, something the Japanese field worker had never been exposed to in his homeland. When the immigrant *issei* found an opportunity for their children to go to school this desire, born of centuries of denial, became over-powering—not for the *issei,* but for their children. The duality of schools, already discussed, was hardly a problem for the older people, although there was a stigma in the non-standard school clearly recognized by those who attended them. By the 1930s most of the *issei* had long since passed the point of no return— that is, return to Japan; they had established their home in America and were disproving the blunt appraisal rendered by Doc Hill of Hawaii: that "a Jap is a Jap" and could not be Americanized.

The older Japanese, in spite of efforts of members of the oligarchy and their spokesman to prove otherwise, were gradu-ally being Americanized. They were not only sending their chil-dren to school, but they were learning some of the American customs their children had learned in school. The strike leader-ship in the 1920s proved far more Americanized than the mild and docile leadership of those who framed the polite letter to the management of the Oahu Sugar Company in 1908. The Japanese no longer wrote courteous notes; instead they pointed bitterly to differentials in pay rates between the Portuguese and the Orientals.

In the urban areas—chiefly Honolulu and Hilo—the changes were even more noticeable than on the plantations, since it was to the cities that the sons and daughters, who had been born in Hawaii, tended to gravitate. They studied at the public high schools, and when the College of Hawaii was ex-panded in 1912 to include a College of Arts and Sciences and became a university with courses that might lead to a doctor's or a lawyer's degree, they jumped at this opportunity for higher learning. To have a doctor or a lawyer in the family raised the entire social status of a Japanese family in Hawaii.

What public education had done for the Japanese in Hawaii was to provide an opportunity for *escape from serfdom*. Many immigrant Japanese had chosen to remain in Hawaii, in spite of the virtual peonage under which they existed in the early days, simply because this avenue of escape was offered for their sons and daughters. Thus, by processes which the sugar planters had somewhat blindly set in motion through indifference to Asian ethnic problems, and their general obtuseness as to their significance, there was emerging a political force that would one day engulf the oligarchy.

The event that triggered the transition from feudal rule to a new Hawaii and finally to statehood was what might be described as the hiatus of World War II. The bombing of Pearl Harbor and the three and a half years of war that followed provided the unexpected catalyst for the fading out of the Big Five.

Although World War II could not have been foreseen, the role played by the members of the Big Five was, in a direct way, of their own choosing, and they can hardly disclaim responsibility for what happened. One of the visible symptoms of the war hysteria that gripped Hawaii—the fear that there was a Japanese spy under every bed—was used consciously and deliberately to enhance the position of the oligarchy. As a result, members of the Big Five who were called in as civilian counselors for the Military Governor became somewhat like Machiavelli's princes who "thought more of ease than of arms." They did all the things they would have liked to do but lacked authority for doing in peace time, such as censoring critical editorials in the non-*haole* press and providing jail sentences for plantation workers who failed to report for work. What they lost was the sense of self-discipline and self-reliance that had been the oligarchy's main source of strength.

One factor that contributed to the decline of the Big Five, less tangible than the political changes, but in the end quite as disastrous, was the leveling off of Hawaii's principal economic base, the export of sugar and, to a lesser extent, pineapples.

In the mid-1930s a number of warnings had been sounded.

Economic experts called attention to the fact that Hawaii's basic exports, sugar and pineapples, were reaching a saturation point. Dr. Romanzo Adams of the University of Hawaii wrote in 1935 that "Hawaii is approaching a condition of closed resources," and Dr. David L. Crawford, President of the University, in an extensive report said Hawaii had expanded to the limit of its economic potential. The reasons were quite apparent. In 1920 Hawaii's sugar exports totaled slightly over half a million tons; in 1930 it had doubled to more than a million tons, and the dollar income for sugar was in excess of $150,000,000. The pineapple industry, just beginning to develop, had moved into position as Hawaii's second industry. The economists also pointed out that the saturation point had been reached in the case of sugar and could be foreseen in pineapples. The Depression of 1929 had begun to take bites out of Hawaii's economy; and it was at this point that a note of pessimism crept into economic appraisals of Hawaii's future.

As the limits for these basic exports, the principal sources of income for the Territory, became foreseeable, the population began to rise. From 250,000 in 1920 it rose to 350,000 in 1930, and by 1940 it had jumped to 423,000. The outcome was inevitable. Hawaii's favorable balance of payments with the Mainland would soon become unfavorable; the Islands would be unable to sell enough of its products to pay for what it needed. As early as 1924 the *Hawaii Hochi*, attacking the sugar planters for importing additional Filipino labor to break the plantation strike, warned that new industries must be developed if the Islands were to sustain their growing population. Its editor, George Wright, argued that by importing additional Filipinos, the planters were "cutting off their noses to spite their faces." They might break the strike, but they would glut the population beyond their ability to support it.

The demand for sugar exports was limited to approximately a million tons a year by 1930, and it remained at that figure for the next thirty years, representing about a fourth of the Mainland consumption. Beet-sugar growers and Louisiana cane sugar planters intended to keep it that way. The only change was in the price, which fluctuated erratically with the economy. In

1950 it dropped temporarily to a total of about $124,000,000 and after returning to $147,000,000 in 1956, it plunged again to $106,000,000 in 1958 due to a long plantation strike. For the first time in history sugar exports fell below the income from pineapples. As James H. Shoemaker, Research Vice-President of the Bank of Hawaii and the Territory's foremost economist, wrote in 1950,

> The lack of balance as between manpower and jobs and the lack of balance in our account with the Mainland are both traceable to the same fundamental cause—since 1930 there has been relatively little expansion in our basic export industries whereas the population has continued to rise rapidly. . . .
> . . . Expressed in its simplest terms, we are faced with the necessity of reducing our imports and standards of living to conform to the level of our . . . productive output unless we take positive action to expand production and our capacity to earn Mainland dollars. . . .[22]

Shoemaker's warnings unfortunately came twenty years too late. The crisis was already developing during the 1930s, partly due to the Great Depression; and only the advent of World War II, which poured defense dollars into Hawaii, saved the Territory from the immediate consequences of its economic problems. The buildup of the military and naval establishments on Oahu had already begun before the United States entered the war following the bombing of Pearl Harbor; but this source would undoubtedly have leveled off and would have served only to delay the crisis, but not to avoid it.

One of the fundamental causes of the economic crisis was the failure or inability of the Big Five to foresee that new industries would be required when the export saturation point was reached for sugar and pineapples. Even the handling of public lands had mitigated against the expansion of the Islands' productive capacity by discouraging homesteading of any lands that might be used for growing sugar and pineapples. Thus the possibility of producing in the Islands commodities that otherwise had to be imported from the Mainland was virtually eliminated. This, of course, tightened the balance of payments since it required an outflow of dollars to buy products for consumption in Hawaii. The growing unfavorable balance of payments coupled with increasing labor troubles, culminating in two serious strikes on the plantations and docks after the war, led to the weakening and downfall of the Big Five.

The missing ingredients were new financial blood, new thinking, and new economic forces. As long as the old-line members of the oligarchy continued to block Mainland interests from coming to Hawaii, this infusion of new blood was difficult if not impossible to obtain. By the end of the 1930s, however, the continued pressure began to break down some of the barriers; and within Hawaii itself there arose a new type of entrepreneur —the "Chinese tycoon," such as Chinn Ho, Hung Wo Ching, Hung Wai Ching, and Hiram Fong, later United States Senator from Hawaii. These enterprising promoters of new businesses appeared shortly after the end of the war and by the 1950s were competing in almost every financial field with the *kamaaina haoles.*

Most of the Chinese who later became sources of financial and political power had meager beginnings. Hung Wo Ching was perhaps the best example. His father had been a cook on an Inter-Island steamer. By hard work and savings, Hung Wo was able to put himself through Cornell University, receiving a doctorate in agriculture. With this educational background, he gained financial support in the Chinese community in Honolulu to build a sugar mill in China. The Communist Revolution wiped him out and he returned to Honolulu virtually penniless.

He might have assumed his backers should share the loss, but instead he personally assured each of those who supported him that he would repay every cent. This required several years, but he paid them back; and as a result his word was his bond among the Chinese of Hawaii.

During World War II Hawaiian Airlines, a subsidiary of the Inter-Island Steam Navigation Company, which was controlled by the Big Five, had refused to employ Orientals. A competing airline, Trans-Pacific, was organized by Rudy Tongg, another Chinese entrepreneur, but before it was certified by the Civil Aeronautics Board it became virtually bankrupt. Hung Wo

Ching, with the backing of the Chinese community, first tried to merge Trans-Pacific with Hawaiian Airlines and was rebuffed. He finally reorganized Trans-Pacific as Aloha Airlines, obtained financing from a San Francisco bank when the Bishop Bank refused to lend him money, and by the year of statehood Hung Wo not only had Aloha Airlines in the black, but he was elected a director of the Bank of Hawaii!

The nonracial aspect of Hawaiian politics was also demonstrated by Hung Wo and his brother, Hung Wai Ching. The latter backed Hiram Fong as a Republican, while Hung Wo, Chinn Ho, and Clarence Ching, the latter also a "Chinese tycoon," were ardent supporters of Jack Burns.

Hawaii's closed economy dominated by the Big Five was rapidly being transformed to an open economy, and the Chinese tycoons were among the salient factors in Hawaii's transition from feudalism to statehood.

It had become evident in the late 1930s that the reign of the Big Five was coming to an end, not only because of certain political changes already mentioned, but due to the ineluctable laws of economics. Their power, as previously noted, deteriorated during the war when they were reduced to the status of Persian eunuchs advising the Caliph of Baghdad.

The phrase "Sugar is King" was virtually obsolete by the end of the war, but there was one last element that helped to extend the tenure of the Big Five at this point, and that was the specter of communism. During the war years the Communists in Hawaii had gone underground, but almost at the moment the war ended they came out again. They furnished a handy target for the oligarchy's last stand—its attack on the militant forces of the labor movement that had begun actively to invade Hawaii in the last half of the 1930s.

The Democratic Convention of 1948 had provided grist for the mill, and the Big Five-GOP coalition was able to divert— temporarily at least—the struggle between the insurgent newly aware citizens and the old guard of both parties to the question of who was guiding the ILWU—America or Russia. The new trend of anticommunism had already begun to dominate the Mainland political scene, in the form of McCarthyism, and the sport of Red-baiting was in full swing; but in Hawaii there was an added incentive for the Red hunters. By turning their guns on both Democrats and ILWU, who were already linked by the efforts of Jack Hall to take over the postwar wreckage of the Party, the Big Five-GOP coalition was able at least for a time to hold its control over the territorial Legislature and win the delegateship at each biennial election in spite of the Democratic victories on the Mainland.

The element they had not reckoned on—or even recognized—was the rising resentment of many factions that were not connected with either the ILWU or communism. This resentment was evident among the emerging citizens—the returning *nisei* war veterans, the angry Hawaiians and Portuguese, the *malihini haoles* from the Mainland, who had not been welcomed very strenuously by the *kamaaina haoles* and had no particular allegiance to the Republicans or the sugar planters. This group had gathered around Jack Burns in the 1948 Democratic Convention and began to create a new political force in Hawaii.

Ichiro Izuka came from the fertile Hanapepe Valley on Kauai, west of Lihue, where his father and mother labored in the canefields for thirty dollars and seventeen dollars a month, respectively. At an early age he witnessed the bloody "battle of Hanapepe," where the Filipino strikers fought the police and National Guard. When Ichiro was sixteen years old he left the plantation to work on the docks at Lihue, loading sugar on Matson freighters bound for the Pacific Coast. He is important in the story of Hawaii's evolution toward its second revolution because he was the first to "blow the whistle" on the infiltration of Communists into the labor movement in Hawaii, and particularly on Jack Hall, militant leader of the ILWU.

In 1937 Ichiro Izuka had become head of the improvised union of stevedores at the Kauai Terminal, and in 1939 he led the dockworkers in an impromptu strike, refusing to load the *Manulani* on a pay scale of seventy-five dollars a month. He described this strike twelve years later in testimony before the House Committee on Un-American Activities as the first "spontaneous" strike in the history of the Islands in which the strikers actually won. They had lost at Waipahu in 1906 and 1909, and in the more organized Japanese and Filipino plantation strikes of 1920 and 1924. In the Lihue strike he said he "got a hint of the kind of pressure the industry can bring," and he learned about labor organization. Policemen came with machine guns and "acted as if we were criminals." Even the supposedly victorious settlement was "phony," he said, because the clause recognizing the union was meaningless.

It was not until Jack Hall and another union organizer, George Goto, arrived from Honolulu to help organize the Lihue stevedores that he began to understand what the labor move-

12

The "Red Menace"

ment was all about. Later, as he told the House Committee, he met others—Jack Kimoto and Robert McElrath, who told him how the Communists were helping labor organize in Hawaii, and so he decided to join the Communist Party. It was only after several years, he said, that he discovered the Communists were using Hawaiian labor groups as catspaws to control the Democratic Party in Hawaii.

Izuka's testimony before the House investigating group, together with that of Jack Kawano, another confessed former Communist, is interesting for its underlying disclosure of the bitterness that was welling up within the ranks of labor in Hawaii, as well as for its impact on the political situation. "I was building up resentment," he wrote in a pamphlet published in 1947. He said he was "ripe for communism." His friend, Jack Kimoto, arranged for him to go to San Francisco to attend a Communist "training school," and he returned just before the war thoroughly indoctrinated in the Communist movement. "We felt like Christian martyrs," he wrote, "pleased with our faith, but not anxious to be caught."

The Communists went underground during the war when the military government took over, but immediately after restrictions were lifted, they surfaced again. Izuka named a number of those he said were active in the movement, including Kawano, then head of the Longshoremen's Union in Honolulu; Robert McElrath, later public relations man for the Communist Party and also for the ILWU; and the Farrington High School instructor whom he described as "a kindly, scholarly man." He also identified his old friend, Jack Kimoto, as head of the *Hawaii Star*, an avowedly Communist newspaper. All but Hall, McElrath, and Reinecke were *nisei*, and most of them were members of the ILWU.

It was not until Izuka, and later Kawano, discovered what they called the "conspiratorial" character of the Communist movement that they decided to break away from the Party and tell the Congressional committees what they knew. But underlying their original acceptance of communism was the pent-up bitterness from the long years of intimidation and violent repression to which they had been subjected.

The disclosure of Communist infiltration into the labor movement in Hawaii had, of course, a far different significance for the oligarchy. It gave them a new target and a new lease on life. Aside from Governor Stainback, who was enraged at the exposure of certain Democrats who seemed to be painted with the Red brush, the Big Five-GOP coalition, virtually bereft of political ammunition during the war, greeted the Communist issue with unrestrained enthusiasm. They denounced Hall, seeing in this new development an opportunity to restore Big Five control of labor which was dissipated when the military took over.

Jack Hall was not particularly intimidated by the Communist issue. It had been raised against him before, and he had ignored it. During the 1948 Democratic Convention several ILWU members who later were accused in testimony before Congressional committees of having been members of the Communist Party were nevertheless elected to Convention committees, and the rank-and-file of labor seemed unperturbed by the exposures. Only Stainback continued to take the Communist charges against Hall seriously, even accusing Johnny Wilson of leaning toward the Red-tainted labor leader. Wilson responded by charging that Stainback was more of a Republican than a Democrat.

Hall, according to Ichiro Izuka's testimony, had been a card-carrying Communist, but this seems to have been simply a matter of expediency; the Reds were helping him organize labor in Hawaii, so he followed the Party line. When their help dwindled—as it did in the early 1950s—his interest in communism dwindled accordingly. To the workers in Hawaii he was an efficient labor organizer, and, as proof of this, they pointed to the fact that between the end of the war in 1945 and the Democratic Convention of 1948 the ranks of organized union labor had swelled from less than 1,000 to more than 45,000. The National Labor Relations Board, under the authority of a new Hawaii Employment Relations Bill, stretched its influence to the Territory for the first time.

The Communist issue was, in a sense, the last gasp of the Big Five in its long domination of the labor force in the Islands.

They had formed an Employers' Council as a wartime measure to help control labor, but when the war ended the Council had almost nothing to do. The Communist menace was about the only thing it could dig up; and they even rallied the distaff side on this issue. Wives of oligarchs formed an auxiliary organization known as "Imua." This is a Hawaiian word meaning "go ahead," and perhaps in modern parlance it might have been translated as "Right on!" but this phrase was unknown in those days, and would probably have been undesirable to the matrons of the missionary families if they had known its later connotations.

Imua worked up all sorts of crusades, with the support of the more vigilante-minded members of the business community and the sterner breed of the military establishment. Led by Mrs. Walter Dillingham, the Imua ladies carried on radio warfare against Communists of all sorts and colors, from Jack Hall and Harry Bridges to Japanese plantation workers, pacifist preachers, and even whacked away at the Teamsters Union, which was known to be strongly anti-Communist. The union leaders, oddly enough, welcomed these assaults; they seemed to think they lent dignity to the labor movement. One labor oganizer was quoted as remarking that "even people who don't know the difference between Communism and rheumatism" were joining in the attack.

The effect was more rhetorical than political. Jack Hall did not even break stride in his effort to control the Democratic Party. What stopped him was not Imua, the Big Five or Red-baiting; it was Jack Burns, who had gathered a small but compact coterie of young men who were becoming skilled in political organization under the tutelage of this Irish expoliceman. These included not only Dan Inouye and other *nisei* such as Sakae Takahashi, Mike Tokunaga, and Matsuo Takabuki, but also Bill Richardson, a part-Hawaiian, and Herman Lum and Chuck Mau, both Chinese. There were other independents who had no direct affiliation with Burns but resented both the old-line Democrats and Jack Hall's ILWU.

Burns's greatest assets were his evident honesty and his understanding of the problems of the little people—the peren-

nial underdogs of Hawaiian politics. His defeat at the hands of
Joe Farrington in the 1948 race for delegate did not discourage
him or his followers. Although Burns did not run in 1950, he
began to plan carefully for the long haul. By 1952 there were
three major factions in the Democratic Party, the new independents, the old guard, and labor; but every sign indicated that the
discord which had for so many years harassed the Democrats
might soon come to an end. The end would come when Jack
Burns eliminated the old guard and Hall from control of the
Party.

Daniel Inouye had programmed his own entry into the political field, not as a candidate for office, but as a party worker
—one of the "men behind the scenes." He had decided to complete his prelegal course at the University of Hawaii and finish
law studies at George Washington University Law School in
Washington. Meanwhile he met a girl.

Since the girl, Margaret Awamura, was to become of considerable importance in his political career, the circumstances under which he met her are worth mentioning. It was in 1947, just
after his return from the war. As he later put it in extremely
simple terms: "I promptly decided I was going to marry her."

The decision was by no means unanimous at first. Inouye
was just twenty-three at the time, but as a returning war hero
and a member of the famed 442nd Veterans Club, he had a
certain status in the *nisei* community. A friend who had squired
Margaret Awamura to a football game introduced her to Inouye.
Although he had seen her on the University campus, he had not
met her. She was petite, with large, lively eyes, and a natural
warmth. His friend introduced her with an air of possessiveness
as his "girl friend." This disturbed Inouye. As he said, "How the
hell could she be *his* girl friend when I was going to marry her?"

They were in fact married in June of 1949 and by this time
Dan Inouye was deep in the inner councils of Jack Burns's growing cadre of dedicated "independent" Democrats, committed to
remolding the political structure of Hawaii. It was not the only
group dedicated to this purpose: there were men like Esposito,
whose father fought the power of the Big Five; Fasi, the ex-

Marine who was not a Burns man although Burns later supported him for Democratic national committeeman against
Johnny Wilson because he feared the Mayor would be under the
influence of Jack Hall; and Gill, the *haole* son of an Island schoolteacher who had gone to Roosevelt High School and later studied law at the University of California. After Hall's bid to rule
the 1948 Democratic Convention had been blocked, this new
coalition of independents was the strongest element in the Democratic Party.

Those closest to Burns were the *nisei* from the 442nd Veterans Club and some like Sakae Takahashi, who had been a
schoolteacher, and Spark Matsunaga, who had studied at Har-
vard, from the 100th Battalion. In addition to Inouye the 442nd
provided Dan Aoki, its president, Matsuo Takabuki, and several
others. Mike Tokunaga, who had graduated from the University
of Hawaii in 1950 with Inouye, joined Burns as an organizer but
did not become a candidate for office. Others, such as Bill Richardson, Chuck Mau, and Herman Lum were neither *nisei* nor
veterans, but they supported Burns's battle against the old
guard and labor for control of the Party. Still others aligned
themselves with Burns as the logical nexus under which an independent party could be formed. Among later members of the
Burns group were Patsy Takemoto Mink, a fiery young lady who
joined Burns in 1954, and earned Hall's enmity when she criticized his political tactics. There were others: Donald Ching, who
grew up in the slums of Palama; Nelson Doi and Masato Doi,
who were friendly to Burns but not members of his group. Thus,
almost by accident rather than design, Burns became the central
figure in a movement to remold the Democrats into a political
force capable of unseating the Big Five from the feudal rule they
had maintained for fifty years.

During the two years from 1950 to the fall of 1952, when
Dan Inouye returned from Washington, Burns had fought Hall
for control of the Party, and in the final showdown it was Burns,
the careful planner, who won. The old-line Democrats such as
Judge Heen, Delbert Metzger, and Judge Coke had retreated
from the battle for control, walking out of both the 1948 and
1950 conventions; and Stainback, the nominal party leader, was

virtually isolated, still waging his lonely war against the Communists. Johnny Wilson, still Mayor of Honolulu, continued to try
to rally adherents to his personal cause, but his prospects diminished as his years increased. When Burns shifted his support
from Wilson to Frank Fasi for National Committeeman in 1952
because he felt Wilson would not resist Hall's pressure, it
marked the end of the line for the old Mayor. It was the last
chapter in a political career that began with the Revolution of
1893, when Wilson's father was the Queen's Marshal.

Inouye and his pretty young wife, Margaret, had left for
Washington in the late summer of 1950 just as the battle between Burns and Hall was reaching its climax. As Inouye said
later, "We agreed that any chance we had of winning the territorial Legislature would go glimmering as long as the Democrats were cursed with the ILWU kiss of death." Hall was seeking
a political power base, not a Democratic victory. Back in 1946
when the Democrats won equal footing in the House with the
Republicans for the first time in a half century, Hall had actually
supported Joe Farrington for delegate!

The decision to sidetrack the effort of Hall and the ILWU
to take over the Democratic Party was more than strategy for
control. It was part of Burns's moderate and thoughtful political
philosophy, and in the case of Inouye it confirmed what Dr.
Fuchs had noted in his reference to the talk with Sakae Takahashi in the hospital in Atlantic City—that Dan Inouye had spoken
"without passion." This approach was characteristic of the new
revolution. The plan to stop Hall was not personal, nor was it
hunger for political power; it was the result of the firm conviction that ILWU support of the Democrats, if it involved a power
base for labor, would be the "kiss of death" for the Party.

During the next two years this was proved with striking
forcefulness in the embroilment of Hall and his followers with
investigations by the House Un-American Activities Committee,
which held hearings in Honolulu in 1950 and later in Washington in 1951. Burns intended to extricate the new Democratic
independents from this link to labor's bid for a power base.

As the revision of Hawaii's political structure—and its economic structure as well—continued through the period from
1954 through 1958 in the struggle to attain statehood, it became

Waikiki of Yesterday: A scene at Waikiki Beach in the early years of this century, with the Moana Hotel, sole remnant of the past, and its beach houses in the background. Under the trees are strollers with straw hats of 1910 vintage, walking along paths later covered by the Royal Hawaiian Hotel, first of the luxury hotels that now cover the old beach area. *Honolulu Advertiser.*

Waikiki Today: This world-famous beach, once the mecca of tourists seeking a tropical paradise, is covered today with massive warrens of modern luxury living. The view is to the south, with Diamond Head in the background, and along the waterfront artificially sanded beaches, resort hotels and high-rise apartments. Ala Wai canal and the huge marina are in the foreground, just beyond the Ilikai and Hawaiian Village hotels, and beyond these the cluster of hotels, with old Moana and the Royal Hawaiian virtually smothered in the forest of new buildings. *Hawaii Vistors Bureau photo.*

Honolulu Harbor about 1882

Honolulu Harbor: This view of the Harbor (taken about 1882) shows windjammers in port, with a scattering of docks and warehouses along the waterfront, facing the city. The Punchbowl is in the background and Nuuanu Valley to the left. Vessel at right is moored at what is now Aloha Pier. *Honolulu Advertiser.*

Judge Sanford Ballard Dole, first President of the Republic of Hawaii and first Governor of the Territory, who was descended from a missionary family and was chosen by the revolutionary party to lead the Provisional Government, formed after the Revolution of 1893. *Archives of Hawaii photo.*

Prince Jonah Kuhio Kalanianaole, known as "Prince Cupid," served as Delegate to Congress from 1902 to 1922. *Archives of Hawaii photo.*

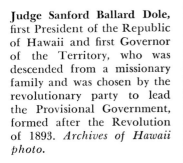

Queen Liliuokalani, last monarch of Hawaii, who abdicated her throne in the Revolution of 1893. *Archives of Hawaii photo.*

Kamehameha the Great, founder of the Kamehameha dynasty, which ruled the Kingdom of Hawaii for almost a century—from 1795 to 1893. He succeeded his uncle, King Kalaniopuu of the Island of Hawaii, in 1782, conquered all the Islands, and died in 1819. The original painting by Louis Choris, a French artist, is the only known portrait of Kamehameha I, who has been called "the Napoleon of the Pacific." *Archives of Hawaii photo.*

Hawaii's Capitol: The new State Capitol, built in neo-Polynesian style with five stories of legislative halls, offices and executive chambers mounted on pillars that are set in a huge pool of water. *Photo by James Y. Young.*

The Old Courthouse: Built in 1842 at a cost of $34,299.50, this was the second largest building in Honolulu and was the site of coronations of Hawaii's monarchs and royal receptions and was even the scene of a riot during the latter days of King Kalakaua's reign. The space was later occupied by Castle & Cooke offices, built nearly a century afterward. The location was Queen Street, between Fort and Bishop, in what became the center of the business district. *Honolulu Advertiser.*

Representative Patsy Takemoto Mink

Senator Daniel Ken Inouye

Governor Jack Burns (left) of Hawaii with President Lyndon Johnson.

evident that neither Burns nor Inouye, who were the chief planners of this evolution, had any desire to eliminate the support of labor. What they wanted was to contain the power of Hall and the ILWU so that it would not dominate the reorganized Democratic Party.

This strategy was an essential element in Hawaii's second revolution, and it illustrates by comparison the potential for success in such a movement when it does not rely on any specific power base—whether it be the power of the sugar planter oligarchy, the Communist-infiltrated labor movement, or by any ethnic or socioeconomic minority seeking to dominate a political organization. In this sense, Hawaii's second revolution was the antithesis of traditional concepts of creating a political power structure, since its success did not depend on any specific power base, but on the electorate itself.

Dan and Margaret Inouye arrived in San Francisco in August, 1950, on the *Lurline* and flew to Washington, where he enrolled at George Washington University. He had his Army pension and the benefits of the GI Bill, and Margaret got a job in the Navy Department Bureau of Docks; and with this combined income they rented a small apartment in Arlington and spent the next two years in the politically sophisticated arena of Washington—an atmosphere that must be lived in at close quarters to appreciate from as far away as Hawaii how the American political system operates.

During this period Inouye divided his attention between law and politics; that is, he studied law at George Washington Law School and worked in politics with the Democratic National Committee. He even found time to attend a school for bartenders. All three disciplines were rewarding.

One aspect of his political education was his participation in a plan to rescue a floundering campaign in Maryland, the seeding ground of Democrats. One of the planners at the Democratic headquarters explained the problem: "Too damned much complacency!" The party strategists in Maryland were already planning what to do *after* their candidate was elected, and as a result there seemed a reasonable chance that he would not be elected.

"The old pros ran the meeting," Inouye said later. "Men who could feel a trend in their guts and who could cut through the verbiage, inflated vote estimates, and apologies with a single somewhat obscene word." The solution offered by one old pro was to send a special force in to tear down Democratic signs in the area.

"Tear down *our* signs?" Inouye was aghast, but as he later explained, his was the voice of a "well-meaning amateur." The old professional said that was precisely what was intended. If the Democrats in Maryland found their signs torn down, it would be blamed on the Republicans, and they would get mad and perhaps wake up and do something about it.

"You're up against a disease," the head of the meeting said. "Complacency. Over-optimism. There isn't anything that can kill a candidate faster and deader."

The strong tactics he described were carried out. Signs were torn down. The Democrats were up in arms, and their candidate won. Inouye admitted the medicine was stronger than he would have prescribed in Hawaii, where those who tore down the signs might be more readily identified, since everyone knew everyone else; but the lesson struck home. It was a good political axiom to head off a problem before it happened rather than after the damage was done.

Inouye dug more deeply into the governmental and political processes in the nation's capital. He watched the intricate maneuvers of parliamentary procedures in Congress, including all the tricks that were played, stalling of bills in committee, swapping votes for one measure in order to get a reciprocal vote on another measure.

"I never saw myself down on the floor of the House or Senate at that time," he wrote later. "The limit of my ambition then was a seat in the territorial Legislature." But what he saw were the processes of representative government at work, and he saw it with the eyes of an idealist. He recalled early training that Miles Cary had provided at McKinley High School—the segregated "Tokyo High" of Honolulu, part of the public school system of Hawaii that the oligarchy had first permitted because it separated the *haoles* from the Orientals, and later sought to restrict and in some cases eliminate because it offered education in American ideals of democracy rather than in the technology of sugar and pineapple growing.

In September, 1952, Dan was graduated from George Washington Law School with the degree of Juris Doctor—a slight advance above the usual LLB degree, but without waiting for commencement exercises he and Margaret headed back for Hawaii to put his new knowledge to work. The day after he arrived he passed his territorial bar examination, and Mayor Johnny Wilson appointed him deputy prosecutor for the City and County of Honolulu, a job Wilfred Tsyukiyama had held some thirty years earlier.

Daniel Inouye returned to Hawaii to find the Islands in the throes of a historic political change, which actually began with the elections of 1952. The shift in the balance of power that virtually displaced the old Big Five-GOP coalition did not occur, however, until the next biennial election in 1954. Nevertheless, the portents were already quite evident.

Several factors contributed to the early phases of this change, two of which involved Jack Burns, Inouye, and the independents to a considerable extent. These were the revival of the so-called Communist menace, not only in the labor movement but in the Democratic Party; and the emergence of Burns, with his cadre of young politicos such as Inouye, as the leader of the Democratic Party. A third factor was the growing split in the Republican ranks between a new liberal wing led by Joe Farrington and the old guard led by Walter Dillingham and the *Honolulu Advertiser* over the issue of statehood for Hawaii.

Initially the outcry against the Communists was inspired by the revelations of Ichiro Izuka in the pamphlet published in 1947, and was directed at the infiltration of Communist organizers in the labor movement in Hawaii. However, by 1950, the "Red peril" had shifted its position; the emergence of McCarthyism on the Mainland served to reinvigorate the anti-Communist campaign in Hawaii, and the target was no longer merely the danger to the labor movement; it involved the statehood issue.

Previously the "Japanese menace" had been the principal argument advanced by forces opposed to statehood for Hawaii, but a vacuum had been created in this area as a result of the wartime record of the *nisei*, who had proved fairly conclusively that they were as American as anyone else in Hawaii. The new

13

The Turning Point

danger cited was the possibility that Russia—not Japan—would take over the government of Hawaii if it should become a state. The opposition had discovered a new vulnerability in the argument against statehood.

This vulnerability to Communist infiltration was sufficient to bring the House Un-American Activities Committee down to Honolulu in 1950 for the first of a new series of hearings. The FBI had converged on the Islands during and after the war and unearthed a good deal of information, based on the revelations of Ichiro Izuka in his pamphlet, and the extent of the Communist apparatus in Hawaii was fairly well documented. The work of Jack Hall in organizing the plantation workers as well as the longshoremen, which led to a crippling dockworkers' strike in 1949, became part of an extensive FBI dossier, and when the House Un-American Activities Committee met in Honolulu on April 10, 1950, it had plenty of ammunition.

Of about seventy witnesses subpoenaed to testify, thirty-nine remained silent under the self-incrimination amendment of the Constitution. Among these was Jack Kawano, the ILWU leader in Honolulu; but a year later he went to Washington at the persuasion of other *nisei*, who were so anxious to rid the Democratic party of the Red bogeyman they helped finance his trip. Kawano spelled out by chapter and verse just who belonged to the Communist Party in Hawaii. The only important labor leader mentioned, aside from Kawano himself, was Jack Hall of the ILWU. This was enough to fuel the fires of anticommunism in Hawaii, however, and the opponents of statehood seized on this as proof of the peril of Communist domination of Hawaii if it ever became a state.

The revelations also had explosive results on the Mainland. The CIO had been sufficiently shocked by Izuka's statements to expel the ILWU from its membership, an action which did not cause much of a stir among the rank-and-file of workers in Hawaii, since most of them were unaware that their union was affiliated with the CIO. They had gone through two and a half months of the longshoremen's strike in 1949, and Alex Budge, head of Castle & Cooke, had formally recognized the right of labor to collective bargaining in Hawaii, so they were quite happy with Hall.

Meanwhile the thirty-nine witnesses who refused to testify before the House Committee, known as "the reluctant thirty-nine," had been cited and indicted by a Federal grand jury for contempt of Congress, a charge that later was overturned by the U. S. Supreme Court; but the Committee had secured enough evidence to indict seven persons, including Jack Hall, under the Smith Act.

The seven—known as "the Hawaii seven"—were tried in 1953 after nearly two years' delay due to legal maneuvering, and all were convicted. The verdict subsequently was set aside by a Supreme Court ruling on the Smith Act itself, and the total effect was more polemical than political. During the entire period Hall spent only a week in jail, because of his inability to raise bail; and aside from the denunciations of the ladies of Imua, who continued to debate the issue extensively on the radio, nothing much happened that had any lasting effect. Johnny Wilson and Del Metzger, two old stalwarts of the Democratic Party, were castigated by the Imua ladies as Communist sympathizers after they testified as character witnesses for Hall, but the Mayor was eighty years old by this time and had about given up hope of becoming governor.

A second factor which contributed materially to the shift in political power, and was becoming evident to nearly everyone except perhaps to some members of the Republican old guard, was the growing strength of the independent faction in the Democratic Party, led by Burns and Inouye. This was so closely tied in with the rising demand for statehood, in which there was a definite split within the ranks of the Republicans themselves, that the two elements can be treated together.

For fifty years many of the *kamaaina haoles* had adamantly refused to consider that Hawaii was ready for statehood, even though the first bill to change its status from that of territory to state was introduced in Congress as early as 1919. During the years preceding and following World War II antistatehood arguments had been voiced by Walter Dillingham and a few diehard members of the Big Five, for reasons that will become clear in the context of later discussions of this issue. But by 1952 Joe Farrington, who became delegate when Samuel Wilder King returned to the Navy during the war, had become convinced that statehood for Hawaii was not only inevitable, but desirable. As publisher of the *Star-Bulletin*, which, under his father, had for years been the voice of the liberal—or least conservative—wing of the Republican Party in Hawaii, he had begun actively advocating statehood immediately after the war.

In many respects the key to the whole situation was the ability of Jack Burns and Dan Inouye to merge the "second-class citizens" into a coalition of independent Democrats who could effectively challenge the Republicans. The Democratic old guard, led nominally by Mayor Wilson but including such party veterans as Judge Heen, a Chinese-Hawaiian of extraordinary political skill and the chief defense lawyer for the youths in the famous Massie Case; Supreme Court Justice Coke, a lifetime Democrat; and Del Metzger, a veteran Democrat who had been influential since the days of Billy Jarrett, was slowly being squeezed out of its political position.

The contest for control of the Democrats had narrowed down to Burns and Hall, and of the two, Burns was the more dedicated to basic principles that for many years had been espoused by the party, such as land reform, greater educational opportunities for students of all races and social classes, tougher tax laws, and strengthening the economy for the benefit of the people of Hawaii, rather than for sugar and pineapples.

The rise of Burns's strength, coinciding with the more liberal position taken by Delegate Joe Farrington, had served to weaken the *kamaaina haole* old guard—the remnants of what had once been the all-powerful missionary-sugar planter oligarchy. This coincidence obviously was not intentional on the part of either Burns or Farrington. What had happened was that the former rulers of the Territory—the Athertons, Cookes, Castles, and Dillinghams, who represented the views of Merchant Street and the basic industries of Hawaii up to the end of the 1930s—had remained intransigent, while the newcomers and progressive elements had moved forward.

While Farrington and his editor in chief, Riley Allen, were voicing progressive views about Hawaii's future, Lorrin Thurston, the son of the former owner of the *Advertiser*, and now its publisher, was still chanting the liturgy of the Big Five: Sugar is King! It was not until the middle of the 1950s that the *Advertiser*, long the spokesman for Dillingham and the Big Five, awoke to the realization that Hawaii was changing and statehood was inevitable, something Farrington had discovered before the war.

What Farrington had observed was the growing strength of the Democrats in the Legislature; and in order to understand the elements that were operating in this sector it is necessary to review some of the basic characteristics of political campaign Hawaiian-style before the war, and the changes that occurred after the war when Communist-oriented labor leaders introduced a more sophisticated type of electioneering and political maneuvering.

In the 1920s and earlier, when the Republicans sat comfortably in their seats in the Legislature with majorities ranging up to fourteen out of fifteen in the Senate and 80 percent of the House, the participation of non-*haoles* in Hawaiian politics was largely personal and oratorical. The Hawaiians took naturally to politics, but it was their own native brand, like *okolehao*, the basic Hawaiian liquid refreshment during Prohibition. They gathered in festive rallies at places like Aala Park, located in the slum district of downtown Honolulu, with the aroma of ginger flowers wafting down from the mountains, and the rank odors of the fish market blown in from the other direction; and all around was the penetrating stench of Japanese and Chinese vegetable markets. It was a melting pot of smells as well as sounds. There they watched hula dancers swaying to the strumming of guitars and ukuleles (originally the *braginha* imported by the Portuguese) and listened to speeches in Hawaiian, a language peculiarly adapted to political utterances with its oratorical resonance and extremely limited vocabulary. It all made for a happy evening.

In the 1930s the political scene had already begun to change, but it was not until after the war that the changes were really noticeable. The rallies were better organized and the good feeling that marked the earlier political gatherings gave

way to sharper and more critical exchanges. The latent bitterness of the Hawaiians and Portuguese after four decades of
being considered second-class citizens began to show up more
openly. It had always been there, but not as visibly. The Republicans, with their conviction that they held an obligation for be-
nign protection of the interests of the *kanakas,* now faced an
influx of *malihini haoles* from the Mainland, and a new and more
hostile group of local politicians. The genial exchange of personalities between speakers of opposite parties was replaced by
more incisive verbal thrusts, such as the attack supplied by
Johnny Wilson's articulate speech writer, Willard Bassett. A
good deal was lost in this change, since the old speeches in
Hawaiian had made use of the double-entendre peculiar to the
Hawaiian language in which a slight change of a single syllable
could create out of a mild political comment a phrase as robust
as an excerpt from Captain Billy's "Whizbang." The audiences,
largely Hawaiian, would roar with each thrust. When the
speeches were made in English, this disappeared.

Meanwhile the smoldering anger, built up over more than
half a century, was beginning to smoke, and would soon turn to
fire. This new style was dangerous to the complacent Republicans, and Joe Farrington was the first to observe this. The new
candidates, many schooled in the harsh discipline of Communist
training schools, were beginning to say things about the Big Five
that no one had dared say before. Many of the speakers were war
veterans who had been educated in Mainland schools under the
GI Bill. They included not only *nisei* but *malihini haoles,* such as
Frank Fasi. It required more than the old friendly repartee for
the Republicans to meet these changing attitudes.

The point on which Farrington broke most openly with the
old guard of the Big Five-GOP coalition was on the issue of
statehood, which could no longer be sidetracked. The statehood
matter had been a sore point for years, and in fact it had first
been advanced by the original revolutionary group prior to Annexation—the elder Thurston, W.O. Smith, W. R. Castle, W. C.
Wilder, and other members of the Citizens' Committee for
Safety who ousted Queen Liliuokalani. The issue had been
dropped when it became obvious that statehood, which would

immediately enfranchise all persons born in Hawaii, was incompatible with the type of government the sugar planters intended to impose on the Territory. There were attempts from time to time to revive the statehood issue, including the efforts of Delegate Samuel Wilder King to introduce a bill in the House in 1935, but this was largely a pro forma gesture to test the attitude of Congress and also to appease the Hawaiians who had supported King. As a matter of policy, the Big Five continued to oppose the idea on the ground that the Territory was "not ready for statehood."

The recent Massie Case was cited as a reason for Hawaii's nonreadiness although actually it should have been used as an argument for unhampered self-government in the Islands, since it indicated that under the existing self-serving rule of the Big Five, impartial justice was virtually impossible.

Farrington, however, began coming out boldly for statehood, both editorially and in speeches. In 1939 the Legislature passed a resolution providing for a plebiscite in the 1940 general election, and statehood for Hawaii was approved by the voters by a margin of 67 to 33 percent. This was lost in the shuffle of military government when war broke out, and it was not until 1947 that Farrington, then the Delegate to Congress, was able to introduce a bill to make Hawaii a state, which passed the House by a vote of 196 to 133, but was buried in parliamentary procedures in the Senate.

Even then the opposition of the Big Five was adamant. Prior to the outbreak of war opponents of statehood had argued that with a population of 423,000 in the 1940 census, Hawaii had a preponderance of 37.3 percent Japanese, with only 15.2 percent Hawaiians and part-Hawaiians, and 24.5 percent Caucasian, or *haole.* This recapitulation of ethnic ratios overlooked entirely the fact that 80 percent of the so-called Japanese group were *nisei* and *sansei* (second generation children of Japanese origin born in Hawaii), and, therefore, were as much American as Italian-Americans in New York or those of Spanish speaking ancestry in California.

While these various elements of change have to some extent been treated separately, the total trend was along one basic line: Hawaii was growing up. The perspective of the Islands had enlarged—politically, socially, and economically. The old clichés about the Japanese peril and the Communist menace were of little significance compared to changes that were taking place in public thinking and *attitudes*. The new Hawaii that Dan Inouye and Sakae Takahashi had talked about in the hospital at Atlantic City was slowly beginning to take shape.

Dillingham, as spokesman for the old guard, continued to warn that the Islands were not ready for statehood, but there were other members of the oligarchy who were beginning to change their viewpoint. Jack Hall was no longer regarded as a menace—except by the ladies of Imua—and as the Territory approached a showdown on the issue of statehood industrial leaders spoke of Hall as a "stabilizing force" in labor-management relations. This nullified one of the primary arguments against statehood, and it appeared that even Imua was running out of ammunition. As a final salvo, they accused Burns of giving aid and comfort to the Communists by associating with Hall! Dr. Fuchs gave an excellent summary of Imua and its contributions in the following comment in *Hawaii Pono*,

> Perhaps the worst service performed by the organization was to obscure the real Communist record in the Islands. In all its attacks it did virtually nothing to explain why Americans should be opposed to totalitarian Communism. By lumping radicals, liberals, labor leaders and Communists together, Imua's arguments, even more than confusing, became boring. Surveys showed that a large majority of Hawaii's voters were actually more indifferent than opposed to the organization. Through its redundant and extreme accusations, it inhibited rational discussion by Hawaii's people of Communist influence in the Islands or anywhere else.[23]

In his analysis of Imua and its failure to raise the real issue of totalitarianism Dr. Fuchs may have overlooked one significant point: Mrs. Dillingham and the other ladies of Imua could have had little to say that would discredit totalitarianism; they and their forebears had lived pleasantly within that kind of society and enjoyed its fruits for more than half a century.

Dan Inouye met with Jack Burns and the others of the inner circle of the Burns group of independents at a local restaurant late in the summer of 1954. The Democrats had agreed to nominate Burns to run for delegate against Farrington, the Republican incumbent, in the general election. Inouye had been named campaign manager for Burns, and they had been planning strategy, not merely for electing Burns, but gaining control of the Legislature. In the 1952 elections a number of new Democratic faces had appeared in both Senate and House—many of them *nisei* and independent *haole* supporters of Burns.

"The time had come," as Inouye said later, "to make our bid for the Legislature." Not once in the history of the Territory had the Democrats held a majority in either branch; and only once—in 1946—had they drawn even in the House.

It was at this point that Burns, as Inouye related it later, "dropped his bombshell." At least it was a bombshell for Inouye. Burns had been saying little while the others, ringed around the room, were discussing pros and cons of strategy. They had whittled down the Republican majorities in both houses in 1952, and they believed the year 1954 was the time to "Go for broke!"

Burns coughed, as he usually did when he wanted to attract attention. Then he said, "Dan, I think it's time for you to run."

Inouye was not quite prepared for the suggestion. He was just under thirty, and his political experience at the time consisted of helping behind the scenes in two campaigns—the one in 1948 when he first offered his services to Jack Burns, and the 1952 campaign, with some precampaign experience in 1950 before he left for Washington. The time he had put in at the Democratic Headquarters in Washington when he was attending George Washington University might be considered training but not experience.

"Why me?" he asked. "There are quite a few others who have been around longer and are better qualified."

"Because you can win," Burns said quietly. "We need winners, Dan."

Dan Aoki, the leader of the 442nd Club, now one of Burns's staunchest supporters, agreed with him. "You've got the right combination, Dan—you've had war service and you're a new face in politics. If we want the vets' vote, we've got to give them somebody they care about—one of their own."

It was settled that Dan Inouye would run for the territorial House. There were others among the independents who were not all *nisei* and not all veterans of the European Theater, who now sought political office. There was Spark Matsunaga of the 100th Battalion and Masato Doi of the 442nd; but there also was Russell Kono from the China-Burma-India Theater, and Herman Lum, a Chinese who had grown up in the slums of Honolulu and become a lawyer. Matsuo Takabuki, from Waialua, ran for the Board of Supervisors, and Anna Kahanamoku, sister-in-law of Duke Kahanamoku who had been Olympic swimming champion in 1912 and later was Sheriff of Honolulu, became a candidate for the House.

Dan Inouye's plunge into the political pool was planned that evening at the restaurant, but it actually occurred one night during the campaign. After announcing his candidacy for the House from the Fourth District of Oahu, Dan proposed that candidates of both parties meet on a common platform to debate the issues and pay jointly for radio coverage. This would not have been a novelty on the Mainland after the Kennedy-Nixon confrontation in 1960, but in 1954 it was a new technique.

Political rallies in Hawaii had often been sponsored by Democrats, because they seemed to get the most fun out of them, although they usually got fewer votes. The format consisted of song-and-dance entertainment with a few lively speeches. These were remembered nostalgically from the days of Prince Cupid and Billy Jarrett, but this was a thing of the past and seldom involved anything but personal issues.

"We understood the real issues," Dan Inouye said, "and we were prepared to talk about them. Educational programs, economic development, land reforms, rehabilitation and reclamation projects—these were the things to discuss. Why not debate them?"

The invitation to join in debates at first was ignored by the Republican strategists. But the Democratic team—six of them on Oahu—toured the city without Republican opposition, hammering away night after night at what they regarded as key issues. Finally the pressure became too strong to be disregarded. The GOP decided to organize a Truth Squad that was assigned to follow the Democratic speakers. The first confrontation occurred at Ainahaina School, on Oahu. The first Democratic speaker had completed about five minutes of his talk when a member of the Republican Truth Squad stepped up and grabbed the microphone.

If the Democrats wanted to debate the issues, here they were: the Communists were linked with the ILWU; control of the Democratic party was held by the ILWU; the Democratic Party had been captured by Jack Hall, with Harry Bridges calling signals from Communist Headquarters in San Francisco!

Inouye sat listening, numbed with sudden realization that everything the man was saying was going out over the air. The program was on radio time, paid for by the Democratic Committee! The Republicans were suddenly reaping the rewards. It was a rather blinding thought.

"I remember getting to my feet and moving over to the microphone," he said. "It wasn't actually my turn to speak next, and I had no idea at the time what I intended to say or do. As a matter of fact, until I began talking everything was blurred in my mind."

His wife, Margaret, sat in the audience watching him, and she was able to give the best account of what happened. "I knew Dan was mad, because the muscles on his neck tightened. They always do that when he gets mad." He reached with his left hand and gripped the microphone, taking it away from the moderator. Then, to get the crowd's attention, he waved what would have been his right arm if it had not been shot off in the war. As it was, all he waved was his empty sleeve. Then he tore up the notes he had prepared ripping them with his teeth, threw them away, and with his left hand again gripped the microphone.

"I can't help wondering," he said, his voice tense, "whether the people of Hawaii will not think it strange that the only weapon the Republicans seem to have in their arsenal is to label as Communists those men of the Islands who have so recently returned from defending liberty on the firing lines in Italy and France. Let me speak for those who did not come back—I *know*

I speak for my colleagues on this platform—when I say that we bitterly resent having our loyalty and patriotism questioned by cynical political hacks who lack the courage to debate the real issues of this campaign."

Then he raised the empty sleeve where his right arm should have been. "I had never before called attention to my disability," he explained later, "because I didn't consider it a qualification for public office." At the moment he was trembling with anger. He lifted the stump of his severed arm and shook it.

"I gave this arm to fight the fascists," he said in a loud, resonant voice. "If my country wants the other one to fight Communists, it can have it!"

There was a moment of silence; then the place broke into an uproar. "It's about time somebody stood up to them!" one man yelled. The man from the Truth Squad left the platform. According to Inouye, this was the last appearance of the Truth Squad and the turning point in the election. Five of the six Democratic candidates in the Fourth District of Oahu were elected to the House. In the final count for the Territory, the Democrats won twenty-two seats out of thirty in the House and two-thirds of the Senate. Inouye led the Democratic ticket with the largest plurality of any candidate. The only really vital loss was in the race for Delegate to Congress. Joe Farrington had died at his desk in Washington in June of 1954, just before the election. His widow, Elizabeth Farrington, was named to fill out his term and was pressed into service for the fall campaign. She won by less than 1,000 votes over Jack Burns. The most ironic twist of the election was on the Island of Hawaii where Doc Hill, who had predicted that "not in a thousand years" would Japanese become Americanized, lost to Nelson Doi, a *nisei* Democrat.

Meanwhile, a new personality was added to the growing strength of the independents. Oren Long, a former schoolteacher, was appointed by President Truman to replace Judge Ingram Stainback as Governor, ending the long list of Big Five-GOP selections who had sat as Democrats in the Governor's chair. It followed a period of increasing friction between Stainback and almost every other Democrat in Hawaii. His unrelenting attacks on communism had been so extreme and chiefly rhetorical that he actually strengthened Jack Hall and the ILWU. Johnny Wilson warned Washington that Stainback would ruin the Democrats in Hawaii if he persisted in assailing the labor leader, and Stainback retaliated by accusing Wilson's speechwriter, Willard Bassett, a former newspaperman, of being in league with the Communists. He even took aim at Chuck Mau, driving him into Burns's camp; and also attacked the venerable Charlie Kauhane, one of the veteran Democrats in the Legislature, whom he accused of being "too friendly" with Hall and his "Communist gang."

Hall thrived on this sort of opposition; and Stainback's close association with the Big Five was no disadvantage to the labor movement. This happy circumstance was eliminated, however, when President Truman replaced Stainback with Long, who had been Superintendent of Public Instruction when Dan Inouye was at McKinley High School and had presented the future Senator from Hawaii with his high school diploma.

Long was quite different from Stainback, a quiet, rather frail man with a scholarly appearance and a reputation for both fairness and firmness. He had been a registered Democrat since 1920 when he graduated from Teachers College at Columbia University, and after a short period of teaching on Kauai he became deputy superintendent of schools for the Territory. Long was instrumental in introducing the English Standard School, which he sincerely believed would raise the standard of English spoken in the schools of Hawaii. He was firmly committed to Miles Cary's educational policies, which in a large measure were the key to Hawaii's second revolution. This educational philosophy had helped create an electorate and the political and social philosophy that produced leaders like Daniel Inouye, Sakae Takahashi, Spark Matsunaga, and other *nisei* who joined with Jack Burns in building a new Hawaii.

One of Long's first acts as Governor was to name Sakae Takahashi as territorial Treasurer, a move that drew bitter complaints from the old guard of both parties, but it was part of Long's build-up of a nucleus of independent Democrats. His tenure as Governor lasted only until 1953, following Dwight Eisenhower's election as President; but in that two-year period he had contributed to a mature, cohesive political force that drew together scattered fragments of an independent Democratic coalition—Dr. Gregg Sinclair, of the University of Hawaii, as well as Vincent Esposito, Tom Gill, Frank Fasi, Patsy Mink, and the Burns-Inouye group.

This alliance, quite significantly, was not built on a collective power base, but on a commonality of belief in a political philosophy that was—in the battered parlance of the Mainland —seeking to "restore power to the people." Long's greatest asset was that as an educator he remained aloof from intraparty squabbles; but even beyond that, he was dedicated to an egalitarian form of democracy more in the tradition of Paine, Jefferson, and De Tocqueville than the power base system advocated by Jack Hall. In this respect, he was one of the important creators of Hawaii's second revolution, which differed from certain more explosive forms of rebellion urged by the New Left a decade later on the Mainland in at least one significant respect: in Hawaii the revolt succeeded. Years after Long had passed through the governorship and the Territorial Senate to become United States Senator from Hawaii, a discerning analyst might have found in his quiet wisdom one of the underlying forces that brought about the success of Hawaii's second revolution.

Part IV/1956-1960
The Fiftieth State

The Republicans in Hawaii faced a situation in 1955 not unlike that which had confronted the Democrats in 1933. President Roosevelt's landslide victory in 1932 had carried Link McCandless into Washington. This gave the Democrats a nonvoting Congressman and a Governor of rather dubious political distinction; but that was all. The territorial Legislature was solidly Republican, as usual. Twenty-two years later the Democrats for the first time had control of the Legislature, but lacked the delegateship and the Governor's chair.

There was one important difference. In 1933 the Republicans were staunchly committed to Big Five policies, and the Big Five were firmly entrenched in the Islands' economy. This was no longer true. Sugar was still "King" but held its throne rather precariously; as many economists had pessimistically warned, the sugar and pineapple industries were nearing the point of saturation. Since they were the base of the Territory's income in Mainland dollars, the balance of payments was shifting as the population increased, and unless some miracle intervened, this was the road to bankruptcy. The miracle occurred in 1941 in the form of World War II, but this was only temporary relief. It occurred again with the Korean War, and it was still temporary.

Of perhaps even greater significance, the Big Five were no longer established in the paternalistic position they had occupied for fifty years. Their stranglehold on the Islands politically as well as economically was weakening; and in fact the Big Five were now really the "Big One"—Castle & Cooke, headed by Alex Budge; or if one included Walter Dillingham, the strongest of the independents and an industrialist rather than a sugar factor, it might be called the "Big Two." Whatever it was, the oligarchy was suffering from both political and economic

14

Changing the Guard

anemia. Its preeminence had been diluted not only by defense spending in the Territory, but by an influx of such Mainland money as the investments of Henry J. Kaiser, who came to Hawaii as a visitor and remained to become its most important financial entrepreneur.

It has been noted that sugar exports, the barometer of Hawaii's economic health until the 1950s, had reached a total of about one million tons a year in 1930 and fluctuated around that figure for the next three decades. The dollar value varied, dropped from $150 million to as low as $125 million in 1950, but moved slowly upward again during the next decade—except for 1958, when an extended plantation strike dropped the figure to about $106 million, based on only 764.9 thousand tons produced. Pineapple continued to climb slowly until it reached nearly $125 millions in 1958, the year before statehood, and temporarily passed the value of sugar exports that year.

However, the population was advancing steadily and as predicted by Dr. Romanzo Adams in 1935, Hawaii was approaching the saturation point in its basic economy. It would have passed that point before the end of the 1930s if it had not been for a rapid increase in defense expenditures prior to World War II. Ten years later the Bank of Hawaii's indefatigable economist, James H. Shoemaker, announced that the trade balance with the Mainland had shifted from "favorable" to "unfavorable." The total inflow of Mainland dollars in 1950, including such "visible" items as sugar and pineapples as well as "invisible" goods and services sold in Hawaii for Mainland dollars, amounted to $513.6 million compared with $545.4 million in expenditures. In other words, Hawaii's balance of payments was on the wrong side of the ledger by approximately $31.8 million. In simpler terms, Hawaii was slowly draining its financial resources. During the half-century prior to World War II there had been an almost parallel increase in sugar and pineapple production and population growth. But after 1932, as Shoemaker noted, there was a "leveling off in output" with a decline in acreage and equivalent decline in employment on the plantations; yet the population continued to grow. Sugar, as has been noted, ranged around a million tons a year and stayed there. Pineapple, which had ex-

perienced a rapid growth in the 1920s, leveled off at about 12
million cases a year. Even with defense money pumped into the
economy by the military establishment the point was startlingly
clear: Hawaii could no longer depend upon sugar and pineapples to support its increasing population.The one underlying
factor that contributed to the decline in the power of the Big
Five, and for which the oligarchy could not be held entirely
responsible, although it contributed to it by its intransigence in
management-labor relations, was the rising power of the labor
movement. Shoemaker put his finger on this in 1954, when he
wrote:

> Management policy in Hawaii from the early beginnings of the
> plantation period tended to prevent the development of strong
> labor organizations in the Territory. Between Annexation (1900)
> and World War II, however, the policy was benevolent, paternal-
> istic and conciliatory. In its simplest terms it was one of strong
> emphasis on employe welfare programs, the betterment of work-
> ing conditions, the gradual increase in wages combined with an
> opposition to labor organization . . .
>
> At the turn of the century, when Hawaii became a Territory,
> wages were comparable to Oriental standards rather than to
> Mainland standards. By the beginning of World War II earnings
> of workers on Hawaiian plantations were *higher than the average
> earnings of farm workers on the Mainland.* [italics added].[24]

This change in the status of field workers—higher wages
and better living conditions—was ascribed by Shoemaker
mainly to advances in sugar and pineapple production technology; and to some extent this was true. But the real stimulus
in the growth of labor power was the introduction of skilled and
experienced labor organizers, a factor muted by most economic
experts; and whenever it was referred to, it was usually coupled
with intimations that the labor organizers were either Communists, or at least Communist-oriented. There was a great deal of
truth in this assertion, since many were trained in Communist
"schools" on the Mainland; but it was the advance of militant
labor that brought the first great pressure on the rather antiquated labor-management policies of the Big Five. As noted
earlier, this break-through of labor was one of the three basic

factors, together with the introduction of a clearer concept of democratic processes through the public school system and the need of economic support from sources other than sugar and pineapples, that led to Hawaii's second revolution.

In his economic review of Hawaii, Shoemaker listed three prewar weaknesses of Hawaii's labor groups: (1) lack of organizing experience; (2) racial conflicts resulting from distrust among the various labor groups (such as the Japanese *vs.* the Filipinos); and (3) a tradition of paternalistic labor relations in the managerial policies of the sugar planters that obstructed union organization. He made the point that "wartime policies of government" instituted by the military establishment were such as to "bring into focus all of those forces tending toward labor organization which had been accumulating prior to the war."

> When wartime restrictions were lifted these forces, and the resentments which military government controls had engendered, resulted in a remarkable shift from a relatively unorganized to a highly organized Hawaiian labor movement. Between 1944 and 1947 the centers of economic power and labor-management relations in Hawaii were decidedly altered. [25]

Thus, while political and racial antagonisms engendered by the oligarchy over a period of a half century were suddenly removed from Big Five control and passed over to the military government, the old system began to break down. The oligarchy was no longer able to control factors that had given them feudal domination since the days of the monarchy when descendants of missionaries and merchant traders first found a way to take possession of the sugar-growing lands of Hawaii.

Putting his finger on the most sensitive spot, Shoemaker wrote:

> It is not surprising that in the early post-War years there were more strikes than in any comparable period in the history of Hawaii. The two greatest strikes were in sugar and shipping. A sugar strike began September 1, 1946, and lasted seventy-nine days. A shipping strike began May 1, 1949, and lasted one hundred seventy-seven days. Neither represented a clear-cut victory for labor or management. Both were costly, not only to the industries involved but to the Hawaiian economy as a whole. [26]

It was during these early postwar years when the deterioration in Hawaii's balance of payments occurred because of the inability of the Islands' two principal industries to sustain their growing population that Shoemaker's clear-cut warning became evident; Hawaii could not continue to live on its income from sugar and pineapples. What Shoemaker and other experts did not foresee—or did not mention—was that the answer to Hawaii's dilemma was already in progress. Outside forces were already moving in. There were also new forces—both economic and political—emerging within Hawaii itself that would build a "new Hawaii" on the crumbling structure of the old sugar planter-Big Five complex. The old guard was changing, and King Sugar no longer was king.

The two factors that contributed most to the resurgence of Hawaii's economy were the expansion of defense spending in the Islands and the influx of Mainland investments, neither of which could be attributed to the financial genius of the Big Five. In 1950 $214 million in goods and services were sold for defense purposes, almost equal to the income from sugar and pineapples. Tourism was also increasing, although not at the rate the Islands would experience in the decade after statehood.

Investment in Hawaiian enterprises was the most visible factor. Hotels sprang up along the Waikiki Beach area and also on the other Islands. These investments were not merely by individuals, such as Henry J. Kaiser, Seth Murchison and other Mainlanders who became interested in prospects of Hawaii; but also by the Standard Oil Company, which began a huge oil refinery near Barber's Point, west of Honolulu; and cement plants and steel mills and similar heavy goods facilities were being constructed, adding to Hawaii's industrial production in areas other than sugar and pineapples.

In addition to Mainland investment, new types of industrial and commercial entrepreneurs were emerging in Hawaii itself, not associated with the Big Five. The so-called Chinese tycoon has been mentioned. Chinn Ho, the grandson of a Chinese ricefield worker and a graduate of McKinley High School in the early 1920s, was one of the first of these. He saw the value of homesites that could be purchased in fee simple, rather than leased from the large landholders; and in 1947 he acquired 9000 acres of former sugar lands of Waianae plantation for homesite development. By 1950 his company's assets rose to $2,000,000; he was challenging major operators in the hotel business. Hung Wo Ching, who reorganized Aloha Airlines, has been cited as an example of the promotional genius of the Hawaiian-born Chinese. His brother, Hung Wai Ching, created a financing empire that ultimately gained him a place on the Board of Regents of the University of Hawaii. Hiram Fong launched his career with a financial group that operated several real estate and insurance agencies, and not only became wealthy but won a seat in the United States Senate, the first of Oriental extraction to sit in that august body, an honor he was later forced to share with Dan Inouye.

The emergence of local business promoters born and bred in Hawaii but not members of the *kamaaina haole* families was one of the basic prestatehood developments, and the rise to financial and political power of the Chinese tycoon was a dramatic symptom of this change. It was a development that would have been unthinkable a quarter of a century before statehood, and a trend certainly not anticipated by the Big Five. However, in justice to their capacity for change, there was no real resistance from the members of the oligarchy, once the open economy was under way.

The Chinese, it will be recalled, were the first aliens recruited for sugar plantations, and they were the first to leave for better opportunities in the cities. In 1853 there were 364 Chinese in Hawaii; by 1910 there were 21,674 and by 1950, including Hawaiian-born Chinese, the total was 32,376. Even more striking, the percentage of Chinese employed in agricultural work had dropped from more than 50 percent in 1910 to about 5 percent in 1950—the largest shift from agricultural labor to professional and business activities of any ethnic group in Hawaii. In other words, the Chinese had followed the rosy road from hard field labor to more remunerative business enterprises more rapidly and more successfully than any other racial group in the Islands. Andrew Lind, professor of sociology at the University of Hawaii, quotes a missionary on this subject,

The Chinese have the very qualities which the Hawaiians most lack—industry, providence, subtlety—all the money-saving virtues are with the Chinese. Idleness, carelessness, generosity, simplicity, all the money-losing virtues are with the Hawaiians.[27]

The rise of Chinese influence, one of the more intriguing aspects of the development of new Hawaii, will be discussed in the review of the decade that followed statehood, and it will be observed how quietly and unobtrusively they worked into positions of economic and political power, starting with less and ending with more than any other descendants of the original immigrant field workers. The Chinese never became a factor in labor struggles, as the Japanese did; they simply headed for the urban centers and in the true Horatio Alger style, usually associated with ambitious Americans, they worked their way up. No one was more unexpectedly and to some extent painfully aware of this in the years after statehood than the *kamaaina haoles* who had blissfully supposed they would always keep the Chinese "in their place."

The changes in the Islands were physical as well as economic and political. Signs of growth appeared everywhere. Waikiki, the Mecca of tourists, was a dramatic illustration. Twenty years before statehood, Kalakaua Avenue was lined with beach bungalows where tourists rented rooms or small apartments and walked to the beach in bathing suits. The only landmark up to 1925 had been the stately Moana Hotel, a square white structure that rose severely among the palms. Then the Royal Hawaiian Hotel was built, with its turrets of turquoise and coral pink. By 1950 the Avenue was lined with glittering pagodas of progress. Old houses were torn down to make room for restaurants and shops. The old Outrigger Canoe Club, once an open pavilion with lockers under it, had become a posh clubhouse, and finally was moved out to Castle's Point to make room for an even gaudier collection of shops and airline ticket offices. Both sides of Kalakaua were lined with hotels with tropical decor and heated swimming pools, towering above the beach—the Princess Kaiulani, the Reef, the Edgewater, the Waikikian, the Hawaiian Village, monuments to Henry Kaiser, Hilton, and

Chinn Ho. They built not only hotels but hospitals, and Kaiser even began constructing an entire city out beyond Honolulu near Koko Head, where mullet ponds and fishing cottages used to offer simple scenes of tropical life for simple tourists.

By the mid-1950s all the old sleepy indolence of Waikiki had passed away. Waikiki Inn had been transformed to Waikiki Tavern, with uniformed maître d' and waitresses replacing Japanese girls in blowzy house dresses and a Chinese busboy in a dirty apron. The old Moana pier, which once jutted out from the banyan tree courtyard, haunted by Hawaiian "music boys" strumming their plaintive melodies just for the fun of it, had disappeared; and if tourists wanted to hear Hawaiian music, they paid for it.

The beach itself was reduced to a flat stretch of naked reef, the sand washed away except for a narrow strip of shoreline and a sanded stretch known as Kuhio Beach where the public might swim. Back streets that paralleled Kalakaua were now lined with high-rise apartment houses, interspersed with pizza parlors, hot-dog stands, and dimly lighted bistros.

The land along the Beach, once the fringe of the Chinese duck ponds that stretched from Waikiki across the flats to Waialae Road, had been drained by the Ala Wai Canal, and the pleasant palm-fringed beach that Mark Twain described as "a paradise for the indolent" had begun to look very much like a section of the Strip at Las Vegas.

Eighty years earlier Mark Twain had predicted this outcome. He wrote in an article in 1873 for the New York *Herald Tribune:* "The traders brought labor and fancy diseases to the Islands—in other words, long, deliberate, infallible destruction; and the missionaries brought the means of grace to get the natives ready. So the two forces are working along harmoniously, and anybody who knows anything about figures can tell you when the last *kanaka* will be in Abraham's bosom and his Islands in the hands of the whites. It is the same as calculating an eclipse of the moon; if you start right, you cannot miss it."

The changes wrought upon this tropical paradise were undoubtedly inevitable. It would have been impossible for a people as naïve and friendly as the Hawaiians, so lacking in the aggressive instincts and ruthless tactics of the white man, to have survived in this strategic location. They occupied a small group of islands in the middle of the Pacific Ocean that within a century of the arrival of the missionaries would become the target of international struggles for trans-Pacific trade routes, with at least three great powers hoping to possess it. They were not suited, either by temperament or military capabilities, to fend off the invasion of the foreigners.

The point that needs to be stressed—and will become evident as the events of the next two decades are unfolded—is that it was equally impossible for the small group of descendants of those missionaries who seized the Islands from the Hawaiians to arrest the course of progress. The second revolution in Hawaii was as inevitable as the first.

The two years of rule by the Democrats, following the elections of 1954 in which they won more than two-thirds of the seats in the House and almost an equal proportion in the Senate, were not years of undiluted legislative achievement. As Dan Inouye later said, there were many Democrats in Hawaii who would "just as soon forget that session of the Legislature." The new Democrats were fresh and eager, but not particularly trained in parliamentary procedures, or the intrigues and strategy of vote-trading and all the other tricks known to the legislative trade.

With Charlie Kauhane, a veteran Hawaiian Democrat, as Speaker of the House, they had a nucleus of experience, but that was about all. Inouye was chosen by the Democratic caucus to be majority leader, a job of which he knew virtually nothing. In desperation he wrote to Sam Rayburn of Texas, whom he had never met, and asked him what the duties of a majority leader were. Rayburn had served in that capacity with the Democrats in Congress longer than any man of living memory.

Rayburn replied to the letter, explaining that it was difficult to define the duties of the office because there was no such office legally defined except by Congressional precedent. The one point he made was that the majority leader had to do what the majority of his party wanted him to do, or quit the job. He also had to be on friendly terms with everyone, including leaders of the opposite party; and in Inouye's case, that meant the new Republican Governor, Samuel Wilder King, who had been delegate back in prewar days when Dan was in high school.

This presented a ticklish problem, because most of what the Democrats were committed to do with their newly won power the Republicans were committed to oppose. A graduated income tax law was enacted, the first in the history of the Islands. Land reform laws were passed to replace the gerrymandered formula of the Big Five-GOP coalition which was designed to avoid obstructing King Sugar. Perhaps most important to the new Democratic majority—most of whom were there as a result of public school education in Hawaii—was the expansion and improvement of the Territory's educational system.

These were the kinds of bills Governor King was likely to veto without reading much more than the titles. Although the Democrats had the muscle to pass the laws, they did not have the power to override the Governor's veto. In the first session, which could last only sixty days, Governor King vetoed seventy-two items of legislation, a record of nullification unsurpassed in the history of the Territory and probably anywhere else.

Majority leader Inouye decided it was time to introduce the good-neighbor policy advocated by Sam Rayburn. He began to hold meetings with the Governor, who was not a particularly bull-headed man but more of a liberal Republican in the tradition of the Farringtons. However, he responded more naturally to Republican than Democratic pressure, so Inouye tried persuasion. He had only moderate success. The repeated spectacle of the freshman Democrats being routed in the Governor's office by each new package of progressive legislation was becoming embarrassing.

King actually held his position as Governor through the influence of Joe Farrington. The first choice for the job had been Randolph Crossley, a *malihini haole* from Kauai who had reorganized a bankrupt pineapple plantation on that Island in the 1930s and had important political connections, including having been a business partner of Herbert Brownell, President Eisenhower's political advisor. He had become chairman of the

Republican Party in Hawaii, and everything had seemed greased for Crossley's appointment as Governor by Eisenhower in 1953, when the old surge of anti-*haole* feeling that had dictated support for King as candidate for delegate twenty years before began to be felt in Washington. Delegate Farrington also knew a few people of political importance and Eisenhower was bombarded with telegrams and personal messages supporting King. As a part-Hawaiian, he would siphon off some of the Hawaiian vote that was swinging to the Democrats, and his negative attitude toward land reform was not much of a factor, since the Hawaiians traditionally displayed little interest in land, as indicated by their mild reaction to the Hawaiian Homes Act. The result, in brief, was that King got the job and Crossley was offered an ambassadorship to an Asian country, which he declined, returning to Hawaii.

Farrington's support of King was not a haphazard selection. He had shrewdly sensed a break in Republican ranks. He had been backed by Jack Hall since 1946, and if he were to retain the support of labor he needed King to offset the growing alliance between the ILWU, with their predominant membership of Hawaiians on the waterfront, and the Democrats. King was not only a liberal Republican but his association with the Big Five was not as obvious as Crossley's.

The choice was a wise one. It moved King into position to assume the party leadership that began to fall apart when Farrington died in 1954. Elizabeth Farrington had served as National Committeewoman from Hawaii and knew Washington, but she was no pillar of political strength. It was upon King that the burden of resurrecting the Republican Party would fall in the years that followed.

Jack Burns was disappointed but not discouraged by his narrow loss to Farrington's widow in 1954. He met with his chief strategists—Dan Inouye, the party's strongest votegetter; Dan Aoki, Matsuo Takabuki, Bill Richardson, George Ariyoshi, and Sakae Takahashi, and also consulted with independents Tom Gill and Vincent Esposito, and with ex-Governor Oren Long, to plan for the 1956 campaign.

By this time the main issue between the Big Five and the

builders of new Hawaii was already defined. It was the long-dormant issue of statehood, which Farrington had recognized as inevitable but which the die-hard members of the *kamaaina haoles* led by Walter Dillingham and Imua refused to concede. Jack Burns and Dan Inouye were aware, perhaps more than any others, that admission of Hawaii as a state would spell the doom of feudal control of the Islands by the expiring oligarchy.

The story of Hawaii's achievement of statehood has many ramifications, in which almost every variety of conniving known to politics was employed. Statehood's final enactment was a case history in devious political cunning, particularly on the part of its long-standing enemies, the *kamaaina haoles* of Hawaii.

The first mention of statehood for Hawaii occurred more than a hundred years before it became a fact. In 1849 an editor of an Upstate New York weekly, William Olund Bourne of the Lewis County *Northern Journal*, who seems to have been knowledgeable in Pacific affairs, proposed that the United States take over this string of tropical islands as a state before England beat us to it. Five years later King Kamehameha III, the young, aggressive monarch of Hawaii, officially proposed a treaty with the United States in which the Islands would be admitted to the Union "on perfect equality with other States."

The proposal came originally from Dr. Gerrit Judd, one of the missionary advisors to Kamehameha III, who was strongly pro-American. Dr. Judd saw wealth in the land and strategic and trading advantages of an American outpost in the Pacific. Kamehameha III died suddenly, however, and his successor, Kamehameha IV, was more inclined toward the English and evinced little interest in union with the United States, so the matter was dropped. When Kalakaua, the High Chief of Kauai, became King in 1874, he agreed to a Treaty of Reciprocity with the United States. This gave the new sugar interests in Hawaii the stimulus of a duty-free quota; and immediately a clique of *haoles* began to agitate for Annexation to the United States, finally overthrowing Liliuokalani, who opposed the plan. The negative attitude of the planters themselves toward actual statehood has been noted; and it was this influence that ultimately

15

Sugar and Statehood

guided the policies of the Big Five in later years.

The political and economic background of the statehood proposal is necessary to understand some of the varying attitudes toward this question after the Revolution of 1893 when the sugar planter oligarchy took over rule of the Islands. At the time of the revolution it was anticipated Hawaii would become a state, but this notion was gradually dropped after a closer study of American laws concerning the rights of citizens. These laws provided far less control of voting privileges under statehood than had been written into the "bayonet Constitution" of 1887. It was felt that while economic criteria for voting rights could not very well be adopted under the American flag, control of elections would be more feasible under territorial administration, with an appointed governor.

During the first quarter of a century that followed Annexation there was little mention of statehood for Hawaii. Prince Kuhio first petitioned Congress for enactment of a statehood bill in 1903 and again in 1919, but these were pro forma gestures which did not even reach the committee stage. The lack of voting privileges in Congress was of little importance to members of the oligarchy; they got what they wanted by more subtle means, and little could be gained by having two senators and one or more congressmen in Washington, who might be more sensitive to the demands of the electorate than the wishes of the Big Five.

There were rumblings of renewed interest in statehood during the Massie Case, when it began to be evident that the prosecution of the five youths for the assault on Mrs. Massie was a frameup designed to appease the Navy. At this point a suggestion was made that a Commission Government might be established, but in a form that was worse than statehood. A Congressman from Illinois lent substance to the matter by offering a resolution proposing that the territorial Government be directed by a High Commissioner sent to Hawaii from Washington.

From time to time members of the Big Five had suggested a Commission Government as more efficient than the territorial rule, assuming the commissioners would be appointed by local

Republicans, or by the same means the Big Five had used to obtain the appointment of Lucius Pinkham and Charles McCarthy during the Democratic administration of Woodrow Wilson. The notion of a government controlled directly by Washington was a different matter, and the oligarchy reacted with horror and dismay. Telegrams were dispatched to Washington protesting such a violation of the Organic Act. The *Hawaii Hochi,* never averse to needling the Big Five, commented in an editorial entitled "Boomerang,"

> For years our local leaders in politics and industry have been trying to frighten the people of Hawaii with threats of a "Commission form of Government." To serve their own selfish ends and whip reluctant citizens into line, they have painted a terrifying picture of this bogey-man. . . .
>
> Now the chickens have come home to roost!
>
> The imaginary "bogey" has materialized into a very vigorous and menacing reality.
>
> The amusing feature of the present situation—if there is anything amusing about it—is that the threat is directed against the very ones who have been using it so long as a means of frightening the people of the Territory into doing their bidding.
>
> The latest measure introduced in Congress is quite different from the "Commission Government" idea. . . . This solution would not deprive the people of Hawaii of their rights. But it would absolutely prevent the dictation of appointments by the local coterie of "big interests". . . . It would strike a fatal blow at the domination of local government by our "captains of industry". . . .[28]

This proposal, which amounted to a carpet-bag government, did not get far at the time, although it reappeared later in the form of a proposed amendment to the Hawaiian residency clause in the Organic Act, which would permit a nonresident to be appointed governor. This frightened the Big Five sufficiently to arouse speculation as to whether statehood might not be a means of fending off such possibilities, but there was still rigid opposition to statehood by most *kamaaina haoles.*

After Delegate King's trial balloon bill in 1935, which hardly got off the ground, a Congressional group journeyed to

Hawaii and spent two weeks, from October 6 to 22, 1937, questioning witnesses and enjoying the celebrated hospitality of Hawaii; but World War II broke out shortly afterward and the issue was dropped for the duration.

Meanwhile Joe Farrington, whose father had advocated statehood for years, both as governor and in the *Star-Bulletin,* became delegate in 1940, succeeding King, and for the first time an energetic effort was launched to bring the statehood matter before Congress. Farrington introduced the bill which the House passed in 1947. This was actually the first time a Hawaiian statehood measure had been brought to the floor of the House for a vote, although Prince Kuhio had introduced two petitions—in 1903 and 1919—and Victor Houston had strongly urged such a bill.

Kuhio had wanted participation by Hawaii in Federal land grants so that Hawaiians could homestead land which the plantations were leasing, and he also wanted Federal funds for education; but these matters stirred little interest among the planters, since they did not contribute to King Sugar. However, when Houston in 1929 suggested that Hawaii might not be able to fight off reduction in their duty-free sugar quota unless they could put voting Senators and Representatives in Congress, this struck a spark, although it did not ignite much action. Harry Baldwin of Maui agreed with Houston that cutting Hawaii's sugar quota was a problem, but the danger of Japanese—or anyone except the Big Five—gaining control of the Territory's elective offices under statehood was far more serious than cutting the sugar quota.

The extent of this miscalculation became evident five years later when Congress enacted the Jones-Costigan Act which ignored Hawaii's treaty rights under Annexation as "an integral part of the United States" and, as far as sugar imports were concerned, ranked it with Puerto Rico and the Philippines as a nondomestic sugar producer, reducing raw sugar imports to allow for increasing production of beet sugar in Colorado.

This posed a dilemma for the sugar planters. They did not want statehood and they did not want to become the pawn of Congress with respect to the sugar quota. At this point the Big

Five decided to toss the trial balloon into the air in the form of HR 3034 petitioning for statehood for Hawaii, to test Congress' attitude on the question. At the same time the territorial Legislature passed a bill creating an Equal Rights Commission, which will be discussed later in the context of Hawaii's final battle for statehood. These two acts revealed the extent of the Big Five dilemma, because if they argued too strongly for statehood they might get it in a form they did not want; and at the same time they realized they needed more political muscle in Washington. It would be fair to state that during the entire statehood campaign there was never any real question in the minds of the Big Five as to what was good for Hawaii; the question purely was, What was good for King Sugar? The extent to which they were dedicated to this view will become clearer as the story of the battle for statehood progresses.

Shortly after the war, when Delegate Farrington was again pressing the issue, the oligarchy finally seemed to have decided that statehood was the lesser of the evils, and began what appeared to be a campaign in support of statehood. A close examination of their actions, however, raises some doubt as to the sincerity of this effort. In 1946, when Governor Stainback was hot on the heels of Communists who had infiltrated labor, he stated before a House subcommittee that statehood for Hawaii was premature, calling attention to the point that this was a "schooling period" for the Territory, adding, "The question we are bringing before you today [is] whether it [Hawaii] is at this time qualified" to be a state.

The Territory by this time had spent nearly a half century being "schooled" for statehood, during which time it had paid more than a billion dollars into the Federal Treasury, with no voice as to how the money would be spent. Its annual contribution in Federal taxes was larger than that of ten states and up to that point there had been nine separate hearings before Congressional committees on the Territory's fitness for statehood.

Stainback would up his testimony by stating, "What we have feared more than anything else was Shintoism [of the Japanese] —the worship of the Emperor of Japan." This was in 1946, *after the war,* and the destruction of Japan's imperial rule had been completed.

A member of the Committee wanted to know whether the Chinese also practiced Shintoism and Stainback said, "No—they have their own Confucianism."

The member of the Committee said, "It would come from the Japanese?" and the Governor replied, "Yes—the Japanese."

A dozen years after this scholarly exchange Stainback—by this time a former Governor—wrote to the *Honolulu Advertiser,* "In the frenzied fight for statehood have our people ever been informed that statehood would not add one cent to our revenues but, on the contrary, would add to our expenditures? That with rising expenditures and increased taxes it would be difficult, if not impossible, to attract new industries to Hawaii as a State, but more likely to drive away some of those already here?"[29]

Judge Stainback's calculations may be as difficult to follow as his understanding of Shintoism and Confucianism, but the purpose of his argument was quite clear: As an obvious spokesman for the Big Five, he wanted it plainly understood that the voters of Hawaii at that time should not be entrusted with the election of their own governor and other territorial officials— whether because of the Japanese "menace," the threat of a Communist takeover, or their failure to understand the arithmetic of public finances. When these various arguments failed to arouse sufficient alarm, he switched to a new tack. Why not try a Commonwealth government? In a letter to Clinton P. Anderson, Senator from New Mexico, he referred to a conversation he had held with Randolph Crossley, the *malihini* pineapple grower from Kauai who made the unsuccessul bid for Governor of Hawaii, quoting Crossley as having said, "If the voters of Hawaii were given the choice of statehood or Commonwealth (a tax-exempt Territory), they would vote three to one for such a tax-exempt Territory."

The source of Crossley's estimate of what Hawaii's voters favored was not mentioned in the letter, but there were already sufficient facts on record to disprove the assumptions. The voters of Hawaii had expressed themselves in favor of statehood by referendum in 1940 and in several polls by ratios as high as 10 to 1. In 1956, the Honolulu Chamber of Commerce had secretly polled its members and found 64 percent in favor of statehood! In a statement to the Senate Committee on Territories, Secretary of the Interior Fred Seaton said unequivocally, "The argument on the Commonwealth status is completely dissipated because the Hawaiians do not want it. They want statehood."

Nevertheless, Stainback's suggestion, which he also incorporated in a letter to the *Advertiser* (dated August 20, 1958), had already begun to take root as a last effort of the *kamaaina haoles* to block statehood. In a statement to the Senate Committee on February 25, 1959—just before the statehood bill was enacted —Senator Frank Church of Idaho said, "Already a Commonwealth Party has been activated there (in Hawaii). I talked with several of its leaders who would like to see Hawaii set loose from the United States, absolved of all Federal taxes, and granted full rights of self-government while the people retained for themselves American citizenship and the continued protection of the American flag. Patterned after the British system, the Commonwealth idea is alien to our American tradition of building one nation, rather than a loose-knot empire."

Meanwhile for twenty years each bill for statehood, as it was introduced in the House or Senate, went through the parliamentary wringer and was lost or sidetracked. From 1935, when Delegate King offered the first of the final series of twenty-two statehood bills, until 1958 just before passage of the final bill, there were no less than thirty-seven documents covering approximately 6,600 pages of printed text on the subject of "Statehood for Hawaii."

In this welter of conflicting viewpoints, both within the Territory and in Washington, it was evident to Jack Burns and his Democratic strategists that the time to strike was now. As he told Dan Inouye, his most successful vote-getter, "We've got to lay our plans for statehood now, or it will be sidetracked for another ten years."

Daniel Inouye possessed a rare combination of two virtues essential for a successful politician. He was a planner, and he could win elections. The phrase "without passion," which Dr.

Fuchs had used to describe Inouye's discussion with Sakae Takahashi at the convalescent hospital in Atlantic City, seemed to characterize the maturity that had replaced the rebel instincts of the one-time barefoot boy of McKinley High School. Burns had the same quality of calm and mature judgment, and the two made an excellent team.

The first thing they agreed upon was the need for dealing with Jack Hall if the election of 1956 were to be assured. The ILWU leader had survived the attack on his Communist affiliations with virtually no scars; and he still was the leading voice among nearly 50,000 members of organized labor unions in Hawaii. However, "dealing with Hall" meant different things to different people. To Hall it meant acceptance of whatever position the ILWU took on any political issue. This was basic training in the Communist school he had attended in San Francisco. To Burns and his "young Turks" it meant seeking a common ground for displacing an opposition that was inimical to the interests of both the Democrats and labor—the old Big Five-GOP coalition.

Hall was not sure he favored statehood, since there were no obvious or immediate advantages for the ILWU, and there might be some disadvantages. There were other labor forces in Hawaii, however, including the Hotel and Restaurant Employees and the Bartenders Union, both guided by Arthur Rutledge and counseled by John Reinecke, who had been one of the Hawaii Seven indicted in the Communist purge of 1951. Hall had to steer a course that would retain his power with labor, and it was about this time that he decided to swing toward the Burns movement.

Burns had already diluted Hall's influence with the Democratic Party and had steered the Party to success in the territorial elections of 1954, although he lost in his own race for delegateship against Elizabeth Farrington, who won the general election that fall by less than 1,000 votes. Burns and Inouye set their sights on the 1956 race as a prelude for the drive toward statehood.

"We need Hall's support to win," Burns had told Inouye and his other advisors. Actually, Hall had little reason to do

otherwise than support Burns and his independents. He had
supported Joe Farrington when he had been a sure winner, but
his widow was a different matter. Elizabeth Farrington had won
the special election after her husband's death in 1954 on a tide
of popular sentiment, but she barely squeaked through the following November, when she won by only 990 votes—69,466 to
68,576, or a margin of 0.6 percent. She was not likely to win in
1956, and Hall—throwing support to the sure winner—switched
to Burns.

Burns had told his strategy group—Inouye, Dan Aoki,
Sakae Takahashi, Bill Richardson, Chuck Mau, Herman Lum,
Matsuo Takabuki, Vincent Esposito, and George Ariyoshi—that
they "had to win this one" because failure would set back statehood for another decade. As it developed, the 1956 election was
the turning point in the statehood battle.

The key to the Democratic program in the 1955–1956
Legislature had been land reform and more money for public
schools. The Democrats had also prepared a sales tax bill that
was designed to put a levy on business, something utterly repugnant to the Big Five-GOP coalition. And they wanted a revision
of Hawaii's antiquated tax assessment procedures, inherited
from the days of the Republic, that would force the old estates
—the Bishop Estate, the Campbell Estate, and other large landholders—to put their land to use or be forced to sell to private
investors.

With overwhelming strength in the Legislature, the Democrats were able to pass the laws they wanted; but just as regularly
Governor King was able to veto them. Under the Organic Act,
the Governor's veto of financial measures could not be overrid-
den. As Dan Inouye expressed it, "The results were far from
happy. An eager gang of idealistic freshman legislators had coll-
ided head-on with a hard core of practical oldtimers, and there
was generated more heat than light."

The frustration of much of the legislative effort of 1955–
1956 brought on new changes in party alignments. Burns's defeat in 1954 was attributed to the lack of support by organized
labor, chiefly by the shifting tactics of Jack Hall, and as Burns

and Inouye had agreed, the Democrats "needed Hall" to win the delegateship in 1956. As a matter of fact, Hall also needed Burns. The fact that Elizabeth Farrington had won a narrow victory over Burns chiefly on the momentum of sympathy for her bereavement, with considerable support from the labor vote that had elected Joe Farrington five times, did not fool the sharp-witted boss of the ILWU. He was not sure his support would swing the election to the Republicans the next time. But he was sure that Burns could win with his support, and probably would win without it in view of the Democratic landslide in the legislative races in 1954.

The result was a coalition between the Burns group and Hall, and although the Republicans recorded some gains in 1956, the Burns-Inouye strategy worked. Mrs. Farrington had lost whatever political charisma she gained from the death of her husband, and Burns was swept into the delegateship. The shambles of the 1955–1956 legislative session was behind the Democrats, and they could even point to a record of good lawmaking that would have gone into effect if it had not been for Governor King's veto powers.

As a matter of record, King's tendency to veto whatever seemed displeasing to the Big Five-GOP coalition eventually proved his undoing. A graduated income tax law was passed again in 1957, and King vetoed it. The Democrats marshalled enough votes to pass it over his veto, and the Republicans were so annoyed at the abuse they took that they advised President Eisenhower to fire King. William F. Quinn, a comparative newcomer from the Mainland, who had failed to win election to the Senate the year before, was appointed to replace him.

The election of 1956 followed a Democratic legislative record that might have been exploited by the Republicans, but the rift between the Big Five old guard and the liberal wing seemed to have destroyed their effectiveness. Hiram Fong had remarked after the 1955 legislative session, "If the Republicans had written the script for the Democrats to foul up everything, in their wildest imagination they could not have written a script like that."

Burns had formed an uneasy coalition with some of the

more independent independents, who were anxious to mold the Democratic Party into a winning political force but were not too happy about Burns. Charlie Kauhane, who had been maneuvered into the speakership by Burns, had regarded this as a mandate to put his entire family on the public payrolls, and this disturbed many of those who were dedicated to a reform policy. He also made the mistake of referring to the House, with its preponderantly *nisei* membership, as "the Diet"—the name Japan uses for its Parliament—and as a result he received little support from the Japanese electorate and was not reelected in 1956. The Democrats shifted support for speakership of the new 1957 House to Vincent Esposito. Elmer Cravalho, who had strong labor backing on Maui, became chairman of the Finance Committee.

As a result of the elections of 1956, there were twelve Democrats to three Republicans in the 1957 Senate, and nearly two-thirds of the House were Democrats. Oddly enough, the voting results showed none of the racial trends anticipated by the Republicans. Younger Japanese and Chinese voted Democratic while the older generations in both groups continued to support the Republicans. The most influential factor was labor, led by Jack Hall. The only basically racial vote was that of the *haoles*, particular in the more exclusive residential districts of Oahu, which were strongly Republican. Another factor that weighed heavily for the Democrats was the voting turnout. Less than 50 percent of the registered voters cast ballots in 1954, an unusually low number. With the Democratic success at the polls that year, the 1956 figure rose to 88.7 percent, and in 1958 it was 89.3 percent.

Dan Inouye picked up a few lessons in politics during those two campaigns. As he said years later, "I had the scars to prove it." The desire to reform was one thing, but getting reforms through the legislative mill was something else. "At the end of that first session, I knew how to go about my job more patiently, and certainly more practically." One basic bit of wisdom the freshman Democrats of that session picked up was that "politics is the art of the possible—if you know how to go about it."

One specific axiom driven home to young Inouye was that

in politics one never takes anything for granted. He had decided that after having served his apprenticeship as House majority leader, he was ready for the speaker's job. He decided before the Democratic caucus to drop a word to his colleagues that he— Dan Inouye—was available. Two others were lining up support: Esposito and Cravalho.

The future Senator from Hawaii had reckoned without the *quid pro quo* that is essential to political success. If a candidate for any office wants something, it is usually taken for granted that he is willing to give something in return. Inouye moved around among his fellow Democrats, hinting that he would accept the speakership if it were offered, and received warm endorsements. In each case there were remarks about what committee posts each of the Democrats would like to have in case Inouye became speaker.

Dan Inouye possessed a natural sense of personal forth-rightness and honesty, so he avoided making definite commit-ments. When the ballots were counted after the vote for speaker, which was secret, there were three votes for Inouye—and one was his own! Esposito was chosen on the third ballot. Inouye was slightly stunned after the vote on the speakership when no less than eight members of his party came to him privately to assure him that they had cast their ballot in his favor.

As in the previous session, Inouye was elected majority leader. With a "substantial majority"—twenty Democrats in the thirty-three seats in the House—the rising power of the new political force began to forge a legislative program that included an increased minimum hourly wage, unemployment compensa-tion, increased funds for education, and new property taxes that would stimulate the development of unused land—all measures that had for years been abhorrent to the Big Five-GOP coalition.

The portents were becoming clear. A new generation of voters with a cross section of ethnic groups was taking control of what had been a *haole* feudal domain for more than a half century. It was preponderantly youthful, the generation that had reached maturity during World War II. The new elements in-cluded not only war veterans who, as one member of the 442nd Veterans Club put it, "had come back from the war with a big chip on our shoulder," but many Hawaiians, Portuguese, Chinese, and Filipinos who were not veterans and had not previously been strong elements in the electorate. The rise of the second-class citizens also included a large number of *malihini haoles* who had come to Hawaii from the Mainland after the war and had no prior allegiance to the Big Five or the *kamaaina haoles*.

The Republicans faced a formidable problem—or rather a set of problems. The first was to find a candidate who could defeat Burns, by now the titular leader of the Democrats, although he held that position in Hawaii largely because of his skills in political maneuvering and the art of compromise. The second problem that confronted the Republicans was that of statehood. The bandwagon had been rolling at a faster pace since the battle against communism had thinned out with the decline of McCarthyism on the Mainland, and the hard core of opposition was finding it difficult to gather much support. The people of Hawaii in 1950 had adopted a state constitution and voted overwhelmingly in favor of statehood, and most of the political frontrunners in the Republican Party had come out strongly for Hawaii's admission as a state.

What made the situation complicated was the fundamental dislike of the entire notion of statehood by the *kamaaina* old guard. Many of those who for political reasons were forced to support statehood sought privately to block it. This required a strategy that was a bit trickier than the tactics the Big Five had usually employed in times of stress; in fact it was a form of political finesse to which the Republicans had never been accustomed.

In addition, they now had a new kind of political representation in Washington in the person of Jack Burns, the tough, astute expoliceman who did not particularly give a damn about the problems of the *kamaaina haoles* or the preservation of their feudal position in Hawaii.

The elements that went into the campaign for—and against—statehood, leading up to its ultimate achievement, were only vaguely visible at the beginning of the decline of the Big Five that started in the latter 1930s. They were still somewhat vague when the campaign gained momentum in the 1950s.

Many of these factors that brought about the disintegration of the oligarchy have been discussed: the breaking down of traditional barriers of a closed economy, the inability of Hawaii's two basic industries, sugar and pineapples, to sustain the growth of population, and above all, the rising power of organized labor resulting from the failure of the sugar planters to rise above the level of feudalism and to regard plantation field workers as something more than serfs bound to the soil. Other factors were more subtle, and in order to evaluate them it is again necessary to retrace the years prior to 1946–1947, when final drive for statehood began.

The war had effectively demolished the basic argument used for four decades—that the Japanese were unassimilable and would constitute a menace if Hawaii became a state. Except for a few such as Judge Stainback, whose learned colloquy on Shintoism, Confucianism, and Emperor worship has been mentioned, the fear of Japan was no longer a factor after Japan had been defeated in the war. The *nisei* themselves continued to be a problem, but it was more political than racial—just as the Chinese problem was more economic then political. It will be noted later that the suspicions of the Hawaiians, Portuguese, and Filipinos continued to be directed at the Japanese in Hawaii, but it was directed at their increasing political influence, not against the possibility that Japan might control Hawaii.

The basic arguments against statehood were:

16

Strategy for Statehood

1. The Communist menace. It was genuinely feared that organized labor, infiltrated by Reds, would be a problem if Hawaii became a state.

2. The fear of Asiatic domination in some form. After the Korean War it was considered that China, rather than Japan, would be the danger point.

3. Hawaii was not ready for statehood. This vague and inconclusive argument was effectively disproved by every political, racial, and historical factor, but it lingered on.

4. There was an alternative of a Commonwealth form of government, which has been mentioned. This possibility was advanced by diehard spokesmen for the oligarchy up to the time the statehood bill was finally passed. It will be dealt with later, although it did not prove a decisive factor.

There was another hidden factor that neither advanced nor retarded the cause of statehood, but should be taken into account. This was the realization that Hawaii as a State was much more of a political entity than it had been as a Territory. It would become, in addition to being a military outpost—where it might have been more effective in territorial status—a political, economic, and diplomatic bridge between the Occident and the Orient. It was the American gateway to trade and political confrontation in the Pacific area.

In assessing these four basic arguments against statehood it may be helpful to restate the accepted criteria set forth on several occasions in Committee hearings in both the House and Senate, under which a Territory may expect to become an American state. These criteria are:

1. That a majority of the citizens of the territory desire statehood.

2. That the inhabitants of the proposed state be "imbued with the principles of democracy as exemplified by the American form of government."

3. That the proposed state have sufficient population, resources, and economic capabilities to support statehood.

These prerequisites for admission were presented in all major committee hearings leading up to statehood, and there was unanimous agreement, among those who discussed them with any measure of responsibility and knowledge of conditions in the Territory that Hawaii met these criteria. In the final hearing before the Senate Subcommittee on Territories and Insular Affairs on February 25, 1959, the Secretary of the Interior, Fred Seaton, stated, "The overwhelming majority of Hawaiians are native-born Americans; they know no other loyalty and acclaim their American citizenship as proudly as you or I. Their economy is self-sustaining. Hawaii is adequately prepared financially for the burdens of statehood."

As to the first point—the desire of the citizens of Hawaii that it become a state—the question was first voted on in the elections of 1940 and by a margin of three to one endorsed by the voters. Later polls, as previously noted, confirmed this by overwhelming ratios.

These points are noted because in the final phases of the campaign for statehood, from 1957 when Jack Burns became delegate to 1959 when the Hawaii Statehood Bill (S 50 and HR 50) was finally adopted, there were many skirmishes on other than legalistic grounds, some of them in outright opposition, others more subtle, as the expiring oligarchy fought to scuttle or sabotage approval of statehood by Congress. This effort continued in spite of publicly avowed protests of many spokesmen for the oligarchy, who claimed to have recanted their earlier aversion to statehood.

In 1931, former Governor Farrington, who with his son, Joe Farrington, appear to have been the only voices of the Big Five that had strongly and consistently supported statehood for Hawaii, presented to a meeting of business leaders in Honolulu a resume of the "thirty years war" for statehood. His paper was entitled "Some Thoughts on Statehood."

"My first thought," he told his audience, "was to entitle this paper, 'Building for Statehood,' but knowing the sentiment of some of the pioneers who in the estimation of their friends may not be so courageous as they used to be, I feared that such a title might cause apprehension if not consternation and suggest to the nervous ones that this paper was intended as a declaration instead of a discussion."

Later in his talk, he suggested that "the elements that may be classified as timid or conservative . . . appear to be actually afraid of a statehood resolution."[30]

This was by no means an understatement. Back in 1893 during the Hawaiian Revolution, as Farrington pointed out, "traditions were trotted out . . . and held back Annexation for a number of years." Actually, it was President Cleveland and his suspicions as to the motives of those who had dethroned Queen Liliuokalani that held back Annexation. But there were quite a few of the revolutionary junta who, as has been noted, were uncertain as to the advisability of full statehood at the time.

Governor Farrington went on, "Generally speaking, many who were active in bringing about the Annexation of Hawaii to the United States feel that we are very comfortable as we are, so why worry. We can secure our tariff favors for sugar by leaning on the beet sugar farmers of the Middle West. Pineapples need more protection, but might live without it. Our friends in the States stand guard over coastwise shipping laws. Altogether, we are comfortable and prosperous."

This was a fairly accurate summary of the viewpoint of the sugar planter oligarchy at the time, although undoubtedly it was not Farrington's view. He had not only supported statehood, but had taken the trouble to write Senator Carl Hayden of Arizona to obtain information on the admission of the last two Territories that had been voted into the Federal Union as states —New Mexico and Arizona—in 1912.

In both cases, statehood was approved by Congress following an enabling act in which the following provisions were set forth:

1. The citizens of the Territories had to vote for delegates to a constitutional convention;

2. The territorial Governor was required to issue a proclamation within thirty days ordering an election to approve admission; and

3. A date was to be set within a ninety-day period for a committee to draw up a constitution that "shall be republican in form and make no distinction in civil or political rights on

account of race or color, and shall not be repugnant to the Constitution of the United States or the Declaration of Independence."

The constitution was to establish provisions for religious tolerance, disclaim all future rights of the people to Government lands in the state, assume liability for all debts of the Territories, require laws for establishing and maintaining public schools to be conducted in the English language, prohibit any law abridging the right of suffrage on account of color or previous condition of servitude, establish a standard of literacy as a qualification for holding public office, and reserve to the Federal Government the right to enforce acts of Congress. In addition, special provisions were to be required for Indian reservations and the sale of liquor to Indians.

If the constitution were approved by a majority vote of the citizens of the Territories, it would be certified by the President under the enabling act and the Governor of the Territory would be required to set a date for a general election of state officials and Senators and Representatives in Congress. President Taft made a special trip to Arizona to advise the people that they need not adopt a "crank constitution as the people in Oklahoma did," in which all sorts of special requirements were thrown into the constitutional pot.

The details of the admission of New Mexico and Arizona are cited because up to the time Jack Burns arrived in Washington as delegate, these two admissions were the most complete of any transitions from territorial status to statehood on record; and Hawaii, as will be seen, had more than fulfilled the basic requirement by the adoption of a proposed state constitution in 1950. As a matter of record, many previous admissions to statehood had been more loosely handled than Oklahoma, which came into the Union in 1907. Nebraska, for example, did not have an approved constitution, the document having been drawn up in a lawyer's office in Lincoln and submitted to the Legislature instead of the people for approval. Voting rights were limited to white males and yet it was admitted by Congress in 1867, eight years before a properly prepared constitution was drawn up. Several southern states went through some astonishing irregularities. In Mississippi only 17,000 of a possible 150,-000 were able to cast a vote for their constitution, and Kentucky was admitted without a constitution, as was Vermont.

During the years 1946 and 1947 Delegate Farrington introduced three more bills before the House and only one—HR 49 —ever got to the voting stage. By that time Hawaii's period of "pupilage," as it was called, exceeded that of every other territory that had applied for admission as a state except New Mexico, which waited sixty-two years. It continued to pay more money into the Federal treasury than ten states, and continued to have nothing to say about how it was spent.

On January 3, 1950, Farrington had offered HR 49 again and once more it passed the House, this time by a vote of 262 to 110. On July 12 it was voted out of the Senate Committee on Territories by nine to one, the dissenting vote being cast by Senator Butler of Nebraska, who must have forgotten how that former Territory became a state. At the same time the Hawaiian Legislature authorized a constitutional convention and on July 22 the sixty-three delegates who had been elected to draft the Hawaiian constitution completed the job and it was approved by the Legislature. The convention included twenty-seven *haoles*, twenty Japanese, eleven Hawaiians, and five Chinese—all American citizens; and politically it was composed of twenty-nine Republicans, twenty-one Democrats and thirteen who registered as nonpartisan.

At this point, HR 49 died in the Senate, which adjourned without voting on the bill.

By 1957, when Burns reached Washington, several additional attempts had been made—HR 49 again in 1953, and S 49 the same year.

In 1954 the Hawaii statehood bill was passed by the Republican-controlled House and was sent to the Senate, which was also Republican-controlled and was prepared to pass the bill, envisaging two additional Senators from a traditionally Republican stronghold. Meanwhile, the Democrats offered an amendment to the House bill which would add Alaska to the statehood package. As a result, the amendment had to go back to the House, where unanimous consent to the amended bill was required. This failed, and the bill went down the drain of parliamentary procedure, dying at the expiration of the 83rd Congress. This was the beginning of the effort to tie Hawaii and Alaska together. Burns was in Washington at the time, with Sam King and Oren Long.

At the time, Burns believed King was sincerely dedicated to statehood for Hawaii, and there was little doubt that Farrington was an advocate of statehood. But Burns was getting a taste of parliamentary procedure; and one of the things that appears to have stuck in his mind was the report that President Eisenhower favored statehood for Hawaii but did not want it for Alaska.

He began to sense the political overtones, not only in Hawaii but in Washington. The additional Senators seemed to be the key: Hawaii was expected to provide two Republican Senators, and the Democrats, to counteract this, wanted two Senators from Alaska. The admission of Hawaii and Alaska had become a political football. This assumed additional significance after Burns became delegate.

There was a second impression that stuck in Burns's mind. This was the distinction between a bill of admission to statehood, which was classified as privileged legislation and did not have to go through usual parliamentary procedure, since the Territory had already qualified itself; and an enabling act, which required approval of the Rules Committee and set forth the criteria under which a Territory could become a State.

By this time many people in Hawaii had given up hope of their homeland ever becoming a state, and those who had opposed statehood consistently for a half century were able to relax. Jack Burns seemed to face a hopeless task.

With Burns in Washington, the mantle of leadership in the Democratic party in Hawaii fell on the shoulders of young Daniel Inouye, who had again led the ticket in the 1956 elections. The record of the preceding Legislature, as he wryly expressed it, was "less than a legislative revolution" which the Democrats had hoped to achieve.

There were two primary objectives for those who had set about the restructuring of Hawaii—the building of a new Hawaii replacing the feudal system of the Big Five and the achievement of statehood. Jack Burns's alliance with labor through Jack Hall was at best an expedient; there was an element of precariousness in all relations with the powerful chief of the ILWU. His arrangements in politics, as in dealings with employer groups, were based entirely on self-interest—that is, the interests of labor. If the Democrats expected to retain their hold on the Legislature and the delegateship long enough to achieve statehood, it would be necessary to build a broader and more permanent base than ILWU support.

Many of the new group of political independents who had won control of the Democratic Party and finally of the government machinery of the Territory, had felt the sting of labor's reprisals. Patsy Mink had launched her political career without support of labor. Later, when she criticized some of Hall's methods, he turned against her. Sakae Takahashi had a similar experience; he had criticized the unemployment compensation bill in the 1956 session of the Legislature as inadequate, and since the bill was inspired by Hall, he turned against Takahashi. Tom Gill, who had been supported for Oahu County Chairman by the ILWU in 1954, refused to take orders from Hall and was scratched off labor's list temporarily, although he was later restored to favor when he broke with Burns in the years following statehood.

In addition to these problems, there was growing discontent with Burns's leadership. While Inouye, Aoki, Takabuki, and others of the closely knit *nisei* faction from the 442nd Veterans Club as well as Bill Richardson, Chuck Mau, Herman Lum, and a few others remained loyal to Burns, there were rumblings of discontent from other sources. Burns was accused of hand-picking candidates for the various legislative races. Oddly enough, the resentment against Burns emanated from both the conservative and radical wings of the Democratic group.

Gill, who leaned to the liberal wing, criticized Burns for being too dictatorial; members of the old guard on the other hand—Bill Heen and Oren Long—felt that he was often unresponsive to their advice. These differences were not serious enough to affect the momentum the party had achieved, but they were portents of trouble to come.

Inouye appeared to be the one member of the Burns group

who had no real opposition within party ranks; and for this reason he was the best man to hold together the wavering elements of the party structure in Hawaii. He had proved to be the best vote-getter, leading the ticket in every election; and he possessed the balanced judgment that in the end would have as much influence as Burns's ironhanded leadership.

Meanwhile the new Delegate from Hawaii was losing no time in pressing forward his program to revive the statehood campaign in Washington, in spite of the feeling back in Hawaii that the cause was hopeless. It was at this point that the lines of strategy—the conflict between Burns and the diehard members of the oligarchy—became plainly visible.

One of the most unusual examples of the subtle and sometimes mystifying efforts for and against the statehood program was the case of Lorrin P. Thurston. The son of the leader of the Revolution of 1893 and publisher of the *Advertiser,* he had been one of the most vigorous opponents of statehood, but suddenly, for no apparent reason, he switched to supporting it. During the 1930s his paper carried most of the arguments against statehood, including the Japanese menace—which evaporated with the end of the war—and the threat of Communist domination of the Islands if they should become a state.

The Hawaii Equal Rights Commission, as previously mentioned, was formed by legislative enactment to counteract such Congressional actions as the Jones-Costigan Act of 1934, cutting Hawaii's sugar quota by ten percent and classifying the Territory as a nondomestic sugar producer. However, it was not actually designed to support statehood; and it was not until 1947 that the name was changed to Hawaii Statehood Commission.

The Commission under its new name was intended ostensibly to be a factor in the promotion of Hawaii's bid for statehood, but since it included in its membership some who had strenuously opposed statehood in the past, there were many in Honolulu who wondered whether they represented a change of attitude on the part of the Big Five, or merely a change in tactics. Thurston was an example of this sudden change. He had previously argued, as his father had, that the people of Hawaii were not ready for statehood, and in effect were incapable of self-

government. Suddenly he appeared as chairman of the Statehood Commission, issuing statements and delivering speeches
that advocated immediate passage of a bill admitting Hawaii as
a state.

By 1957, when Jack Burns was in Washington reviving the
statehood bill, Thurston had not only gotten on the bandwagon
but was one of Hawaii's most ardent spokesmen for statehood.
The publisher of the *Advertiser*, which in 1940 had insisted
editorially that Hawaii should not become a state until its people
—primarily the Japanese element—were Americanized and had
later warned of the peril of Communist control of the Islands,
argued before the Democratic National Committee meeting in
San Francisco on March of 1957 that "in no State in the Union
is communism under more constant surveillance" than in Hawaii.

He also noted that the constitution of the proposed state,
adopted in 1950, would make it "the first under the American
flag to include in its charter disqualification of any Communist
from holding any public office whatsoever."

The reason for Thurston's apparent shift in viewpoint was
not made clear in any of his public statements, although one
report, partially confirmed by Burns, indicated that the delegate
had spent several hours with Thurston's editor, the late Ray
Coll, and that it was Coll who persuaded Thurston that statehood was inevitable and the *Advertiser* should change its stance
and support it editorially. Whatever the reason may have been,
Thurston became one of the central figures in the curious
strategy involved in the final—and successful—effort to achieve
statehood for Hawaii.

Jack Burns was in Union Station in Washington on his way to Philadelphia to attend an Army-Navy football game when somewhat accidentally he met Senator Richard Russell of Georgia, who more than any other man in the Senate was regarded as the voice of the South.

"It had been more or less assumed in Hawaii that opposition to statehood for Hawaii would come from Southern senators and congressmen," Burns said later. "I was surprised when the Senator asked me how the Hawaii statehood bill was coming along. We chatted for a few minutes, and I had the distinct impression that he was not opposed to statehood for Hawaii. I also got another intimation, that he would like to see Hawaii's bill acted on separately, not tied to the Alaska bill."

In 1957, three years after Hawaii's application had first been joined with the Alaska bill, the two proposals for statehood for Alaska and Hawaii were introduced separately by Senator James E. Murray of Montana as Acts of Admission and not, as heretofore, Enabling Acts. This was possible, since both territories had adopted state constitutions and fulfilled the initial requirements for statehood. The bills were labeled S 49 and S 50, and Senator Murray pointed out that in deference to the wishes of the delegates from Alaska and Hawaii the bills would not be joined as a single measure.

In November, 1956, shortly after his election as Delegate, Burns had dinner with Delegate Bartlett of Alaska in Washington and they had discussed the introducing of both Hawaii and Alaska bills as "Acts of Admission" rather than "Enabling Acts." Both territories had met all necessary requirements and the bill

17

The End
of an Era

to admit was "privileged"—in other words, it did not have to pass through the Rules Committee. They agreed upon this procedure, and also agreed to separate the two bills.

This strategic switch was extremely important, because it later developed that opposition to the Alaska Bill by certain Congressmen would have killed it in the 85th Congress without the privileged status. When the bill came up the in 1958 the House parliamentarian, Dr. Lewis Deschler, ruled it had privileged status.

Burns had made the decision to split the bills, having in mind the intimation he received from Senator Russell that the Hawaii bill should be separated from Alaska. There were two major factors involved. First, there was a belief among supposedly knowledgeable people in Hawaii that Southern Congressmen were blocking statehood because of a latent feeling that the people of Hawaii were mostly nonwhite and therefore unfit to govern themselves. Burns, after his talk with Russell, did not believe this.

While many people who lived in Hawaii, including members of the Hawaii Statehood Commission, were certain that Southern Senators and Representatives would oppose statehood for Hawaii because they did not want dark-skinned Hawaiians or saffron-hued Asians sitting beside them in the halls of Congress, Burns felt that Russell, who could speak for the South more accurately than members of the Hawaii Statehood Commission, harbored no such feelings.

Burns had a second reason for wanting to disengage the two bills. There were members of Congress who were opposed to admission of Alaska for reasons that did not apply to Hawaii. The argument that joining Hawaii and Alaska in the application for admission would double the affirmative support had a negative aspect; it might double the opposition.

There were additional reasons in Burns's mind that favored keeping Hawaii's bill split from Alaska. Hawaii had certain advantages Alaska did not have. For example, it was much better off economically than Alaska, which had less population and less industry. There were differences in tax burdens, both Territory-wide and per capita. Hawaii paid $140 million in Federal taxes in 1956 and Alaska paid only half that amount. In per capita tax burden, Hawaii ranked higher than thirty-six states. Its gross territorial product was over $1.2 billion, more than twice that of Alaska. Its population of more than a half million was larger than that of ten states, and twice the population of Alaska.

Burns decided not only to ask that the bills be split, but he agreed to press for the passage of the Alaska bill first! His reasoning was simple and logical; if Congress passed the Alaska Bill, there could be no possible argument for not admitting Hawaii, which was far more qualified. In addition, the primary argument that had always been offered—that they were "noncontiguous territories"—would be nullified with passage of the Alaska Bill.

The two statehood bills, cosponsored by twenty-six Senators, were put before the Senate, and at Burns's suggestion, the Alaska Bill was acted on first. This set off a storm of protest in the Islands. Governor William Quinn, the *malihini haole* who had come to Hawaii in the early 1950s and run unsuccessfully for the territorial Senate prior to his appointment as Governor, protested vigorously. Burns was accused of "betraying" Hawaii's interests. Thurston, as chairman of the Statehood Committee, urged Burns not to delay the Hawaiian bill, and the *Advertiser* said he was "naïve" to suppose that acceptance of Alaska as a state would have any effect on the Hawaiian case.

Burns knew his way around Washington, and he had detected certain signs that convinced him he was on the right track in separating Alaska from the Hawaii bill. He must have been aware also that the real opposition to Hawaii's statehood did not come from the South—as was popularly supposed in Hawaii— nor from Washington. It came from Hawaii itself, from the *kamaaina haoles*.

In retrospect, there appear to have been two possible ways in which the Hawaii bill could have been scuttled. One was to keep the two bills tied together, and if the opposition to Alaska was sufficient to kill its bill, Hawaii would go down with it. The other was to press for immediate action on Hawaii if the Alaska bill, separated from the Hawaii bill, should pass both House and Senate, on the theory that the Congressional timetable near the end of the session would make it virtually impossible to get the

Hawaii bill out of Committee. Congressmen and Senators would be heading for home to mend their own political fences, in which case Hawaii would be bypassed again. Burns estimated that the Alaska bill would not be acted upon until midsummer, and he was right. It was signed by President Eisenhower on July 7, 1958. The Delegate from Hawaii had already assured Congress that he would not press for the Hawaii bill until the following year, and had actively worked for Alaska's admission.

This drew further protests from Honolulu. A delegation from Hawaii, including members of the Hawaii Statehood Commission led by Lorrin Thurston, came to Washington to urge Burns to push for immediate action on Hawaii's bill as soon as the Alaska bill passed. Burns was adamant. He recognized that pushing the statehood bill near the end of the session would be the one sure way to kill Hawaii's chances. He said, "No. Wait until next year." Members of Congress were getting ready to finish some of their own legislative chores and get home for the fall campaign. They would have little time to consider anything as remote as Hawaii's statehood aspirations.

Burns, attacked by the Republicans for supposedly having botched the job, returned to Honolulu that fall to campaign for his own reelection. He ran on one plank: "Send me back to Washington to finish the job. If we don't get statehood next year, you'll never hear from me in politics again."

The battle in Hawaii was bitter. Republicans, fortified by what happened in Washington, charged Burns with having committed an irretrievable blunder in not pressing Hawaii's case. When he pointed out that Senator Johnson, the majority leader, and Sam Rayburn, Speaker of the House, had both assured him that Hawaii's bill would be taken up early the following year, Burns's Republican opposition accused him of working with Hawaii's enemies. Both men were from Texas, they pointed out, and "Hawaii will never get statehood while Southern Democrats control key positions of leadership."

Meanwhile Dan Inouye and the "Burns boys" were having problems back in Hawaii. The territorial House had undergone one of its customary factional disputes and seemed unable to organize itself. The 1958 Legislature had been elected for the first time along the lines anticipated in the Constitution for statehood approved by the voters in 1950, expanding the House from 30 to 51 members and the Senate from 15 to 25. The Democrats had a 33 to 18 majority in the House and a 16 to 9 majority in the Senate.

When the Democrats met in caucus in December 1958, there was little agreement as to committee chairmanships and other offices, but finally disputes were resolved in the Senate. The House was a different matter. Vincent Esposito, leading an insurgent group of Democrats with Tom Gill, gathered 18 votes, enough to organize, but leaving the other 15 Democrats out in the cold. When the House convened in 1959, just about the time Burns was giving the Hawaii bill the last nudges through Congress, the territorial House was deadlocked. The Gill-Esposito group had enough votes to control the Democratic side of the House, but not enough to control the House.

This lasted long enough to threaten the smooth passage of the statehood bill in Congress. Senator Henry M. Jackson of Washington, who was spearheading the Hawaii bill, was asked to come to Honolulu to address the Legislature, but he spoke only to the Senate, since the House was not organized. He began to wonder out loud if Hawaii was really "ready for statehood," as the Big Five die-hards had said it was not.

The significance of this division in the ranks of the Democrats became more noticeable later, during the decade following the achievement of statehood. But to Burns it presented an immediate problem. While he was in Washington carrying on the battle for statehood, with Dan Inouye and the cadre of Burns boys trying to hold the line in Hawaii, there were increasing signs of disaffection, much of it engendered by the shifting tactics of Jack Hall and the labor vote. There was also a growing bitterness among Hawaiians that the Japanese *nisei* were moving into positions of power. On the outer Islands—Kauai, Maui and Hawaii—many of the old party lines were breaking down. Doc Hill was still the most powerful politician on Hawaii, but he owed his strength to the contacts he had made as a jewelry peddler on trips through the plantations, selling cheap jewelry and picking up votes. He owed nothing to the *kamaaina haoles;*

he could as easily have been a Democrat as a Republican. To
understand Hawaiian politics, one had to realize that organiza-
tional rules that prevailed on the Mainland were meaningless in
Hawaii.

A creeping change had come over Hawaii's political structure. When Nelson Doi defeated Doc Hill in the race for the
territorial Senate in 1954, it was merely a portent of things to
come. A new generation was sweeping into power—and not on
a political broomstick wielded by the medieval practitioners of
the Big Five-GOP coalition and the plantation managers. It was
a cross section of ethnic groups. Names such as Oren Long,
Herbert Lee, Sakae Takahashi, David Trask, Ray Adams, Tom
Gill, Dave McClung, Spark Matsunaga were lumped together as
Democrats, with few racial overtones and strong group motivation. The *nisei*, for example, who had been largely led into Jack
Burns's camp by Dan Inouye in the late 1940s, had emerged as
the most powerful single group in the Territory, and both parties fought for their support.

The former commanding officer of the 100th Battalion,
Farrant Turner, a Republican, sought vainly to draw his boys
back into the Republican fold, but failed. The effort of the fading
GOP to bring out a candidate to face Burns in the fall election
in 1958—while antistatehood forces were desperately trying to
get the Delegate out of the way so they could wreck Hawaii's
statehood chances in Congress—was unable to muster a candidate to oppose him! Turner, who was Secretary of the Territory
under the newly appointed Governor Quinn, tried to woo voters
from the 100th Battalion away from Burns by putting pressure
on Wilfred Tsukiyama, once the leading Japanese politician in
the Territory, to run against Burns, but Tsukiyama refused.
Arthur Woolaway, a Republican national committeeman and a
member of the planter oligarchy, beseeched Hebden Porteus, a
lawyer and an officer of Alexander & Baldwin who had trailed
Inouye in the 1956 House race, to run against Burns, but he
respectfully declined. It was finally Farrant Turner upon whom
the dubious mantle of GOP leadership was draped, with a promise by Governor Quinn that he would be taken care of if he lost
—which he did.

The significance of all this was not in the growing power of the Democrats, nor in the political charisma of Jack Burns—because he had little of that. It was the waning power of the Republicans pitted against the insurgent neglected citizens aroused by postwar angers that Dan Inouye and his fellow *nisei* veterans felt against the unfairness of the oligarchy's domination of the lives of everyone in Hawaii. Inouye, because he seemed to express this feeling most articulately, became the spearhead of that revolt. Even Republican *nisei,* such as Lawrence Goto, city treasurer of Honolulu for many years, ran under the Democratic banner in 1958; and so did Adrian DeMello, a lifelong Republican who filed for the Honolulu Board of Supervisors as a Democrat. It was not racial influence that motivated the voters. Portuguese, Hawaiians, Filipinos, and even Chinese who were formerly Republicans began to vote with the Japanese *against* certain groups as contrasted with being *for* their own groups. Labor candidates ran stronger on Maui and Kauai than those formerly backed by the Baldwins and Rices, because they were opposed to planter control. Dan Inouye's ability to lead the ticket in every political contest he entered was based more on the fact that he represented the rise of the second-class citizens than his Japanese blood. It was in this respect that he was becoming a symbol of the new Hawaii.

Inouye made what he regarded at the time as "the most important political decision of my life," although later he was confronted with a few that were much tougher and far more important. He decided to shift from the House race and run for the territorial Senate. As he later wrote, "In our Islands there is a great prestige attached to the Senate. True or not, that body is considered to be occupied by Hawaii's statesmen, and I sincerely felt that to be elected a territorial Senator would cap my career. . . ."

In the election Dan Inouye again ran ahead of his ticket, joining a growing group of powerful Democrats in the Senate: Patsy Mink, who had shifted from the younger independents to the more conservative Burns wing; George Ariyoshi, who became one of Burns most trusted lieutenants; Frank Fasi, who wobbled between outright support of Burns and the independent independents but usually stayed with Burns on the vital issues. Wilfred Tsukiyama, who had rejected the Republican nomination for delegate, barely won a Senate seat in the fifth Oahu district.

Burns, elected by a substantial majority over Turner, was thus returned to Washington to resume his fight for statehood with a coalition of somewhat divided Democrats behind him, and few of the newer and more liberal Republicans willing to challenge him. Neal Blaisdell was returned to the office of Mayor of Honolulu as a Republican, but as one political observer noted, "he sounded more like a Democrat in his campaign."

Of even greater importance in the light of earlier arguments about Hawaii's racial problems and the threat of a Japanese takeover of the Islands, there was no pronounced Japanese strength on the outer Islands. The *nisei* had been the first to back Burns in the electoral revolt of 1948, but they did not rule the elections. In fact, the results were quite mixed. On Hawaii Doc Hill ignored Republican leadership, although he ran on the GOP ticket, and won handily with Hawaiian support. Jimmy Kealoha, a Chinese-Hawaiian, defeated his Democratic *nisei* rival in the Senate race. Hawaiians as a group were still suspicious of the Japanese, and so were the Filipinos. As Andrew Lind pointed out in an excellent study of Hawaii's ethnic problems, there was a more ominous side to this development. When the barriers of racial inequality were broken down, Hawaii became exposed to new problems, and to many of these they had no established immunity. There were dangers in an open society that had not been suspected. They were not the same perils feared by Judge Stainback and the ladies of Imua, and the extent of this difference was revealed in the decade following passage of the statehood bill.

Burns was finally called in to straighten out the immediate split in the Democratic ranks. He had met Senator Jackson after the latter returned from his visit to Hawaii, and Jackson had said, "I'm not sure you're mature enough in Hawaii for statehood at this time." Burns, fearing the intraparty factional dispute might imperil the statehood measure, spoke to the Esposito-Gill group and suggested a more reasonable approach. Finally he called in one of the Republican leaders and asked him to deliver the minority vote, with the understanding that there would be no "coalition" but the minority would receive proportional representation. This solved the problem temporarily but left a residual bitterness that had its effects in the elections following statehood.

On September 19, 1958, a visitor from New Orleans, George Lehleitner, who had worked for years for passage of the Alaska statehood bill, was interviewed by the *Star-Bulletin* concerning his views on Hawaii's chances of becoming a state. He cited three errors of judgment on the part of the people of Hawaii. First, it was wrong to believe Alaska's admission was a guarantee of statehood for Hawaii. It would be folly to assume that admission would be automatic. They would have to work for it. Second, it was also false to assume business interests could pressure the verdict in Congress. Not even the oil industry could do it in Alaska. Third, he stated, people in Hawaii were wrong in suspecting that Southern members of Congress would block statehood due to racial hostility or the Communist menace. He said, "No one in a position to know has the slightest fear of a Communist menace in Hawaii." He noted that more than 1300 editorials had been printed in Mainland newspapers in support of statehood for Hawaii, and almost an equal number had supported statehood for Alaska, even though the Communist menace in Alaska had been raised as a specter. He added, "There is no Imua in Alaska."

Lehleitner said he suspected that stories of the Communist menace in Hawaii emanated chiefly from Hawaii, and he named specifically "a former Governor, a Justice of the Supreme Court of Hawaii, and certain prominent business and professional men" in Honolulu, including members of Imua. These people, he said, were the real opposition to statehood for Hawaii.

This drew a roar of protest from Imua, which had expanded its pursuit of the Communist menace, and now included men as well as matrons of the *kamaaina haole* families in its membership. L. G. Phillips, the current chief of Imua, immediately retorted, "Who is this man? What ax is he grinding?" Without necessarily identifying the Imua ax that had been sharpened several years earlier by Mrs. Walter Dillingham, the wife of Hawaii's most consistent opponent of statehood, Phillips accused Lehleitner of butting into Hawaii's business, and denied that the New Orleans businessman knew what Southerners thought about the situation. Lehleitner replied by referring to a statement made by Joe Farrington in 1935 when he quoted Senator John T. Morgan of Alabama, a Southerner who was an expert on Hawaii, as having said in 1897 on a visit to Hawaii, in which he spoke at Kawaiahao Church, "That Hawaii is going to be a state is certain. Whether it will come at the time of Annexation is a question."

This was some sixty years later, and the question was about to be answered, regardless of the opposition—overt and covert —of the ladies and gentlemen of Imua or the Hawaii Statehood Commission.

Dan Aoki, the stocky First Sergeant of Dan Inouye's "E" Company in the 442nd RCT, was in a position to know better than most the maneuvers necessary to achieve statehood for Hawaii; and in particular he was in a position to understand Delegate Burns's strategy because he was with him in Washington throughout the last intensive phases of the campaign. "The Delegate had one capability that few people gave him credit for," Aoki said. "He knew how Congress worked and he knew how Congressmen thought. He did not talk a great deal but what he said counted, particularly among the members of the committees he worked with in both the House and Senate."

Burns had introduced the two Hawaii bills—HR 50 and S 50—and they were referred to the Committees on Interior and Insular Affairs, but according to the strategy agreed upon with the Alaskan delegate the latter's bill was to receive priority. It had passed the Senate without amendment and was sent to the House. Meanwhile, the House subcommittee was holding up the Hawaii Bill pending action on the Alaska Bill. Unexpectedly Representative O'Brien of New York, chairman of the parent Committee on Interior and Insular Affairs, moved to discharge the Hawaii Bill, which would have put it directly before the House for a final vote on admission.

This, in Burns's view, might have killed the Hawaii Bill; and he remonstrated with O'Brien. The latter said that Jim Haggerty, the White House press secretary, had suggested the move in order to get movement on the Alaska Bill—which Burns knew the President did not favor. He pointed out to O'Brien that the result might be to wash out the Hawaii Bill.

At this point, the parliamentary wheels began to turn. Burns received a call from the Senate policy secretary, Bobby Baker, asking why the Hawaii Bill was being pushed, and he promptly replied that it was not—and asked Baker to assure Senator Lyndon Johnson, the majority leader, that this was the case. Burns and O'Brien then went to Senator Russell to assure him that the two bills would be handled separately, and Russell at that point remarked that whoever thought up that strategy had found the *only* way to achieve statehood for Hawaii.

Burns looked at him, recalling the conversation at the Union Station, and said, "Senator, I'd like to thank you for contributing to that strategy."

There was one more base to touch—the majority leader, Senator Johnson. Burns and O'Brien visited his office. After the Hawaii bill had been reported out of the House Committee, any member of the House could call it up for a final vote. Burns suggested that if he, as Delegate from Hawaii, should ask for a vote to recommit the Hawaii bill to the Committee, it would pass. Johnson was silent for a time; then he nodded.

Later Burns learned that Johnson had called Sam Rayburn, the House majority leader, and asked him not to recognize any member for the purpose of a motion to bring the Hawaii Bill, which was an Act of Admission and therefore privileged, before the House for a vote. This bypassed the effort to kill the Hawaii Bill.

The Alaska Bill went through the House and Senate as privileged legislation and was sent directly to both houses for a final vote. Meanwhile, Burns was assailed by members of the Hawaii Statehood Commission, who had come to Washington to guide him, for not pushing hard for enactment of the Hawaii Bill.

"I don't give a damn which bill goes through first—whether the Hawaii bill is forty-ninth or fiftieth—as long as it passes," he told them. "What I want is statehood for Hawaii."

It would be unfair to assume that all members of the State-hood Commission were motivated by a desire to sabotage the Hawaii Bill, although the two things they advocated—tying Hawaii to the Alaska Bill, and, when this failed, trying to rush passage of the Hawaii Bill at the close of the session—were actions most likely to kill the Hawaii Bill. Many who formerly opposed statehood, and now supported it, were undoubtedly guided by honest convictions. It was improbable, for example, that Lorrin Thurston would have spoken so strongly in support of statehood if he wanted it defeated. But there were a number of members of the Statehood Commission who had advocated every move likely to jeopardize statehood for Hawaii, and there was a growing suspicion that what George Lehleitner said was true—that the real opposition to statehood came from Hawaii itself.

After the election, Burns moved steadily ahead on the course he had set for himself. He had been correct in his assessment of the Congressional attitude toward Alaska; there were more opponents of Alaska from the South than had been expected—as George Lehleitner had told the people of Hawaii—and yet it had passed. Had the opposition to Hawaii's bill, led by Congressman John Pilion of New York and Senator James Eastland of Mississippi, been joined to those opposing Alaska's admission, the bill would have failed. Pilion had expressed fear of the influence of the ILWU in Hawaii's political control and insisted that admission of the Territory as a state would be like "inviting agents of the Soviet government to sit in our Congress." Eastland took the same position.

To counteract this, Burns arranged for a special subcommittee of the House Committee on Insular Affairs, led by Representative Leo O'Brien of New York, to visit Hawaii between November 24 and December 8, 1958. O'Brien reported that "on the basis of a comprehensive and exhaustive study . . . your subcommittee believes that Hawaii is entitled to statehood by every fair test and precedent." He said it would be "unthinkable" for Congress to "delay further the fruition of Hawaii's magnificent dream." He quoted almost everyone, from Harold Rice to Mrs. Ben Baker, public relations director of the Girl

Scouts, as being in favor of statehood for Hawaii. Senators John Carroll of Colorado and Frank Church of Idaho, who had joined O'Brien in the pleasant excursion to Hawaii, corroborated his views.

Burns still had a few hurdles to clear. The House Committee did not act immediately on HR 50, and he decided to shift to the Senate, which had a similar resolution —S 50—before it.

Aoki, who was with Burns at the time, recalled how converted pro-statehood supporters from Hawaii—Thurston, Governor King, and the others—had swarmed into Washington to join Delegate Joe Farrington in 1954 to help block the Alaska bill, so Hawaii could "go through first." Burns, when he became Delegate, had said, "To hell with the number—I want statehood for Hawaii." His last chance was in 1959.

When Senator Eastland visited Hawaii in 1957 to find out whether Harry Bridges, the West Coast boss of the ILWU who had been mixed up with communism for two decades, really ruled Hawaii from San Francisco, he ran into opposition of powerful labor forces in Hawaii. Jack Hall, presumably to give the Senator a taste of what he was looking for, called a mass meeting of ILWU members in Hawaii, which Bridges attended. At the meeting Hall said, "We are going to tell Mr. Eastland what we think of him," and promptly called a walkout of his Longshoremen's Union while Eastland was holding hearings in Honolulu.

This rather graceless act, which Governor King called "presumptuous, insulting, and uncalled for," gave Eastland some of the ammunition he wanted. Although he insisted while in Hawaii that he was "not going to discuss statehood—we are here for internal security," Eastland fired away at the opening of the Senate subcommittee hearing in January, 1959, chaired by Senator Jackson, again calling attention to the "Communist menace" if Hawaii became a state.

Judge Stainback also continued his attacks, which had begun with statements at earlier hearings that Hawaii was going through a schooling period for statehood but apparently had not yet graduated. His latest ploy was to suggest a Commonwealth form of Government in which the Islands would be tax-free and—although the ex-Governor did not highlight this point

—would be controlled from within the Islands, a form of rule to which Hawaii had been accustomed for a half century.

Burns marshalled sufficient support to counteract most of these arguments, summed up in the O'Brien report which was introduced by Senator Carroll. After taking up one by one the classic objections to statehood, including the Communist menace, the report pointed out that (1) it was no longer necessary to contend that a half million people in Hawaii were not entitled to two Senators and respresentation in Congress since Alaska, with half that population, received both Senate and House representation; (2) it was no longer necessary to prove that Hawaii could support itself economically, since Alaska, far less advanced economically, had been accepted; and (3) the "alleged precedent" of noncontiguous territory had been nullified by the Alaska bill.

One point made by Senator Jackson has been mentioned earlier, not as an argument but as a situation that would result from Hawaii's admission. He said,

> When Hawaii is admitted it will come into the Union not just as the 50th State, but as our diplomatic State—our diplomatic representative, if you please—next door to over half the population of the world. Hawaii in the Pacific represents for America and the free world what West Berlin stands for in the Atlantic community —freedom. Hawaii is a living example of the real fruits of freedom. Here the Occident and the Orient have met in a climate of mutual trust, understanding and respect. By precept and example they have given us in the Pacific the kind of environment which will have great meaning throughout the Far East.[31]

Leaving aside the extravagance of expression to be found in all such political statements, the remark introduced an element that probably was of greater importance—and impact— than all the arguments for or against the admission of Hawaii to statehood. It established the principle of an American outpost in the Pacific that was political, economic, and diplomatic, rather than military. Hawaii, as a state, became an accredited ambassador to all of Asia. This was headier stuff than the Big Five could have handled, and it is possible some of the resistance to statehood on the part of *kamaaina haoles* grew out of this knowledge.

Hawaii, as a state, could no longer be retained as a feudal fief-dom in a mid-Pacific tropical paradise. It was on equal terms with all other states, with inalienable rights that could no longer be controlled or suppressed.

Burns had one more river to cross, which was largely of his own making. Although the Hawaii statehood measure was an Act of Admission and did not require approval by the Rules Committee, Burns decided in deference to that body to ask that the bill go through the Committee. As Aoki had said, Burns "knew Congressmen and he knew how they thought." At that time Representative Howard W. Smith of Virginia was chairman of the Rules Committee and he ruled it with an iron hand. He was known as "Judge Smith," a man who seldom smiled.

A Congressman asked Burns one day in the cloakroom, "When are you going to get your rule, Jack?"

Smith happened to be passing at the moment, and Burns said he hardly thought it proper to tell the chairman what to do. Smith, glancing at him, muttered something that sounded like "Humph!" and walked on.

In order to avoid a conference between the House and Senate over minor differences in the two bills, HR 50 and S 50, Burns introduced the Senate bill into the House. This required unanimous consent, and Congressman Pilion of New York, the archenemy of statehood for Hawaii, objected. Burns went to him and found that he had objected because Congressman Rogers of Texas had stated he would also oppose the bill. With their votes, the Republican opposition on the committee could block the bill.

Later, the Congressman, William Jennings Bryan Dorn of North Carolina, who was a friend of Judge Smith, said to the delegate, "Why don't you take one of your hula maidens to Judge Smith? It would probably soften him up."

Burns laughed, but he immediately wired Honolulu for a hula skirt and some *leis*. Then he recruited into service a young lady from Hawaii, Leilani O'Connor, who was working in Washington. He telephoned Dorn and said, "I've got the hula girl—you finish the job."

On a wintry day in March, Congressman Dorn escorted the

young lady from Honolulu, wearing a fur coat over her hula dress, into Judge Smith's office and she placed a *lei* over his head. The Judge shook hands, but hardly cracked a smile.

This was on the day the Rules Committee met to act on the Hawaii statehood legislation. Burns noticed that several members of the Committee were walking down the corridor *away* from the Committee meeting room. Among them were Pilion and Rogers. It struck the delegate that this might be a subtle way of reducing opposition. The Hawaii Bill was voted out of the Rules Committee and when it reached the House it was passed on March 12, 1959, by a vote of 329 to 89. The Senate had adopted the same bill earlier, 76 to 15. President Eisenhower signed Hawaii's statehood bill on March 18.

Later Burns met Judge Smith in the House cloakroom and shook hands, thanking him. A congressman, passing by, asked, "Is this the payoff?" Judge Smith grinned. "I've already been paid," he said. "Just the other day."

Part V/1960-1970
The New Frontier

There have been varied explanations, some critical and others apologetic, as to why the Big Five lost control of Hawaii after more than a half century of feudal rule of the Islands. One mildly critical review by Joseph Barber, Jr., *Hawaii: Restless Rampart,* attributed it to a "conflict of interest" with the military establishment, but this was written prior to the war and before the actual collapse. Others have blamed it on the war itself. Dr. Fuchs offers a number of reasons, including failure of the sugar-oriented economy to advance with political and economic changes, and the apparent inability of the oligarchy to recognize the influence of the public school system, an instrument of democracy, on the closed society of Hawaii.

Machiavelli once expressed the axiom that those who are unfit to rule usually cease to rule, but few students of Hawaiian history seem to have applied this principle directly to the oligarchy; that is, the theory that the Big Five simply were unfit to rule. However, in assessing the performance of the Big Five over the years, one cannot help being struck by the extraordinary ineptness with which they met their varying problems. These problems were in three basic categories: racial, political, and economic (including labor). Again quoting Machiavelli, the classic authority on feudal government, he noted three classes of intellect: "one that comprehends by itself; another which appreciates what others comprehend; and a third which neither comprehends by itself nor by the showing of others." The first he described as "excellent," the second as "fair" and a third as "useless." While it might appear too harshly critical of the oligarchy to classify it as "useless," the record speaks for itself.

18

The Politics of Change

As an example of the oligarchy's fundamental unfitness to rule, one may start with the sugar planters' most important problem: the means of dealing with labor they were forced to import from Asia. Their methods were quite simple. They herded Asian workers together as if they were serfs, with no regard for their ancestral traditions, customs, or comfort. This was described by a Department of Labor surveyor as "effective control of the work force," a euphemism for serfdom.

While basic ethnic groups were segregated as Chinese, Japanese, and Filipinos, the plantation managers made no effort to distinguish between intraracial groups with varied backgrounds. Chinese imported through the city of Canton were regarded as Cantonese, or just Chinese, even though they might have been Hakka from the hills of Kwangsi or Chiang-Thai from the mountains of Yunnan, who spoke entirely different dialects. Japanese from Okinawa and Naichi from the major islands of Japan were mixed with *eta,* the lowest class of peasants, even though they did not mix in their homeland; all were simply regarded as Japs. Differences among Filipinos were even more pronounced. Ilocanos and Visayans hated each other, and those who spoke Tagalog dialects despised both; yet they were all Filipinos on the plantations. The result was a polyglot mixture that reflected either the ignorance or indifference of the planters to traditions or conditions under which these imported laborers lived. It was this treatment that drove many to seek some means of escape from the plantations, and, ultimately, to revolt against the planters.

Having lumped these differentiated fractional groups into what amounted to racial conglomerates, the planters thus created races that really had not existed before; and as these groups grew together, so to speak, they developed an anti-*haole* feeling because the latter were the only people they recognized as a race, and also as their oppressors. The earlier European labor groups—Portuguese, Swedes, Germans, and other Caucasians, along with the Hawaiians—had already moved off the plantations into villages and the cities and became part of a larger grouping of what might be regarded as second-class citizens, ignored, humiliated, and politically repressed. These were gradually welded with the Asians into a dissident political force ready to join any leaders who might attack the Big Five.

Taking these larger Oriental ethnic groups in order of their appearance in the Islands, the first to arrive were the Chinese, who came to work in the canefields in the 1850s and quickly moved to the towns and cities, setting up small businesses, and ultimately the larger operations of the Chinese tycoons of the 1950s and poststatehood period. They did not stir up racial rivalries and quickly became as Americanized as the *haoles*. The second wave—the Japanese—would have been ideal field workers if the sugar planters had made any effort to understand their agrarian background and way of life. Instead, they described them as unassimilable and fit only for plantation work; and this attitude and treatment built up the deep racial resentment of the Japanese—particularly the *nisei*—that exploded following World War II. The theory that the *nisei* could never become a real part of the American community was effectively disproved by the war, yet it required a political revolt to drive the point home to the Big Five.

The treatment accorded the Filipinos has been discussed briefly, and will be taken up later in the context of the rising influence of the Filipino voters in the electorate during the decade following achievement of statehood. It is sufficient to note here that the Filipinos were never a racial problem. They lived by themselves, "strangers and afraid," as Dr. Fuchs described them. They could hardly have been regarded as a menace, as the Japanese were considered. They did not mix readily with other people, and most of them planned to return to the Philippines as soon as they had saved enough money; but the low wages and poor living conditions on the plantations drove them to the docks of Lihue and Honolulu and ultimately into the arms of Jack Hall and the ILWU.

In brief, as sociologists Lind and Adams indicated, the sugar planter oligarchy created its own racial problem, and as Professor Lind pointed out, "Gaps still remain between Hawaii's professions of racial equality and its actual practice."

Senator Inouye had put his finger on the two critical defects in the oligarchy's method of control. The first was unwillingness or inability to understand the Oriental mentality, particularly the Japanese; and the second was the failure to recognize the importance of the public schools as a breeding ground of democracy.

The first point may be applied generally to the oligarchy's attitude toward all alien races. Japanese and Filipinos were the largest ethnic groups on plantations, although the Chinese up to 1882 constituted 50 percent of the field labor, with the Hawaiians about a fourth, and the rest made up of a scattering of Portuguese, Swedes, Germans, and other Caucasians. By 1900 the Japanese furnished three-fourths of the plantation labor, but instead of trying to understand their ethnic background, the planters herded them into special areas and referred to them as "an unruly lot" or "an Asiatic menace," particularly after they began to organize a labor movement.

The second element noted by Inouye was the apparent inability of the planters to realize that the public school system was an escape from serfdom for the Japanese, a chance to improve their lot. For the plantation managers it was simply a nuisance. In both examples there is an underlying similarity: lack of interest on the part of the ruling group in the background and mental habits of those whom they expected to govern. In a sense it was similar in a reverse way to Arnold Toynbee's theory that a dominant minority begins to lose control, and the society it dominates begins to disintegrate or revolt, when an "alien faith" is introduced. In this case it was not so much the injection of an "alien faith"—although this was the purpose of the missionaries—as it was the unwillingness or inability of the oligarchy to permit plantation workers to participate in the democratic principles enjoyed by the *haole* elite and extolled in the public school system.

Dr. Adams pointed out in a study of the educational problems of Hawaii in 1928 that the "Orientals of Hawaii (chiefly Japanese and Filipinos) have had to accept a position of inferior privilege." Professor Lind noted in a similar study that the sugar planters appeared actually afraid of the economic competition that might develop if the Japanese and the Chinese were allowed to become educated in the American schools. Although they permitted and even encouraged the establishment of foreign language schools on plantations in the early years, this was merely to shunt them off into segregated groups of their own racial origins, and avoid public schools. This permissiveness was withdrawn in the 1920s when reference to the so-called Japanese menace became popular among the *haole* elite and laws were passed to regulate the language school problem.

Throughout the period of Big Five domination of the Islands, most of the earlier racial disputes on plantations were created by the *haoles* themselves in their effort to "keep the Orientals in their places." These efforts were successful for a time, except among the Chinese who ignored the superiority pretensions of the *haoles,* left the canefields, and set up their own businesses. But among the Japanese and Filipinos, and particularly among the Hawaiians, the seeds of discontent were planted and nurtured on the plantations. In later years there was also a tendency among *kamaaina haoles* to regard many newcomers from the Mainland—the *malihini haoles*—with similar contempt, and this drove the latter into the camp of the Asians, Hawaiians, and Portuguese. Although the Portuguese were grouped in census figures as Caucasian they were never regarded as *haoles* among the *haole* elite.

Reduced to rather simple terms, the problems that plagued the oligarchy in later years were not racial in their essence, but were created by the attitude of the sugar planters and their business associates in Honolulu toward all groups outside the closed society of the *haole* elite, the *kamaaina* families and those who joined them by marriage. The Big Five failed to recognize the truth of the old Hawaiian adage quoted earlier—that "a canoe is not swamped by the outside wave, but by the inside wave." While this was mentioned in connection with the events of World War II, which drove Daniel Inouye and his fellow war veterans into political activity and precipitated the second revolution in Hawaii, it can also be applied generally to the factors that brought about the disintegration of the power of the Big Five. Again quoting Toynbee, he refers to a comment of the Swiss psychologist, C. G. Jung, that "great innovations never come from above; they invariably come from below . . . from the much-derided silent folk of the land."

The ineptness of the oligarchy lay in its apparent inability to deal with people and problems outside its members' own limited social, economic, and political experience. Most of the forefathers of the planters had come to Hawaii as missionaries, to bring Christian morality to the natives; yet their descendants appeared to regard plantation workers as hardly human, and little better than domesticated animals. Despite their claims of having introduced new technical skills in the production of sugar and pineapples, and their impressive contributions to the economy of Hawaii, they could not advance beyond the feudal mentality characteristic of Bedouin sheiks. And when their system seemed to be collapsing around them, they resorted to such fumbling strategy as the campaigns of Imua against the Communist menace in an effort to torpedo statehood, which they feared would—and did—destroy their feudal system.

Statehood for Hawaii, as Senator Morgan of Alabama pointed out at the turn of the century, was inevitable; but it was actually helped along in its final stages by the crude maneuverings of old-line remnants of the declining oligarchy. It was even a bit ironic that in the report of Congressman Leo O'Brien's committee, which made the junket to Hawaii in 1958 to counteract Senator Eastland's activities a year earlier, introduced as a final basis for approving statehood, there should appear these words,

> In addition, there is an organization of patriotic men and women known as IMUA with the dedicated purpose of keeping the public informed in anti-American activity. It has an office, a staff, all available information and files, and through the use of radio, television and newspapers, it keeps the public informed, not only as to activity of Communists and the threat of communism, but also on facts concerning the activity of those known to be or to have been connected with the Communist movement. It is probably safe to say that the public in Hawaii is kept better informed on the threat of communism than is the public in any similar community on the mainland.[32]

This type of vigilante espionage was the last, and one of the least effective, of the final frantic efforts to block statehood. In any event, Hawaii was vindicated in Congressional eyes as being ever alert against menaces in any form, and the Communist issue disappeared with the advent of statehood, along with Judge Stainback's worries about the Emperor of Japan having his representatives seated in the American Congress.

The economic aspects of the oligarchy's downfall were forecast in the 1930s, when it became apparent that sugar and pineapples, with a small amount of support from tourism, could not sustain Hawaii's growing population. Again, the Big Five seemed disinclined to accept warnings, as they had ignored warnings with respect to the public school system and the inability of a nonvoting delegate to hold the line in Congress against the attacks on Hawaii's sugar quota. It was not until the end of the 1940s that the shift in balance of economic power became inevitable, and a few members of the Big Five saw the light.

However, as noted earlier, compensating factors were already coming into play. Dr. James Shoemaker's warning in 1950 was based on the unfavorable balance of payments that was in evidence during the years after World War II. He had said specifically that "in terms of current income and expenditures we are going in the red." At the time members of the Big Five were on notice that sugar and pineapples could no longer support Hawaii's growing population. In terms of goods sold to the Mainland and purchased from the Mainland, the Territory was going downhill. However, the sale of goods and services in Hawaii, chiefly in Federal expenditures for defense and the trickling tourist trade, was covering the imbalance.

By the early 1950s reliance on sugar and pineapples was no longer necessary. In this respect, the old cry of the Big Five that Sugar is King has become an economic anachronism. Not all of the Big Five were so myopic as not to realize this, and long before statehood was achieved diversification of Hawaii's large companies was taking place. Alex Budge of Castle & Cooke, one of the old-line members of the oligarchy, was among the first to recognize this and began to look around for Mainland investments. Others followed. At first the Big Five control of the agencies was maintained through closely held stock and inter-locking directorships, but economic talent had to be imported from the Mainland to run the businesses, and stockholder bases were broadened.

The plantation labor force had been drastically reduced. In 1930 there had been nearly 50,000 employed on the planta-tions; in 1940 the total was about 35,000, and by the year of statehood it was reduced to slightly over 15,000. Much of this was due to automation, although curtailment of sugar lands diverted to other uses by homesite developers such as Chinn Ho and Clarence Ching was a significant factor.

Meanwhile two new sources of income, more permanent than Federal spending, were being tapped, and these became the foundation of Hawaii's economic growth in the years follow-ing statehood. The first was increased investment in new facili-ties in the Islands; and the second—which in some respects was related to the first—was the increase in tourist travel, which was euphemistically described as the visitors industry.

Hawaii in the decades before and after statehood—from 1950 to 1970—passed from an agriculturally based economy to one of extensively diversified industry. The construction of ho-tels and apartments has been mentioned, as well as the new refineries, cement plants, and other industrial enterprises. The building boom was probably the greatest since the dizzy days in Florida in the 1920s. Tourists—or visitors—began to flock to the Islands as a means of escape from troubled times on the Mainland. The Beach at Waikiki, reduced to a gravelly patch of sand between high water and the reef, still lured people who wanted to get away from the nervous disorders of living in the continental United States, with all the violence, rioting, assassi-nations, and outbursts of youthful dissent, together with in-creased drug addiction, that began to develop on the Mainland in the 1960s. Where does one go in times of stress? To Hawaii, of course, to bask on beaches, play golf, and live amid exotic tropical scenery. Tourism, which brought only 40,000 visitors to the Islands in 1950 and 172,000 the year before statehood, rose to 1.2 million ten years later, in 1968.

With increased tourism came the building boom. A substantial portion of this was for homesites of those who intended to remain in Hawaii. The resident population ten years after statehood was 769,000, plus military personnel, compared with 499,000 in 1950 and 645,000 in 1959. In addition, there was an in-migration of approximately 35,000 annually from the Mainland and 5,000 people from other countries who planned to remain in Hawaii permanently. Investment in Hawaiian enterprises jumped from $175 million in 1958 to $463 million a decade later. Federal expenditures also rose from $421 million to $911 million in the same period. Hawaii was on the move.

Daniel Inouye, the first person of Japanese blood to be elected to Congress, was described by Jack Burns as "able to reach people." Many years after Inouye became the first Congressman from Hawaii, and later the first United States Senator of Japanese ancestry, Burns said, "Inouye feels what people feel, and he makes them feel what he feels."

There was probably no simpler explanation of Dan Inouye's uncanny ability to win elections, leading his ticket in every campaign in which he was engaged. He was able to do what the members of the oligarchy could not do: he could reach people, understand them, and thus gain their confidence. He himself was one of the second-class citizens of Hawaii, and he understood their frustrations and needs.

In certain respects, the young *nisei* war veteran was not unlike another young man of about the same age whose personal charisma was enabling him to scale far greater heights than Inouye. This was John Fitzgerald Kennedy, who became President of the United States a year after Hawaii's admission to statehood. In many ways the two were alike. Both were fired with an inner desire to "make the world a better place" and both possessed—or developed—strong political motivation. Inouye also had a great sense of restraint, an inborn instinct for self-effacement that came of his racial origin as well as an upbringing far different from that of Kennedy. The events that followed the admission of Hawaii to statehood illustrate this point.

Inouye had fixed his eyes, along with many others in Hawaii, on the political aspects of Hawaii's new position as a state —such as, for example, the United States Congress to which Hawaii's Senators and Representatives could now be elected. His first thought was to run for the House. He was aware that Jack Burns had a personal desire to return to Congress as a Senator from Hawaii, and although Burns had not announced his plans, Inouye decided on his own responsibility to try for the single seat in the House open to Hawaii in the first special election in 1959. He drew most of his savings out of the bank —about $5,000—and made plans for his campaign.

Meanwhile Burns decided his job was to remain in Hawaii and consolidate the gains of the Democratic party, which was already showing familiar signs of internal conflict. The Gill-Esposito faction still maintained tentatively friendly relations with Burns, but Tom Gill deeply resented what he regarded as Burns's autocratic rule of the party. The arrangement between Burns's independents and the ILWU was by no means a permanent political fixture, either. Jack Hall had backed a number of candidates in the 1958 election who were not "Burns boys," and his relations with Burns were more of convenience than principle.

Burns could have had that first Senate seat for the asking, but he chose to remain in Hawaii and run for governor. Later he explained this. "I had never actively sought public office," he said. "In 1948 it was an eleventh hour decision. Bill Heen was slated to run for Delegate, but did not want to file because he was sure Joe Farrington could beat him. I filed to fill the gap." He stayed out of the delegateship in 1950, and William Borthwick, the Democratic candidate, failed to make a dent in Farrington's popularity. Burns ran again in 1952 and 1954, but it was not until 1956 that "Old Stone Face," as he was called, finally broke through. In this case his goal was clear; he believed that as delegate he could pilot Hawaii to statehood.

Burns had always been more interested in political planning and organizing than in running for office, and the governor's office in Hawaii, with new powers under the state constitution, seemed to be the best place for executing political strategy.

When Burns's decision became known, Inouye changed his

own plans and announced his candidacy for one of the two senatorial posts. Patsy Takemoto Mink, the young lady who had broken with Jack Hall two years earlier over her criticism of ILWU methods, told Inouye she planned to file for the House seat, since Inouye was now a candidate for the Senate. He tacitly approved. The decision was unfortunate for both of them. Burns had decided on the two men he wanted to run for the Senate: Judge Heen and former Governor Oren Long. Both filed for the primary race, leaving only two choices open for Inouye: to contest the two veterans in the primary, relying on his vote-getting powers, but perhaps splitting the Burns faction in the party; or to run for the single House seat, in which case he would have to repudiate what had been a virtual endorsement of Patsy Mink.

"This was not a happy choice," Inouye said later. "Nothing in politics stays private and personal, and soon the newspapers, sensing my dilemma, began to make public property of an intensely personal question: What is Dan Inouye going to do?"

He decided to stay out of the Senate race and try for the House; and the hardest job was to explain this to Patsy Mink. He talked first with Burns, who told him the opening chance at the Senate seats "belongs to Long and Heen." Young Inouye called his family together—his wife Margaret, and the parents of both—and announced his decision. "I'm going to withdraw from the Senate race and announce my candidacy for the House."

Telling this to his family was one thing; telling it to Patsy Mink was another. He called her on the telephone. "I'm going to withdraw from the Senate race in favor of Governor Long and Judge Heen," he told her. "I'll announce my candidacy for the House today." There was a long silence. Then he said, "Patsy, I'm sorry as hell it turned out this way. I didn't know Long and Heen would get into this thing. I meant it when I gave you my blessing."

She said, "I know you did. I'm disappointed, but I think I understand." Then she added that she would not withdraw —even though beating Dan Inouye in an election in Hawaii had thus far been proved to be virtually impossible. "Too many people have worked too hard for me just to pull out. So I guess we're in for a primary fight."

It was not much of a fight. Inouye defeated Patsy Mink easily in the primary and won the general election by a landslide. But in some respects it was a bitter political pill. He had, in fact, jumped the gun when he announced his candidacy for the Senate. Although there is some indication in his book that Burns gave him the "go" sign when he announced his candidacy after Burns decided to run for governor, the fact that Burns himself asked Inouye not to run against Long and Heen would appear to contradict this. Those close to Burns have denied that he had at any time supported Inouye's early ambitions for the Senate.

In retrospect, it was probably a fortunate choice for Inouye. His political charisma was enhanced, and his ability to win elections was fast becoming a legend in Hawaii. In the long run it provided another example of the similarities in political personality between Inouye and Jack Kennedy. Like the latter, Inouye seldom made the same mistake twice.

In June of 1959 Hawaii voted in a special election, as required under the bill enacted by Congress, to accept admission to statehood. The margin was overwhelming—17 to 1—in spite of the earlier concern of the Hawaii Statehood Commission. Everyone was on the bandwagon by this time, and every county voted solidly for statehood, except the tiny Island of Niihau, farthest north of the major Hawaiian Islands, which had only 107 registered voters. There were two aspects of Niihau's vote worth noting. It was entirely owned by the Robinson family of Kauai, one of the oldest missionary-planter dynasties, and as such its inhabitants were solidly Republican; and the voters were all Hawaiians. In a sense, this was a symbol of the undying resentment of many Hawaiians against statehood, which they felt severed the last strand in their attachment to Hawaii Nei—the old Hawaii of Polynesian kings.

There was another symbolic significance in Niihau's dissenting vote. The Republicans were not as defunct as the 1958 election returns might have indicated or as the Democrats might have hoped. The decision Jack Burns made to stay in Hawaii and run for governor was a temporary disaster. The Republicans, who now bore little resemblance to the old Big Five-GOP coalition, ran their appointed territorial Governor William Quinn against him. In the Senate contest they put up Wilfred Tsukiyama, who had been the leading Republican *nisei* the year Dan Inouye was born, to run against former Governor Long; and in the other race, in which Frank Fasi had defeated Judge Heen in the primary, they ran Hiram Fong, one of the rising new Chinese tycoons who had become wealthy in the financing business, against Fasi.

The general election in 1960, following a special election in 1959 to fill out terms in the expiring 85th Congress, was extremely close. Quinn, an articulate *malahini* lawyer with less than ten years' residence in Hawaii, dragged out an old issue—land distribution—which he called "the new Mahele." Apparently he was unaware that the term "Mahele" was odious to Hawaiians who read history; the Great Mahele a century earlier had been the distribution of land by Kamehameha III that resulted in the *haole* plantation owners acquiring most of the fertile sugar lands in the Islands. However, the memories of Hawaiians were notably short on the subject of land and on Quinn's promise to provide plots of government land at fifty dollars an acre they voted heavily for him, and he won by a margin of 4,139 out of 168,287 votes cast—a percentage of 51.2 to 48.8. Jimmy Kealoha, the Chinese-Hawaiian Republican leader on the Big Island of Hawaii, who had once been a Democrat, defeated Burns's man, Mitsuyuki Kido, for Lieutenant Governor.

In the senatorial races, Tsukiyama failed to lure the *nisei* vote as expected, and Oren Long won; but in the other contest Fong ran ahead of Fasi, carrying many of the predominantly Democratic precincts. The most surprising reversal for the Democrats was the loss of the new State Senate, fourteen seats to eleven, and even though they held a solid majority in the new House—33 seats to 18—it was at least a temporary indication that the Republican party had not expired. The most solid victory, as usual, was Dan Inouye's landslide over Fred Titcomb. He had defeated Dr. Charlie Silva, a dentist, in the special election in 1959, and no established Republican was willing to risk his reputation in a contest with Inouye the following year. Titcomb was buried in an avalanche, 135,829 to 46,812.

Possibly the most significant aspect of this election was that any resemblance between the Republican Party in Hawaii in 1960 and that of a decade earlier was entirely coincidental. Not a single member of the old Big Five-GOP coalition was elected to any of the major offices; and those Republicans who were elected were acknowledged liberals.

Ben Dillingham, grandson of the original Ben Dillingham who had arrived in Hawaii as a seaman in 1865 and married into the missionary Smith family in 1869, was Oahu county chairman and campaign manager, but his political strategy was hardly the deciding factor. He harped on such worn-out themes as the "capture" of the Democratic party by the ILWU, the "Communist menace," and the "yellow peril," while Quinn talked about unemployment compensation, taxes on unused land and—his most telling point—distribution of public land at low prices. He seemed uninformed about the Hawaiian Homes Act, the land fraud perpetrated in the name of rehabilitation in 1920, a point on which his future constituents seemed equally ill-informed.

What the election proved in general was that the Republicans were still alive if they could come up with a few meaningful planks in their platform similar to those Joe Farrington had advocated in the 1940s and that the Democrats had tried to enact into law in the 1950s—bills usually vetoed by Republican governors.

When Sam Rayburn, Speaker of the House, was informed of Burns's defeat in the first state election in Hawaii, he said, "If I'd known the people of Hawaii were going to do that to Jack Burns, I'd never let the Hawaii bill get off my desk."

The joy of the Republicans was short-lived, however. Two years later, in 1962, after Governor Quinn had failed to deliver on his $50-an-acre land program, the Hawaiian electorate turned him out, voting in Burns for the first of three terms he was to serve as governor by a plurality of 114,308 out of 196,615 votes cast, or a percentage of 58.4 to 41.6.

Oren Long retired after the first term in the Senate, and

Dan Inouye was elected to fill the vacancy defeating—of all people—Ben Dillingham. The vote was 136,294 to 60,067, Inouye again getting the largest vote on the Democratic ticket. The result was symbolic of what had happened to Hawaii. The grandson of an immigrant Japanese field worker, who grew up in the slums of Honolulu, had defeated the scion of the most powerful family in the oligarchy—the son of Walter Dillingham, who had been Hawaii's leading industrialist a decade earlier, and Mrs. Walter Dillingham, the founder of Imua. The election of Inouye as junior United States Senator from Hawaii put the final period in the story of the second revolution in Hawaii, as far as its political aspects were concerned.

The Democratic sweep of 1962 was the end of one era, but also the beginning of another. The 1960s were a decade of change that encompassed not merely the political shift in power and the virtual eclipse of Big-Five control of Hawaii's political system, but an even more significant shift in the balance of economic power. This involved a drastic reassessment of several basic factors, the most important of which were a new appraisal of Hawaii's underlying racial problem, an evaluation of the new financial forces that emerged in the 1950s and became dominant in the decade after statehood, and the rise to power of what some students of the situation were inclined to describe as "a new power elite." The dissidents of the 1950s were becoming the new Establishment of the 1970s.

Tom Gill, a squarish-looking man, fairly athletic in appearance and approaching fifty, with the face of a born fighter, was the Hawaiian-born son of a Honolulu newspaperwoman who had allied himself with Jack Burns in the early years of the second revolution, but never quite joined the "Burns boys." The nearest he came to being a member of the Burns group was in 1962 when he was on the "unity" Democratic ticket and won in the race for the House, Hawaii having been awarded a second Congressional seat. Spark Matsunaga won the other seat in an election in which they easily defeated Albert W. Evansen and Richard Sutton, the Republican candidates, and Dan Inouye overwhelmed Ben Dillingham in the Senate contest, again topping the Democratic ticket. Burns defeated Quinn for the governorship with Bill Richardson as his running mate.

Prior to that, Gill had opposed Burns's selections of several Democratic candidates, upsetting Tadao Beppu, a Burns man, for Oahu county chairman as early as 1954. Gill then had the support of the ILWU, but like Patsy Mink, he broke with Jack Hall because he would not take orders from him.

Two years after the 1962 election, Gill tried for the Senate and was beaten by Hiram Fong, seeking his second term. The vote was 110,747 to 96,289. In the 1966 election Gill challenged Burns in the primary race for lieutenant governor, defeating Kenneth Brown, whom Burns, then seeking his second term as governor, had backed. Gill won in the general election, but the open hostility between Gill and Burns nearly cost the latter the election. Burns refused to campaign with Gill and the two, running as a team before a change in the state election laws separated the offices of governor and lieutenant governor on the ballot, barely beat Crossley and George Mills, 108,840 to 104,-

19

The New Establishment

324. After that Gill and Burns parted company.

This intraparty split has been described in some detail because it was a basic factor in the development of the so-called Gill-Esposito independent faction in the independent wing of the Democratic Party. Sitting in his office in Honolulu, overlooking the Federal post office building and the old Palace Plaza—a triangular strip of land that existed as a park in the days of the Hawaiian Revolution of 1893 and has now become a public parking area—his brown eyes glinting with sardonic humor, Gill outlined to a visitor in his office what he thought had happened to Hawaii's second revolution. Gill himself was no longer actively seeking office (this was in 1971) but he was a powerful influence in the rising strength of the Gill-Esposito faction. He was attorney for several labor groups, including a newly organized Hawaii Federation of Teachers, and had represented the Teamsters Union; but his main strength lay in his consistent opposition to what he regarded as Burns's autocratic rule of the Democratic Party. Reminiscing over events, he said, "Politics is like a time wheel. You watch it turn and pretty soon the same spokes come up again. For nearly fifty years, from the end of the century to the end of World War II, we lived under a sugar factor hierarchy. Our economic and political lives were controlled by sugar, pineapples, and shipping, and by the agencies that controlled them. These included only a small handful of people who were descendants either of missionaries or of adventurers who had dispossessed the Hawaiian kingdom.

"This hierarchy was a closed society. It talked to itself. It spoke to the people through chosen instruments, the principal one being the Republican Party. It enforced its mandates with methods that were often ruthless and always self-serving. It was paternalistic and fundamentally racist. Those who wanted something more than the hierarchy was willing to give—better wages, racial equality, in short, the normal demands of people in a democratic society—were called Communists. Young men who were not of *haole* racial origin, who came back from fighting America's war, were not willing to accept a passive role any longer. Many were armed with better education than their fathers had, or that might have been their lot if it had not been for the GI Bill of Rights.

"At first they had no place to go. The society in which they had grown up was closed to them. The power structure would admit only those who would adapt themselves to the hierarchy. But there were weaknesses in the old structure, and it began to crumble visibly, and finally collapsed. There were new faces in the Legislature, young men who were a bit dazed at finding themselves suddenly in the seats of lawmakers, but full of new ideas and burning with a desire to right old wrongs.

"In the early days the old order fought with old weapons but these failed. Although the newcomers to the territorial Legislature had many of their bills vetoed by the Governor, they had breached the walls of the hierarchy." Gill smiled reminiscently. He had been one of these "new men." He went on: "They discovered that changes in laws do not in themselves change society, although they may shake it up a bit.

"The old order still controlled the castles of commerce. They still owned the land and the banks and most of the industry of Hawaii."

Up to this point Gill was repeating what has already been covered—the events leading up to the second revolution and the reasons for the collapse of the Big Five. He then made a comment that expressed his own political philosophy. There was probably no member of the political independents who brought the new Hawaii into being who was more consistently a rebel than Gill. He had grown up in Hawaii with sound *haole* credentials, yet he had avoided joining the *haole* elite and avoided equally being tagged as a "Burns boy." He was a political maverick.

"Someone of the old order made a canny discovery," he said. "They decided many of these new young men did not really want to change things, or destroy anything. They just 'wanted in.'"

Whether or not this assessment was close to the truth or merely an expression of Tom Gill's tendency to rebel remains to be determined; but there was no doubt that the second revolution in Hawaii had shifted the political power base from the Big Five to the new Democratic alignment, led by Jack Burns. As Gill expressed it, Burns was "firmly in the saddle" and his election to the first of three terms as Governor in 1962 cemented that position. In Gill's view, it was merely a "turn of the time wheel."

"In the mid-fifties there obviously were strong motivations at a high level," he continued. "Some of it still persists. But as many of the 'young Turks' grew older and fatter—not only around the waist, but in some cases between the ears—making over the old order became less important than simply 'making it.' "

However, there were elements other than political and economic advantages to be taken into account, and many of these were not included in Tom Gill's admittedly simplistic evaluation of the second revolution. One of these was Hawaii's new status as a state, and its increasing importance in the Pacific community of nations. It was no longer merely a tropical paradise. Governor Burns recognized this in his first inaugural address on December 3, 1962, in which he said:

> I am committed to a program for developing in Hawaii a center for stimulating exchanges between peoples of the Pacific Basin, for providing services that would facilitate that exchange, and attract future Pacific traders to come to Hawaii for negotiations . . . Hawaii is at the hub of the great wheel of the Pacific.[33]

This was not the "wheel" to which Tom Gill had referred; but it expressed in prophetic terms what Senator Jackson of Washington had said when he placed the Hawaii statehood bill —SR 50—before the Senate Committee on Interior and Insular Affairs four years before: "When Hawaii is admitted it will come into the Union not just as the 50th State, but as our diplomatic representative to over half the population of the world."

Gill may have overlooked this point in his personal relations with Burns's Democratic power base, with which he was then at odds; but it was an element Burns did not overlook, and to which he and Senator Inouye, who had become Hawaii's most articulate spokesman on the national scene, had firmly committed the new State Administration.

Burns noted in his inaugural speech that there was "embodied" in the people of Hawaii "the very blood of Pacific peoples."

There was in the new State of Hawaii "an understanding of the cultures and needs of the many people" that rim the Pacific. "Through the long history of immigration to these shores, the Hawaiian people themselves became outnumbered," he went on, "but they still conquered with their warmth, their spirit of aloha, of brotherhood. They have given all our people the potential of becoming the greatest ambassadors on the face of the earth."

The habit of exaggeration is not unusual among politicians, and the Governor may be pardoned the extravagance of drawing the folk spirit of the Hawaiian people into his diplomatic vision. The actual record does not bear out the theory that the "spirit of aloha," which the Hawaiians possessed to an unusual degree, ever conquered anything as practical as a politician. However, the sense of what he said presents a significant aspect of the change of Hawaii from the feudal domain of a small group of sugar planters and pineapple growers and their business agents to a full-fledged state in the American Union. This will be dealt with in more detail in the final chapter of this book, but it is noteworthy that Burns singled out this point as the theme of his first address as Governor of Hawaii.

"The conclusion is inescapable," he said. "There must be a dramatic upsurge in Pacific trade, in commerce, in understanding, in trust, in good intent. Let us welcome this challenge, confident in our potentialities and in our ability to meet each obstacle with wisdom and courage."

One of Burns's first acts as Governor was to expand the new East-West Center, a federal project adjoining the University of Hawaii established in 1960 during the first year after statehood when Quinn was governor. Its purpose was to provide facilities and personnel for studying various problems of the Pacific Community from the vantage point of Hawaii, both physically and racially centralized. A second step, initiated some years later, was to organize a group for the purpose of studying Hawaii's own social, political and ecological problems leading up to the year 2000. The group was headed by George Chaplin, editor of the *Honolulu Advertiser*.

Daniel Inouye, as Hawaii's first Congressman and later as

Senator, had become the island state's chief spokesman in Washington. He recalled in later years many of his early problems, and a few of the triumphs, in the job of introducing Hawaii into its new legislative status.

"The inner workings of Congress are quite complicated, and even mysterious, to the freshman legislator," he said. "My first introduction came in an unexpected and extremely gratifying manner. I received a telephone call one day and the man at the other end wanted to know whether I was 'Congressman Inn-oo-way' or 'Inn-way.' " The new Congressman from Hawaii explained that his name was pronounced "In-no-way." The caller, who spoke with a distinct Southern drawl, was the Speaker of the House, Sam Rayburn of Texas. He laughed and said, "Well, I'm going to start calling you 'Dan' because I'm damned if I can pronounce your last name."

Rayburn told Inouye he would like to have him drop over to his office and he would show him around the Capitol. "He said he wanted to welcome me personally," the Senator said later. "I guess this was the first time a freshman Congressman from a new state was welcomed that way."

As they walked through the galleries and the library, and finally through the House and Senate chambers, the young man from Hawaii recalled the day he had been introduced to the House by Representative Leo O'Brien of New York, sponsor of Hawaii's statehood bill, and Speaker Rayburn had administered the oath of office. The scene was recorded in the *Congressional Record*, at O'Brien's request.

"The House was about to witness the swearing in of the first American of Japanese descent to serve in Congress," the *Record* said. " 'Raise your right hand and repeat after me,' intoned Speaker Rayburn. The hush deepened as the young Congressman raised not his right hand, but his left hand. There was no right hand. It had been lost in combat in World War II."

The day Rayburn took Inouye on a tour of the Capitol he asked him if he knew who the best known member of Congress was—"after me, of course."

Inouye shook his head. "No," he said. "Who?"

The Speaker looked at Inouye and said, "You."

"I asked him why in the world it should be me," the Senator said. "Sam Rayburn replied, 'Just think of it, son. How many one-armed Japanese do you think we have in the Congress of the United States?'"

Sitting in his paneled office in Suite 442 in the Old Senate Office Building, the Senator from Hawaii was able to contemplate with some humor the differences between the *modus operandi* of national politics and the more provincial character of politics in Hawaii. Twenty years before—   , when he was completing prelegal studies at the University of Hawaii prior to going to law school in Washington—he had received a telephone call from a prominent member of the Big Five. He asked the young law student to call at his office.

"I went down to his office," Inouye said. "He offered me a job in one the major agencies in Hawaii—at 700 dollars a month. That isn't much by today's standards, but it was astronomical then, particularly for a young man just entering law school." Inouye refused politely, explaining that his current interest was completing his education. Even when the advantages of returning to Honolulu with a ready-made job awaiting him were outlined Inouye still refused. The offer was more than the simple practice of "buying up" promising young men. Inouye was already advancing in Democratic political councils, and with the help of his young wife, Margaret, an elocution instructor at the University, he was acquiring capabilities in the use of the English language far superior to the pidgin English he used when he failed the oral tests for the English Standard School.

Eighteen years later, on September 11, 1968, the junior Senator from Hawaii stood on the podium of a crowded auditorium in Chicago and in polished language, without a trace of the Oriental accent so familiar on the streets of Honolulu, he delivered in ringing tones the keynote speech of the Democratic National Convention. He pleaded for unity and understanding of all races as a "commitment" of his Party. He spoke of "more than a hundred years of systematic racist deprivation" in America. The speech was not an exercise in political semantics. "The keynote address at the national political convention traditionally calls for rousing oratory," he said. "I hope I may be excused from that tradition tonight because I do not view this as an occasion for flamboyance or levity."

In one sense, that speech was a declaration of principles of Hawaii's second revolution. It was also a personal statement of Dan Inouye's own revolt, which began when he returned from the war with one arm missing and decided the time had come to redress a few old wrongs—and to do it through democratic processes:

> As an American whose ancestors came from Japan, I have become accustomed to a question . . . "Why can't the Negro be like you?" First, although my skin is colored, it is not black. . . . It does not ignite prejudices that have smouldered for generations. Second, although my grandfather came to this country in poverty, he came without shackles. Third, my grandfather's family was not shattered [by having] individual members of it sold as chattel or used as security on loans. And fourth, although others of my ancestry were interned behind barbed wire during World War II, neither my parents nor I were forced by convenants to live in ghettos.[34]

While Dan Inouye was addressing this statement, involving the meaning of democracy, to an entire nation, political wheels were turning back in Hawaii where the second revolution was not only virtually completed, but was going through what might be described in military terms as the consolidation phase. There were even those who thought a third revolution might be in the offing. The suspicions expressed by Tom Gill that displacement of the oligarchy by the "young Turks" of the second revolution might be a prelude to the setting up of a new Establishment to replace the Big Five were being voiced by others who had taken part in the political revolt of the 1950s.

In expressing the conviction that the basic principles of equality and justice were a solemn commitment of the national government, and that they had not been resolved, Senator Inouye was speaking to the nation; and his warnings of the failure to keep these commitments were prophetic for the Democratic Party, but the results of the general election that fall are, of course, a matter of history. In Hawaii Dan Inouye once again rolled along far ahead of his ticket, defeating the Republican candidate, Wayne Thiessen, by an overwhelming margin of 189,248 to 34,008, a ratio of nearly six to one. Spark Matsunaga and Patsy Mink were returned to the House, defeating Neal Blaisdell, the successor to Johnny Wilson as the perennial Mayor of Honolulu who made a try for the House, and George DuBois, a little-known Republican. Blaisdell, incidentally, gave up the Mayor's job, which went to Frank Fasi, in order to run for Congress.

Two years earlier Burns had run, much against his desires, with Tom Gill to win his second term as Governor, beating Randolph Crossley, the Republican "white hope" from Kauai; but this was the last time Gill ran on the Governor's ticket. The breach between the Gill-Esposito faction and Burns became virtually irreparable after the 1966 elections.

By 1970 the Governor had a new partner as lieutenant governor—George Ariyoshi, who had joined the Burns group in 1956 when Burns was first elected Delegate to Congress, and had advanced rapidly in the second revolution that carried Hawaii into statehood. Ariyoshi became Burns's obvious choice to succeed him as Governor when he should decide to retire from the gubernatorial race. A rather slender, well-groomed and extremely articulate man, Ariyoshi, along with Dan Aoki, became more closely associated with the Governor than any others of the original cast of "Burns boys," with the exception of Dan Inouye, who was in Washington.

There were others beginning to break with Burns. Sakae Takahashi, who provided the early incentive for Inouye's entry into politics, was another who had moved away from the Governor. His own political record had placed him in a position where he could have gotten "a piece of the action" if he wanted it. He was named Treasurer of the Territory in 1951 by Governor Long and won a seat in the territorial Senate in 1954; and when his former commander of the 100th Battalion, Farrant Turner, tried to get Takahashi, along with Spark Matsunaga and Howard Miyake, also "his boys," to switch to the Republican side in 1956, Takahashi spurned the offer and supported Burns for the delegateship in 1958.

Yet Takahashi broke with Burns in the late 1960s and

joined forces with the Gill-Esposito dissidents because, like Gill, he thought Burns was becoming "too aloof and autocratic." Sitting in his law office in the Central Pacific Bank building at the corner of Smith and King streets, the old Chinatown section of Honolulu, Takahashi detailed his reasons in somewhat the same terms Gill had, except that he did not agree that the group that remained loyal to Burns simply "wanted in."

"There is too much wheeling and dealing going on," he said. "The State government is working too closely with special interests, such as big land developers, big contractors, hotel interests, the ILWU, and even the sugar planters." He cited certain instances. The Governor had permitted a delay in enforcement of antipollution regulations on the Island of Hawaii, requiring sugar mills to stop pouring waste into the ocean, which they continued to do in spite of the findings of a Federal commission that this practice was causing widespread pollution of the shorelands. The ILWU had joined with the Governor in agreeing to the delay requested by the sugar mills.

"It looks too much like a deal between the ILWU and the sugar planters, with Burns's approval," he said. "I don't like it."

Takahashi had been one of the first to introduce antipollution legislation in the territorial Legislature and even had to get help from Republicans to support the issue. "A new economic elite has taken up where the Big Five left off," he said. "It's simply a new Establishment."

The one member of the Burns group who did not seem to have aligned himself either with the burgeoning new Establishment or with the Gill-Esposito group was Inouye. He still was the strongest candidate the Democrats could offer in any race, and he seemed to have held to a position of neutrality in the growing split between the Governor and Hawaii's version of a new Left.

Inouye actually stood midway between the two opposing forces—the Burns faction and the recalcitrant group led by Tom Gill and Vincent Esposito. He did not appear to fit into Gill's assessment of the reasons for the "angry young men" of the 1950s joining Jack Burns's crusade—the simplistic explanation that they "wanted in." Nor was he closely aligned with labor, including the more moderate unions controlled by Arthur Rutledge who had been the originator of Unity House, a group that included hotel and restaurant employees and bartenders, or the AFL-CIO builders unions, headed by Jack Reynolds. Inouye became an independent on his own, and to some extent was a target of shafts from both sides. He was not too warmly regarded by the men around Burns, since he was a silent threat to Burns's domination of politics in Hawaii; and he was also criticized by Gill and others for straying too far toward the conservative wing of the Democratic Party.

In reality, Inouye had begun to stand apart from local politics. He was the one man from Hawaii who represented, in a political sense, the national interest. He had been closely associated with the late Sam Rayburn, who guided his first faltering steps in Congress; and he had been considered by President Johnson as possible vice presidential timber in the 1968 race, before Johnson withdrew. Jack Anderson, the Washington columnist, reported early in 1971 that a group of Senators "had tried to persuade Hawaii's popular Senator Inouye to challenge Senator Edward Kennedy for the Whip job." They had taken a secret poll of the Senate and found that Inouye could have defeated Kennedy easily, but "Inouye decided he didn't want the job."

In 1970 Senator Inouye was instrumental in the decision to run a *malihini haole* from the Mainland—Cecil Heftel—against Hiram Fong for the senatorial seat then occupied by Fong, who was seeking reelection. Fong promptly accused Inouye of introducing racism into the campaign, although the avowed purpose was to avoid the complaint voiced by many in Hawaii that only candidates endorsed by the 442nd Veterans Club could get anywhere in the Democratic Party. While the support of a Hawaiian-born *nisei* for a Mainland *haole* against a Hawaiian-born Chinese could hardly be classified as racism, Fong made such a point of this that he refused to allow Senator Inouye to escort him up the aisle, a tradition in the Senate, when he took his place on the Republican side early in 1971, after he had beaten the politically unknown Heftel by a margin of only 7,566 votes.

The one point Dan Inouye had made indelibly clear in the

record of his personal and political views, expressed over the years, was that racism was not a significant factor in the change that had taken place in the Hawaiian political scene. The second revolution had been led by an Irish Catholic expoliceman; it had achieved its initial goal—the displacement of the Big Five-GOP coalition—by a conglomerate collection of disenchanted *nisei* war veterans, angry Hawaiians, and Portuguese who would no longer accept second-class citizenship, and an admixture of *malihini haoles* and rising Chinese businessmen who had no ties to the Big Five, plus the power of Jack Hall and the ILWU.

Dan Inouye put this into fairly concise language in a letter to a Chinese student from Hawaii, Mrs. Bina Chun, who was writing a thesis for a degree in political science at the University of Kansas on the subject of "Japanese influence" in Hawaii's political transition. Senator Inouye wrote,

> First, I think the title . . . "Japanese influence" . . . can be a little misleading. Any influence the people of Japanese origin may have had on Hawaii politics has come through institutions of government which can be duplicated throughout the United States. . . . It has seemed to me that after World War II the social and economic needs of Hawaii's people had advanced to a point where wide-scale changes were in order. It happened that a number of people of Japanese origin were at that time prepared and motivated to move into politics and to espouse causes which former political leaders had ignored. People of other racial backgrounds felt the same as they. But those Americans of Japanese origin who became a political force did so only because the majority of the people backed them.[35]

The drastic upsurge that Governor Burns predicted in commerce and trade in the Pacific, in his inaugural address of 1962, had meanwhile been obscured by certain other events, such as the escalating war in Southeast Asia which was rapidly drawing the United States into new confrontations in the Pacific which would impose new burdens on the diplomatic outpost created by statehood in Hawaii.

The Islands' own economy was also undergoing a drastic facelifting process. One of the most dramatic illustrations was a meeting between two giants of industry, Walter Dillingham, representing the old-line oligarchy, and Henry J. Kaiser, who was wrangling with Dillingham over the building of two large cement plants northwest of Honolulu—Kaiser's Parmanente plant and Dillingham's new Hawaiian Cement Company. The Mainland entrepreneur accused Dillingham of using "underhand tactics" in blocking his enterprise, in a face-to-face meeting at the Waianae School, and Dillingham replied by calling Kaiser a "visitor"—a word of utter opprobrium in the lexicon of *kamaaina haoles.* Both plants were built, however, at a cost of 12 million dollars each. Standard Oil also opened a new refinery on Oahu. A second tunnel was bored through the Koolau mountains, a $10 million project originally conceived by Mayor Johnny Wilson, linking Honolulu with windward Oahu; and Hawaii Western Steel was put into operation, producing cold rolled steel for the first time in the Islands.

The unfavorable balance of payments with the Mainland was no longer a problem. Hawaii was building its own industries at a pace that absorbed any imbalance in monetary exchange with the Coast, and as pointed out by Wesley Hillendahl, the new economic expert for the Bank of Hawaii who had succeeded Dr. Shoemaker, Hawaii was now an open economy. Insurance companies, for example, were investing more funds in Island enterprises than they were taking out in premiums, something unheard of during the reign of the oligarchy.

Members of the Big Five had diversified to an extent that would have seemed incredible in prewar days. Castle & Cooke, headed by Malcolm MacNaughton, had begun to buy into Mainland firms; at the same time it was liquidating some of its Hawaiian enterprises in both sugar and pineapple. The old Grove Farm plantation on Kauai, founded in 1864 by George Wilcox, son of a missionary schoolteacher, abandoned its pineapple fields when the industry began to decline after the war. MacNaughton brought in a newcomer, Henry C. Cornuelle, who took over the disorganized Hawaiian Pines and rebuilt the industry until it again led the world in production of canned pineapple. Cornuelle, incidentally, was one of the new managerial imports without *kamaaina* connections, who later became head of the far-flung Dillingham operations. He was the son of a Presbyterian minister and had studied philosophy at the University of Colorado before coming to Hawaii.

Hutton Smith, who succeeded the aging George Sumner as President of American Factors the year Hawaii became a state, followed the course set by Alex Budge, decentralizing operations of his company. Sumner himself was one of the elder statesmen in Hawaii's economy, but he saw the writing on the walls in time and extended Amfac's activities to land development and broadened the company's managerial policies even before Smith took over. Smith began to widen the scope of Amfac's land development program, utilizing dormant sugar lands on Kauai and Hawaii for massive development projects, and even established a branch of Liberty House, Hawaii's oldest and largest department store, in San Jose, California.

Others of the Big Five, with the exception of C. Brewer & Co., Ltd., the oldest and smallest of the original sugar factors, began to look abroad for opportunities. Brewer expanded, but within the limits of the Islands, converting sugar lands to other uses. By the end of the decade it had phased out the 9,000-acre Kilauea Plantation in the Hanalei district on Kauai and converted it into Metcalf Farms. This was a project for raising disease-resistant seed corn that could be sold to Mainland feed growers at a high premium to counteract leaf-blight in certain corn-growing areas.

By the mid-1960s a reverse process of expansion was under way; that is, Mainland firms, inspired by the success of some of Kaiser's enterprises in Hawaii, began to look to the new state for interesting investments. Alexander & Baldwin considered moving its headquarters to San Francisco, and Dillingham was threatened with a takeover by its growing preponderance of stockholders outside Hawaii. American Factors became one of the first Hawaiian firms to be listed on the Big Board in New York, and combined its industrial expansion with both tourist hotels and homesite developments. It also worked out a huge land development in Western Australia for raising sheep and growing grain; and as a result it became a prime target for Mainland investment.

While Hillendahl forecast increased stability and long-term improvement in Hawaii's economy, he also pointed to the more immediate impact of a downward adjustment, particularly in the construction industry and the "current downtrend in Hawaii as a consequence of conditions nationally." He expressed concern over too much government interference, but added that notwithstanding this factor, "the outlook for Hawaii is for continued growth."

In a monthly review of economic conditions in Hawaii early in 1971 he noted, with admirable restraint, that

> history has taught us that all governments tend to proliferate, and in so doing engage in spending programs which generate a chronic excess of total demand over total supply of goods and services. To the extent that the increment in demand exceeds the capacity of the economy to generate true savings this excess must be supported by investment based on debt. This excessive demand is reflected in overinvestment in both private and government sectors . . . The resulting overexpansion in debt is accompanied by overexpansion in money and credit, which by definition is inflation.[36]

What Hillendahl was warning against was what might be termed overreaction to the poststatehood boom; and in effect he was pointing out that while the release of Hawaii from the limitations of Big Five control might improve the economy, it was not as much of a liberation from the basic rules of economic growth as some of the more euphoric members of the business community might have anticipated.

His words of warning had begun to emerge into reality by the end of the first decade after statehood. Increased taxation had forced some of the plantations out of business, and agricultural lands formerly devoted entirely to sugar and pineapple were now diverted to other uses. Among these were not only production of seed grains, sorghum, potatoes, and other farm products, but also large hotels with luxurious fittings and expansive golf courses.

Whether these would result in long-range benefits for Hawaii as a whole would depend largely on how well the new open economy of the Islands would survive the pressures of the new Establishment that was rapidly being created at the State capitol to replace the old monolithic oligarchy.

Race relations in Hawaii have always been something of a mystery to the outsider, and the reasons are not hard to discover. For more than a century this tropical paradise that Mark Twain described as "the loveliest fleet of islands anchored in any ocean" has been referred to as a melting pot, the assumption being that all races in the Islands "melted" together in one big happy family. The concept on the face of it is illogical and absurd. As a matter of semantics as well as ethnology—as Professor Lind pointed out—people do not "melt." They may merge interests, or join forces, or even learn to live together, but separate ethnic groups have separate cultural as well as racial characteristics. This concept of Hawaii as an exceptional deviation from the common course of racial development was passed on to tourists in large doses of advertising, however, and was accepted uncritically by those who never strayed very far from their base at Waikiki Beach.

The inference drawn from the advertisements, and in some carefully screened sociological studies of Hawaii, seems to have been based on the single fact that the varied ethnic groups in Hawaii were not fighting each other, as they so often did in other parts of the world. Whatever hostilities existed actually were *intraracial,* such as the ill-feeling between Ilocanos and Visayans from the Philippines, or the Okinawans and the Naichi from Japan. There was no racial problem per se, and this has puzzled those who are accustomed to racial antagonism.

The ethnic pattern in Hawaii can best be put in perspective by tracing racial developments in the Islands. These fall into two distinct eras: the century of prestatehood rule by the monarchy and later the oligarchy from the middle of the nineteenth century when the first alien field workers were imported, to the

20

The Takabuki Incident

middle of this century when plantation field forces were reduced to insignificant numbers; and the poststatehood era. During the first period the melting pot concept was more or less a fiction of the tourist mind, because there was actually nothing to melt. Up to the time of the arrival of foreign ethnic groups in Hawaii, beginning with the missionaries, the Hawaiians as noted earlier had no word for race. People were either Hawaiians, called *kanakas,* or strangers, known as *haoles.* The most striking illustration of this native simplicity of viewpoint is to be found in the Hawaiian expression for Negro. It is *haole eleele,* which literally translated in its modern meaning would be "black white people."

During this prestatehood period, or more precisely up to the end of World War II, the lid on the so-called melting pot was kept tightly closed by the oligarchy. Visitors to Hawaii had no reason to suspect that the various races were not living happily together as described in the tourist advertisements. The tourists came to bask on Waikiki Beach, and only curiosity or the desire to buy gaily colored fabrics at cheap prices lured them as far away as the Aala Park area, where Musa-shiya the Shirt Maker and C. Q. Yee Hop had established exotic trading marts with lower prices than on the Beach. They seldom saw nearby River Street or "Tin Can Alley" or the slums of Palama and the School Street area where Dan Inouye was born. And except by express invitation they never saw the plantations.

It was quite natural therefore that up to the beginning of the second revolution Hawaii should still be regarded as some sort of miraculous mutation in which rules of racial antagonism, with which the rest of the world was painfully familiar, would be inoperative. As a matter of fact, there was little antagonism among the ethnic groups themselves, although the Hawaiians remained suspicious and hostile toward the Japanese, whom they regarded as inimical to their economic interests; and the Filipinos retained similar suspicions after the disastrous plantation strikes of 1920 and 1924.

The point that was never brought home to tourists and only indirectly mentioned in most of the scholarly sociological and political studies of the islands was that the racial situation in

Hawaii was normal and similar to what might be found anywhere people of different ethnic origins live in close proximity to each other. As Senator Inouye pointed out, conditions in Hawaii as far as Japanese political influence was concerned could be "duplicated throughout the United States." Whatever conflict existed was the result of the private attitude of the *kamaaina haoles* toward everyone else, a caste system in which there were only two opposing classes—the members of the old families and the second-class citizens.

This situation prevailed until the latter group which, as noted earlier, included not only Asians and Hawaiians, but Portuguese and even *malihini haoles,* revolted in the years after World War II. Their revolt was a political challenge triggered by returning *nisei* war veterans who had shed blood for the common cause of America and democracy, and now made common cause with other ethnic groups against the oligarchy. In Sakae Takahashi's words they had earned an even break and intended to get it.

The tendency to cite Hawaii as an example of a place where many races live in harmony, comparing it favorably with the Mainland of the United States where racial differences provoke violence and hatred, does not usually take into account the different ingredients. Among these are the background of inmigration of those ethnic groups that came to the Islands as compared with the importation of the Negro to America, for example. A comparison of the two modes of revolutionary conduct carries an indirect assumption that the elements of confrontation were similar, whereas they were not. In the United States as a whole the same principles should apply, but in actual fact, on the Mainland an initially disadvantaged group was seeking to establish its place in a supposedly democratic economic and social system by physically uprooting sources of injustice and inequality. The confrontation was between the former white master and the former black slave.

In Hawaii no such confrontation occurred. The Hawaiians themselves invited the missionaries into their councils, and the monarchs of Hawaii were guided by such men as Dr. Gerrit Judd and the Reverend Mr. Richards. This was not in any way similar to the situation on the Mainland. The Japanese and Filipinos were not slaves, dragged from their native lands by Arabs and Portuguese, who sold them to the English who sold them to American plantation owners. They came as volunteers, bonded for the terms of their contracts; and it was only when they arrived that they encountered the feudal situation imposed upon them by the sugar planters.

There was actually no motivation for racial conflict as between the various segments of the population of different ethnic origin. For this reason Hawaii was widely heralded as "a shining example of the American way" to use President Eisenhower's words, although its governing system bore little resemblance to "the American way."

Earlier it was remarked that the apparent sublimation of the racial problem in Hawaii was due to a form of tolerance rather than acceptance of alien groups who were regarded as inferior by the *haole* elite; and that this gave rise to an equalitarianism rather than equality among races. The planters obviously did not want to eliminate the "inferior" racial groups since they constituted their field labor force. Thus, they learned to live with them without an outward demonstration of superiority, although anyone who has lived in the Islands will understand this did not represent the real feelings of the *kamaaina haoles*. Professor Lind quotes a South African social psychologist at a conference on race relations in Honolulu (in 1954) as saying in exasperation, "The only real difference between race relations in South Africa and in Hawaii is that where I come from we openly admit that we discriminate on the basis of race, whereas your hypocritical code won't permit you to admit that you do."[38]

This misses the point entirely. In Hawaii the discrimination was not on a basis of race, but of economic and social distinctions. It is interesting to note that Dr. Romanzo Adams, the first sociologist to study Hawaii's complex racial situation without necessarily being guided by the oligarchy's views, came to the conclusion that the private attitudes of racial superiority adopted by the *kamaaina haoles* were actually irrelevant, since racial customs in Hawaii tended to be the *"mores* of race equality" and therefore the attitudes of the old missionary families were of little importance. This would have been true if these attitudes were based on racial values, but they were not. They were purely and simply the attitudes of masters toward serfs, as expressed in the Masters and Servants Act of 1850 and carried through the entire period of the oligarchy's rule; and the so-called racial problem in Hawaii was not racial at all.

This became quite clear when Hawaii changed from a territory to a state. It is in this context that the comparison between the melting pot aspects of Hawaii's second revolution and the violent upheavals elsewhere in the United States becomes pertinent.

This leads to the suggestion that there may have been a massive miscalculation in evaluating so-called racial questions, not only in Hawaii but elsewhere. Even racist hostility on the Mainland, which seems to stem from the hatred of blacks for whites, and vice versa, may be due to economic, sociological, and psychological differences rather than purely ethnic conflicts. Senator Inouye's reference in his keynote speech in 1968 to "more than a hundred years of racist deprivations" may have had more significance for the sociologist and economist—and the politician—than it had for the racist.

It may appear to be an oversimplification to imply that the conflicts that have been regarded as racial are not really racial, but economic, political, and sociological; yet the case of Hawaii's transition in its second revolution may offer support for this theory. When Hawaii passed from territorial status to statehood, the control of the Big Five passed out of the picture. This was a *political* change, wrought by political means; but the underlying causes were *economic* and *sociological;* they *were not racial.* And the revolution was nonviolent.

It was after statehood and the collapse of the oligarchy that the real racial and cultural characteristics of the varied ethnic groups in Hawaii began to emerge—*not before.* The attitude of superiority on the part of the *kamaaina haoles* no longer had any real significance, except perhaps to themselves. The cultural characteristics and ethnic background of the many groups who made up Hawaii's racial mix began to surface. When the caste system imposed by the oligarchy was lifted, racial identity became more apparent. The Chinese established their own societies, not for the purpose of contesting for social status vis-à-vis other racial groups, but for such things as mutual aid. The Japanese revived traditional cultural activities. Professor Lind, in an analysis of poststatehood racial conditions in the Islands, notes that "prejudice, as the overt expression of uncritical sentiments of derogation or hostility toward other groups, was least evident in Hawaii during the period of plantation dominance when racial distinctions were marked but also most commonly taken for granted as a natural and essential part of the established order."[38]

He adds that following World War II "when the barriers to equal opportunity across ethnic lines have been most rapidly falling, and especially during the decade following statehood" many Islanders became "most acutely aware of racial tensions."

Actually, what many observers saw in this emergence of racial differentials was a sinister sign of racism that *seemed* similar to the black versus white racial antagonism evident on the Mainland. Whether this was a true evaluation of this emergence may be determined in a review of the so-called Takabuki incident that occurred at the end of the decade following statehood. The point to be determined is whether it was similar to the confrontation between blacks and whites on the Mainland; and if it was not, what was the difference?

On June 17, 1971, the announcement was made that the Chief Justice of Hawaii's Supreme Court—Bill Richardson, who had been allied with Governor Burns throughout the second revolution—had appointed Matsuo Takabuki, one of the young Turks of the political revolt organized by Burns in the late 1940s and a member of the *nisei* 442nd Veterans Club, as trustee of the Bishop Estate. Takabuki was appointed to fill a vacancy left by the death of Herbert Keppler, a *haole* member of the five-man board. Appointment as a Bishop Estate trustee carried with it what amounted to a $50,000-a-year income, originally for life, although in the Takabuki appointment it was stipulated that he should resign when he reached seventy.

The Bishop Estate, it will be recalled, was created by the will of Princess Bernice Pauahi Bishop from the extensive lands she held as the lineal granddaughter of King Kamehameha the Great. The income from the Estate's large landholding was to be devoted to educational purposes for the "children of Hawaii." This was generally conceded to mean the children of Hawaiian blood, and the Kamehameha Schools were founded on the basis of that income, admitting only those who were at least half-Hawaiian. The will actually did not specify this distinction.

The appointment aroused a storm of indignation on the part of Hawaiians, which was probably the most definite outbreak of purely racial feeling in the Islands since the Revolution of 1893.

The day after the announcement was made public, a mass meeting was called in Kawaiahao Church, established by the missionary group from the *Thaddeus* 150 years earlier, and the center of the rapidly dwindling Hawaiian religious community. The Reverend Abraham Akaka, pastor of the church and leading religious spokesman for the Hawaiian people, bitterly attacked the appointment of Takabuki, a man of Japanese ancestry, as a trustee of the Islands' most important source of private educational funds for Hawaiians. An ad hoc committee was set up, including such militant Hawaiians as the Reverend William Kaina, State coordinator of Hawaiian churches; Arthur Trask, son of former County Attorney and territorial Senator David Trask; John Allen, president of the Kamehameha Schools Alumni; and Pae Galdeira, head of The Hawaiians, an activist group. A demonstration of protest was held, Hawaiians marching around the statue of Kamehameha I, which stands in front of the old territorial courthouse building, with its motto, *Ua mau ke ea o ka aina i ka pono*—"The life of the land is preserved in righteousness"—emblazoned in gold letters beneath the cast iron figure of the "Napoleon of the Pacific." The bells of nearby Kawaiahao Church tolled dolefully.

Various Hawaiian groups, who frequently fought each other in minor matters, were now united in a common cause. The vacant trusteeship on the Bishop Estate Board must be filled by a man of Hawaiian blood, who understood the needs of the Hawaiian people. Pastor Akaka called it "a dark day for our native Hawaiian people" who, he said, had become "strangers in their own land."

At first glance, the dissent of the Hawaiians seemed to be clear and logical. Their most important remaining link to the past—the Bishop Estate, which provided schooling for children of Hawaiian blood—was now in the hands of "strangers" who were not merely *haoles,* but now included a Japanese. On closer examination, however, there were many interesting aspects of the situation that bear upon the question: Was this really a racial confrontation?

First, there was the appointing officer—Chief Justice Bill Richardson, of the Hawaii Supreme Court. He was part Hawaiian, reared in the slums of Palama, an early recruit in the second revolution, and a descendant of one of Queen Liliuokalani's loyal followers. There was also the fact that nearly all previous appointees as Bishop Estate trustees had been *haoles,* with a few exceptions, such as John Clarke, a part Hawaiian named in 1932; Edwin Murray, also part Hawaiian; and the current board chairman, Richard Lyman, who was part Hawaiian. The most significant exception was Hung Wo Chung, of Chinese descent and a Chinese tycoon into the bargain. No serious protest had been made against the *haoles* or Hung Wo. Why had there been no objection to the latter, to whom the same criteria could be applied that were now being applied to Takabuki?

In commenting on the vehemence of the protest that followed Takabuki's appointment, the *Honolulu Star-Bulletin* remarked editorially that the protest, while understandable in view of the desire of the people of Hawaiian blood to see more of their race recognized on a trust estate set up especially for the education of Hawaiian children, "ignores two basic points." These were that the Bishop Estate had not been financially successful and needed good business management and experience to be able to provide the financial assistance needed to meet the needs of Hawaiian children; and that Takabuki, who had quit politics, was "an exceptionally talented individual whose business background suggests he may be just the man to help overcome this failure."

There were a couple of other points the *Star-Bulletin* did not mention. One was that Takabuki's current business activities were linked closely with the affairs of Chinn Ho, the first of the Chinese tycoons, who had become chairman of the board of the *Star-Bulletin* and was heavily involved in land deals—the most important phase of the Bishop Estate's activities. There was also the point that Bill Richardson was one of the original "Burns boys" and so was Takabuki. The suggestion was made that Governor Burns was paying off a political debt. The issue was not with Takabuki; it was with Governor Burns and the new Establishment.

The real issue was not support for or opposition to the Takabuki appointment. What was significant was the *nonracial* aspect of this confrontation, which was regarded by many as an outbreak of racial hostility similar to those that had occurred on the Mainland. Actually, there was no real similarity. It was a *political* and *economic* issue in Hawaii, and all the essential elements of controversy were within that scope.

The Takabuki incident itself was not of lasting importance, although it was taken to court by the Ad Hoc Committee in an effort to block the appointment. Tom Gill represented the Hawaiian group in the action brought against the Supreme Court, which had the power to appoint Takabuki, and the Bishop Estate itself; but Gill's plea was turned down by the Circuit Court on the grounds that the Court lacked jurisdiction and the plaintiffs, including several students from the Kamehameha Schools, lacked standing in the court.

The hearing also lacked a measure of judicial decorum. Judge Yasutaka Fukushima described Gill's argument that the Hawaiian plaintiffs were not given the benefit of due process by holding public hearings as "a lot of garbage" and at one point he remarked that Gill himself did not seem to "understand democratic processes." Meanwhile the bells of Kawaiahao continued to toll their doleful message to the people of Hawaiian ancestry.

The Takabuki Case was the most stirring issue that had confronted the Hawaiians since the Massie Case in 1932, and although it was regarded by many as a sudden surge of racial unrest in the Islands, it could also have been interpreted as part of an awakening of racial groups as the result of the release from the domination of the oligarchy with its equalitarianism. The Hawaiians were expressing, for the first time in eighty years, a demand for racial identity. The appointment of Takabuki was merely an excuse for protest. The charge of unassimilability had been drummed into the mixture of alien races living in Hawaii for half a century, until it seemed to be a sin to express ethnic identity. The melting pot theory actually was a subtle effort to suppress that racial identity. The anger of the Hawaiians was simply an expression of this demand for recognition of racial identity, which was denied for *political* purposes.

During the rule of the oligarchy, retaining traditions of their homelands on the part of Japanese, Chinese, Filipinos, and Koreans had been regarded as un-American and the language schools—Chinese and Korean as well as Japanese—were considered potentially subversive. Except for the early years on the plantations, when language schools were a convenient substitute for public schools, these educational deviations were opposed and in some cases laws were enacted restricting them.

While many of these legislative strictures were later removed by higher courts as being unconstitutional, the suspicions engendered by the existence of language schools—and in some cases justified by the attitude and actions of Shinto priests —persisted. As a result many of the younger generation of *nisei* and *sansei* evaded an overt expression of attachment to the traditions of their homeland, although they retained these feelings inwardly.

Dan Inouye, who went through these experiences when the language school question was most intense—the latter 1920s and early 1930s—presents a clear picture of this sort of inner tension in his book, *Journey to Washington*. He writes of an incident that occurred in the language school he attended as a boy, in which he was confronted with what he described as the "jingoist little speeches" of the Japanese *issei* instructor.

> The trouble I got into at the Japanese language school . . . crystalized for me, once and for all, the matter of who I was and where in this cultural melting pot I was headed. Most of my contempo-

raries quit at the end of the tenth year, by which time they had a fair grounding in Japanese history and tradition. In deference to my grandparents, I suppose, I was enrolled in the eleventh grade and sat through excruciatingly long afternoons listening to lectures on the sacredness of the royal family and being admonished to preserve the centuries-old customs of my people.[39]

He found himself in an argument with the teacher over the adequacy of Christianity as compared with Shintoism, and when critical references were made about the Christian bible, he rose and objected. As a result, "all in one cataclysmic afternoon, I unburdened myself of my smouldering resentment and in consequence was flung bodily from the classroom, never to return."

These experiences, which young Inouye had known all too well in his schooldays, were seldom understood by those who studied the problems of Hawaii's melting pot from a distance; and it was only when the advent of statehood shifted the focus of control from the *haole* elite to the second-class citizens that they became apparent.

Today the suppressed but always latent links with the traditional ethnic past have been exposed by the removal of suppression from both sides—from the indoctrination by the elders of the ethnic groups on one hand, and from the stigma attached to alien ancestral traditions by the *haole* elite on the other. The result has been the emergence of a true melting pot in which the realities of race relations have become in fact what they had always been potentially—a multiracial but free society. Professor Lind notes this tendency in an interesting comment in his study, *Hawaii: The Last of the Magic Isles,*

The renewed interest of third and fourth generation Chinese, for example, in the mutual-aid societies established by the immigrant generation is undoubtedly stimulated in part by their desire to share in the inflated economic value of the property belonging to these organizations, but there is also present a mounting pride in the history and cultural achievements of their ancestors. So also the Hawaiian-born citizens of Japanese ancestry who participate in such traditional institutions as *kumi* and *tanamoshi* (primary group organizations for mutual assistance and credit) or the sects of Japanese Buddhism may derive some material benefits from their associations, but the psychological returns on an additional basis of group self-respect may be even more important.[40]

The sudden surfacing of these symptoms of ethnic identity leads to the possible conclusion that while racial identification in Hawaii since statehood is more apparent than under the rule of the oligarchy, it is also less dangerous because it is no longer suppressed. A *nisei* or *pake*—the Hawaiian word for Chinese— no longer evades reference to his ancestry, but openly finds in it a source of pride. Racial hostility under such circumstances becomes irrelevant. The fact that a person is of Chinese, Japanese, Korean, or Filipino descent is no longer considered a stigma, but rather as the identification of racial heritage.

This acceptance is visible in the revival of cultural celebrations such as the Chinese Ching Ming festival, the Japanese Hana Matsuri celebration, and Rizal Day among the Filipinos. These are no longer regarded as oddments for the attraction of tourists, but are legitimate cultural revivals, attended by many ethnic groups that do not necessarily participate, but enjoy the festivals and dances. The East-West Center has become an outlet for this cross-cultural exchange and the wider understanding of art forms peculiar to varied ethnic backgrounds.

Thus the comparison with the demonstrations of racial unrest on the Mainland, suggested earlier, can be explored in terms of the racial harmony provided by the Hawaiian melting pot, and the conclusion may be quite valid that in Hawaii the racial problems such as appeared in the Massie Case, and farther back in the Revolution of 1893, were really not racial but economic and political.

The Takabuki incident may have aroused what many regarded as a racial confrontation on the part of the Hawaiians, but it was not racial in its essence. The real issues were political. And it opened a Pandora's Box of political repercussions. Among other things, it exposed certain ramifications of Hawaii's new political-economic system that had been described by Tom Gill, Vincent Esposito, and others—including Sakae Takahashi, a former Burns man—as the new Establishment.

Jack Burns's career, from the time he left the police department, indicated he was neither personally ambitious nor self-serving. His prestige was based on his ability to organize a political machine, and on his personal integrity. But power has a tendency to whet the appetite, and there is little doubt that as Governor, Burns was engaged in consolidating the position of the second-class citizens who had been elevated to political parity with the *haole* elite by the second revolution.

Mayor Frank Fasi of Honolulu, who had been in and out of the Burns circle of adherents during the decades preceding and following statehood, made this point in an article and editorial comment in his small tabloid newspaper, the *Honolulu News*.

"One thing is certain," the article, written by Brian Casey, a former *Advertiser* reporter who had been head of the City Information Bureau under Mayor Neal Blaisdell and later worked for Fasi, said. "The potent political organization of Governor John A. Burns took another giant step forward [in the Takabuki appointment] in its drive to dominate Hawaii's economic scene in both the Governmental and judicial structure." Fasi, in an editorial in the same issue, wrote,

"It is time that people realize that Hawaii's electorate made Takabuki's appointment possible. The political system pro-

21

The Emerging Races

duced this appointment. Those who object can retaliate in only one way with success—at the ballot box in 1974."

Fasi did not attack the appointment specifically, stating "there is no argument that Takabuki has the technical qualifications necessary to be a trustee." But the Casey article asked questions on certain sensitive points:

"Will Mr. Takabuki combine his direct lines with powerful financial, political, and labor resources with land power to use his position for the benefit of his political cronies, or for the Hawaiian people?

"Why is Takabuki willing to give up the income he now makes—more than twice the income he will receive—to become a trustee of the Bishop Estate?

"Is he prepared to sever his financial and legal interests with Chinn Ho and those who are developers of land in Hawaii?"

It was generally accepted that a *hui*—the Hawaiian word for a combine, or club—had been organized to back Burns politically. The group included not only Chinn Ho, whose Capital Investment had become one of the most profitable land development enterprises in Hawaii and who had built the luxurious Ilikai Hotel at the western end of the Waikiki Beach area; but also Clarence Ching, head of Loyalty Enterprises, another land development firm; Hung Wo Ching, who was engaged in land development; and certain major contractors such as Lloyd Martin of Reed and Martin Construction Company which built the $30 million State Capitol building. This group, together with the ILWU labor organization, which Robert McElrath, the one-time member of the Hawaii Seven who had been linked with the Communist Party in Hawaii, now headed, and Jack Reynolds of the AFL-CIO unions in the Islands, had backed Burns in his bid for governorship in 1962. Burns, running with Bill Richardson as Lieutenant-Governor, beat Quinn, the fading GOP hopeful. One of Burns's supporters in that race was Arthur Rutledge, the head of Unity House, the headquarters of Local 5, the hotel workers and bartenders, and the Teamsters.

Rutledge was a pleasant, rotund man who had arrived on the Hawaiian labor scene almost coincidentally with Jack Hall and began to put together an alliance of small unions, in which truck drivers, electrical workers, typographers, and dairy farmers were brought together, breaking up many of the company unions. As the power of Jack Hall began to be allied more closely with Burns, Rutledge began to criticize what he described as deals. This view was also taken by Dr. John Reinecke, another of the Hawaii Seven, and also by Tom Gill. Although Rutledge had entered the labor movement in Hawaii about the same time as Hall, he had not sought to establish his unions as a political power base, as Hall had. As a result, his comments on the rise of Jack Burns to political power, with the aid of Hall, may be regarded as fairly objective. He gave Burns credit for having molded a new Hawaii, but like Tom Gill he had observed a "dangerous trend" toward a new Establishment replacing the Big Five.

The focus of much of this political and economic maneuvering was the increasing importance of land development, chiefly the building of new hotels for the visitor industry. The forces that were molding this new economic complex were formidable, and the new Democratic administration was well aware of this. It could readily dominate Hawaii, as the sugar industry had once ruled the Islands. The rising tourist trade was rapidly becoming Hawaii's greatest source of income. The influx of tourists, by the end of the 1960s Hawaii's biggest industry, had increased at a rate in excess of ten percent annually. In 1948 there had been 36,397 tourists who visited Hawaii, bringing in $18.9 million. Ten years later—the year before statehood—there were 171,588 tourists who spent $82.7 million. Ten years after statehood —in 1968—the arrivals totaled 1,209,417 and the income from these was $460 million. A year later the arrivals rose to 1,369,058 and the income was $510.5 million. By the end of the second decade of statehood it was conservatively estimated that Hawaii would draw a billion dollars a year from tourism—five times the combined revenues from sugar, pineapples, and all other agricultural products.

Even more significantly, from Arthur Rutledge's viewpoint, the construction industry and the number of hotel rooms had soared upward during the decade after statehood. In 1969 the overall value of building permits was nearly a half billion dollars, more than six times the total for 1948 and three times the volume in 1958. Hotel rooms increased from 1,980 in 1948 to 26,923 in 1968.

In the days of the oligarchy the hotels were controlled by Matson Navigation Company, the Inter-Island Steam Navigation Company, Territorial Hotels, and von Hamm-Young—all controlled in turn by the Big Five. Wages of employees averaged $50 a month for Filipinos, $56 for Japanese, and $102 for *haoles*. Rutledge had brought together not only hotel employees and bartenders, but the Teamsters Union and Brewery Workers Union; and with this complex of labor organizations he had supported the rise of Jack Burns and the Democrats to power. However, by 1970 there was a definite demarcation between the ILWU and affiliated labor groups, such as Rutledge and the Unity House unions; and the former appeared to have the inside track with the State Administration. Jack Burns, one-time police detective, was in the process of welding together the new Establishment. He even brought in Reynolds, the AFL-CIO leader, as his official labor negotiator.

What was at stake was another contest between the political haves and the have-nots except that Governor Burns and his powerful leadership at the State Capitol and in Washington were now the haves and Gill, Esposito, and Takahashi were on the outside. Mayor Fasi, playing his customary role of both sides against the middle was obviously not motivated by the same reasons that stimulated the objections of Tom Gill in his remarks about the Burns organization. Fasi had a power base of his own in the City of Honolulu. But he had kept a wary eye on the growing strength of the Burns organization since the early 1950s, and he viewed such actions as the Takabuki appointment with distrust. There was a growing concern among many others who had formerly backed Burns that the power base at the State capitol was being strengthened to a point that might forecast a replacement of the old Big Five oligarchy. They foresaw a new ruling group headed by Jack Burns, now strongly backed by the new alignment of certain elements of labor, notably the ILWU, and the increasingly powerful Chinese tycoons.

Among those concerned, although not necesssarily for the same reasons, were the people at the other end of Merchant Street. As previously noted, the balance of payments was no longer regarded as the principal index of Hawaii's economic health as it was in prewar years when the Islands depended on income from sugar and pineapples, and to a lesser extent the tourist trade. Mainland investments more than compensated for the unfavorable balance that had worried Dr. Shoemaker. Construction and tourism were the economic barometers of the 1960s. Wesley Hillendahl, who succeeded Shoemaker as chief economist at the Bank of Hawaii, issued an extensive report on construction early in 1971, noting that both industrial and commercial segments of the building industry had declined in 1969 and 1970, and were due for a further drop the current year. This obviously reflected a decrease in the tourist business. Of greater significance from the standpoint of tourism, the occupancy rate of hotel rooms dropped from 85 percent in 1968 to 69.6 percent in 1970.

Part of this was due to readjustment from the excessive building boom during the earlier years of the poststatehood decade, when hotel construction was rising to meet the needs of the tourist trade. But construction in general seemed to have reached its peak at the end of the decade and then began to decline, with the single exception of single-family housing which climbed steadily, indicating a constant influx of *malihinis* from the Mainland who planned to live in Hawaii.

In his review of economic conditions in the Islands early in 1971, Hillendahl wrote,

> Moderation in the rate of growth of many sectors of Hawaii's economy is expected to occur during 1971, including the visitor industry, manufacturing and agricultural activity. Construction is expected to show a decline from the 1970 volume. Consequently, the growth of job opportunities will also diminish. . . .[41]

In short, Hawaii was coming to the end of the poststatehood honeymoon, although as Hillendahl explained, it was more of an adjustment than an arresting of progress. In his view, Hawaii's economic future was assured. Mainland investments were continuing to pour into the Islands. The third largest state portfolio of the Equitable Life Assurance Society was Hawaii, involving such massive enterprises as the Ala Moana Shopping Center, advertised as the world's largest, and the Ilikai Hotel and shopping complex, one of the largest hotel and apartment structures built in Hawaii during the poststatehood decade—a monument to the enterprise of Chinn Ho and Capital Investment. In 1968 the restructuring of Hawaii's downtown section included the opening of the Financial Plaza, a block of buildings at King and Bishop Streets, housing the Bank of Hawaii, the thirteen-story American Savings & Loan Tower and the twenty-one-story Castle & Cooke building. This complex had become the center of Honolulu's business district, replacing the old Fort-and-King intersection where the first and only shot in the Revolution of 1893 was fired. As a matter of fact, there was no longer an intersection; it had become a paved promenade of shops and restaurants, with no street traffic on the surface.

The new $30 million State Capitol building had been completed the same year—a structure of pronounced neo-Polynesian architecture, erected on columns with an open square in the center, surrounded by spacious halls of the State Legislature, the Governor's suite, and a multitude of libraries and offices for the Speaker of the House, the President of the Senate, the majority leaders, and so on. In a certain sense it was an answer to one of the first issues raised by Dan Inouye when he was elected to the old territorial House for the first time in 1954. He objected to the two houses of the Legislature holding sessions within the former throne room of Iolani Palace, and particularly to the Speaker of the House—the venerable and mercurial Charlie Kauhane—squatting on the throne once occupied by Queen Liliuokalani herself!

"Why don't we pitch a tent outside the Palace and hold our meetings there?" he asked, suggesting that it would be more appropriate than desecrating the throne room of the deposed monarchs of Hawaii. The suggestion got little attention at the time from the legislators, but the ultimate answer to Inouye's objection was far more impressive than a tent. It indicated how far Hawaii had progressed along the lines of emancipation from traditions established by the oligarchy and the Big Five-GOP coalition, who had no hesitation in establishing their seat of power in the royal throne room!

Anyone who had lived in Hawaii during the first years of the Territory, with unpaved streets except in the downtown area where the trolleys rolled along steel rails, drawn by horses at first and later electrified—and there were few of the residents of Hawaii in 1970 who had lived in those days—would have had a traumatic experience observing the new State Capitol. The shining walls of the central city, granite and concrete buildings, towered above the archaic Young Hotel which once was the pride of downtown Honolulu. Glass-walled modern structures obscured the old landmarks, such as the alley where John Good drove the wagonload of rifles and small arms out of the E.O. Hall hardware store to equip the tatterdemalion "army" of the revolutionary junta nearly eighty years ago.

Mark Twain's prophecy had come true with a vengeance. The "paradise for the indolent" was bustling with signs of the "long, deliberate, infallible destruction" he had predicted a hundred years earlier for the mid-Pacific tropical paradise, once the white man took charge. Hawaii, from the standpoint of its ancient heritage, had indeed become "the disenchanted isles."

In the midst of these signs of metamorphosis of the old port town of Honolulu, where windjammers and brawling sailors were the only foreign elements in the early years of the nineteenth century, into a metropolitan oasis in the middle of the Pacific Ocean, one element seemed inconsistent with Hawaii's visible progress and it was interpreted by many observers from outside the Islands as a symptom of racial upheaval. This was the long-delayed resurgence of the Hawaiians themselves.

On Sunday morning, June 6, 1971, the members of the congregation of historic Kawaiahao Church, most of them elderly Hawaiians, were astonished as they filed into the gray building erected by missionaries who landed in Honolulu in the *Thaddeus* in 1820, to see a word painted in large green letters on the doorposts of the antique building. It was somewhat similar to the graffiti often found on the walls of subway latrines in New

York City, advocating Black Power and other causes; except that in this case the word was *Huli!* the Hawaiian term for "Overturn!" The green of the paint was also reminiscent of the color of Irish rebellion. The word itself was the slogan of a small group of young Hawaiians known as "Kokua Hawaii," which means literally, "Join together for Hawaii."

The incident had nothing to do with the Takabuki appointment since it occurred about two weeks earlier. And it was not an invitation to violence. It was an expression of a sentiment that had been gathering momentum during the first decade after statehood—a change in Hawaii's status which, it will be recalled, many Hawaiians opposed because they thought it would sever the last links of the Hawaiian people with their past. Kokua Hawaii's purpose was, in a sense, to regenerate in the Hawaiian people a pride of ancestry.

A young Hawaiian instructor in religion at the University of Hawaii, Larry Kamakawiwoole, was the leader of Kokua Hawaii; and he frankly admitted that the painting of the word *Huli* on the portals of the staid old Kawaiahao Church was the work of his followers. It was intended, he said, to shock the older Hawaiians, going into the old church, into a realization of their obligations to their racial past.

"What Hawaiian has not accepted the values of Western civilization?" he said. "On the other hand, what Hawaiian does not feel wistful about the loss of the purity of Hawaiian life?" When he was asked why the word was painted on the doorway of the Hawaiians' most venerated place of worship, he replied, "Perhaps it is a symbol, a reminder of what the church can become. Perhaps the church today is too comfortable and too secure in its life-style. From our perspective the word *huli* means a kind of conversion, not an overthrowing of the order of things. Where does the church stand in times of crisis for the Hawaiian people?"

The words painted on the doorposts of Kawaiahao Church were regarded by many as a sign of racial unrest, an outburst of antagonism similar to those that had been occurring during the same years on the Mainland. Yet if the observation of Dan Inouye had real meaning—"The Hawaiians have no malice in their hearts—which may explain their inability to cope with the 'strangers' who came to the Islands to instruct them in Christian ethics"—the word *huli* may have had a different significance.

Young Kamakawiwoole had referred to the change in life-style of the elder Hawaiians, and the need to reestablish Hawaiian racial unity. He spoke of "the point of separation between the old and the young."

Again the question arises, as in the Takabuki incident: What was the reason for the outburst of Hawaiians after two centuries of comparative passivity? Was it racial antagonism, or the need for racial identity?

The passive racial characteristics of the Hawaiian people were dealt with earlier. Craighill Handy, in a study of Hawaiian cultural revolution written for the Institute of Pacific Relations in 1931, noted that "in the course of many centuries of isolation the native [Hawaiian] civilization had not only reached a condition of stability, but was probably static."

This again brings into focus the comparison between the forms of revolt that have taken place, almost within the same period of years, on the Mainland and in Hawaii—one relying on violence and the other on the more orderly forms of change. Would violence have brought about the change for the Hawaiian people themselves? It seems not. The coalition formed by Jack Burns, Dan Inouye, and the other rebellious young men of the 1950s—including a number of Hawaiians—had achieved its goal within the framework of processes that Senator Inouye had pointed out could have been "duplicated throughout the United States."

Would the Hawaiians have improved their position in this revolt by a more violent form of rebellion? Even Larry Kamakawiwoole and his militant Kokua Hawaii followers did not believe this. "By militancy," he said, "I don't mean rock-throwing. I mean changing the system, speaking out. Maybe it's time for this kind of militancy. Maybe the Hawaiians will have to become more militant to get what they want."

The specific things Kokua Hawaii wanted were more equitable laws regarding the use of land. This had been the Democratic war cry in the 1950s when Dan Inouye was majority leader in the House, and the brash young reformists in the Legislature, led by Inouye and Sakae Takahashi, tried to force land into use by taxing the large landholder, such as the Bishop Estate. But this purpose had been lost in the shuffle of the new Establishment. In Kalama Valley on Oahu, where many Hawaiians had settled on land under lease from the Bishop Estate, small farms had been moved to less favorable locations to make way for land developers—including the builders of golf clubs and hotels— and the pigs and crops were dying in a new environment. In a full-page advertisement in the *Advertiser* the "friends of Kokua Hawaii" had quoted from a song written during the Revolution of 1893:

> *Hiki mae ka 'elele o ka loko 'ina*
> *Palapala 'anu me ka pakaloa,*
> *A 'ole 'a'e kauika pulima*
> *Maluna oka pepa o ka enemi*

Which in translation said: "When the evil-hearted messenger comes with his greedy document of extortion, no one will fix a signature to the paper of the enemy."

In a statement of purpose, Kokua Hawaii said, "We must use our land to house and feed our people and learn to rely on ourselves—not on the Mainland. As a start, we demand that Kalama Valley be saved for the local people and that the tourist and high-income development planned by the Bishop Estate and Hawaii-Kai be stopped."

The historic role of the Hawaiians had always been one of passive acceptance since the arrival of the white man two centuries earlier. Except for a few incidents, such as the killing of the members of the crew of the American schooner *Fair America* in retaliation for rope-whipping a Hawaiian chieftan on Hawaii, and the killing of Captain Cook in Kealakakua Bay on the Kona Coast after Cook had shot a Hawaiian, the native Hawaiians had showed little tendency to violence. There had always been a distinction of caste between the rulers and the ruled, as demonstrated by the Masters and Servants Act of 1850 (patterned, as noted, after American laws governing the treatment of sailors). The Hawaiian people were not unused to despotic rule. The *alii* did not mix with the common people. But gradually, since annexation by the United States, the Hawaiians had achieved a measure of belief in the virtues of democracy, obscured as it may have been by the nondemocratic aspects of the oligarchy's rule.

Larry Kamakawiwoole's reference to "the point of separation between the old and the young" may have been the root of the rebellion advocated by Kokua Hawaii, just as it was the difference of viewpoint between the Japanese *issei* and *nisei*—the old and the young—that triggered the revolt of the Japanese-American war veterans in the postwar period. In this respect, the "revolt of youth" may be as significant in Hawaii as it appears to have been on the Mainland, but again with essential dissimilarities in style.

Part VI

Hawaii 2000

Early in 1969—the tenth year of statehood—a program was undertaken in Hawaii that probably has no counterpart anywhere in the world, and in point of fact, there probably is no other place in the world that would—or could—have undertaken such a plan. It was known as "Hawaii 2000" although officially designated as "The Governor's Conference on the Year 2000."

The idea of evaluating the new island state's present situation and its future in the Pacific community began with a speech delivered in 1967 by George Chaplin, one-time chief of the Pacific edition of *Stars and Stripes* during the war, who had come from New Orleans to Honolulu in 1958 to succeed Ray Coll, the venerable editor of the *Advertiser* who died "in harness" at the age of ninety-six. Chaplin, a mild, scholarly looking man, had foreseen the need of planning for the future, looking ahead at Hawaii's potential position in the Pacific as it might be in 2000 A.D. He urged an immediate study of the state's assets in population, racial mix, industrial and agricultural capacity—in short, as he put it, "examining Hawaii's future economic, political, cultural and social systems" for the purpose of "identifying the objectives we desire and the action necessary to reach those objectives."

Like most people with new ideas, George Chaplin had talked himself into a job. Governor Burns immediately appointed Chaplin to head up the project and by 1969 the Legislature had enacted bills authorizing the Governor's conference. Ten statewide task forces were named with three additional groups from the outer islands of Hawaii, Maui and Kauai. They

22

Hawaii's 30-Year Plan

were to study everything from ecology to the economy.

Chaplin's group differed from most conferences of this nature not only in the scope of its activities—the development of a thirty-year plan—but in the fact that the task forces consisted mainly of laymen rather than academic experts in the various fields. Chaplin had asked, in effect: What will Hawaii be like thirty years from now? If we are to achieve practical planning for what we expect the Islands to be in the year 2000, why not start now? Experts were selected to head up the task forces in ten basic fields, with technically qualified men to guide the work of each task force; but the job of preparing for the Conference was to be done by a cross-section of the public, and particularly by young people who would be the middle-aged and elder statesmen of Hawaii in 2000 A.D.

Chaplin had pointed out that most conferences consist of scholars and experts who spend their time talking to themselves. His plan was to get them to talk to each other and to the man in the street.

At first the project was greeted with scorn, it was regarded as not only unrealistic, but virtually impossible. Who could tell what Hawaii would be like in 1975, let alone 1999? One of the task force leaders, Dr. George S. Kanahele, then head of Hawaii's International Service Agency, described it as "just another talk-fest." Some of leftist persuasion, such as the Students for a Democratic Society (SDS), accused the Governor of embarking on a "capitalistic plot" and called it a "militaristic, imperialistic adventure" for the purpose of conquering the Pacific community during the next three decades.

Governor Burns, however, had evidently taken seriously the remarks of Senator Jackson when he referred to Hawaii as "not just the 50th state, but our diplomatic state . . . next door to half the population of the world." In his inaugural message in 1962 Burns had noted the Islands' "unique position as the hub of the great wheel of the Pacific." With the approval of the Governor and the authorization of the Legislature, George Chaplin plunged into the job of digging out all possible information on everything from economy, transportation and housing, scientific and technological developments, arts and education, to the Islands' life-style and Hawaii's place in the community of the Pacific.

At the time of the Conference, which was held in August, 1970, Hawaii's most enduring problems were the same that confronted the Islands as a Territory in the 1930s—the ethnic mixture and its influence on the political and social pattern; the growing population and its effect on the Islands' economy, and the influence of militant labor. New factors had been injected into both situations, however, in the years following World War II. For one thing, Japanese were no longer the dominant ethnic group in Hawaii; the *haoles* were. In 1960 the number of white people in the Islands had risen to 32 percent, about the same as those of Japanese origin; but by the end of the decade, largely due to in-migration of *haoles* from the Mainland, it was 47 percent, and the Japanese had dropped to 28 percent.

The most astonishing racial shift, for example, was among Filipinos. Initially the Filipinos, with the highest ratio of males to females in the Islands, had remained more or less static, with about 63,000 or 17.1 percent of the population in 1930 and approximately the same number in 1960. Suddenly the Filipino influx rose to about 93,000 in 1970, although the percentage of total population, due to the general increase, was only 12.1 percent. However, it was a new type of immigrant from the Philippines. There were fewer unskilled laborers, fit only for work on the docks or in the canefields. Many were of semiprofessional status, or clerical employees, and they brought their wives, intending to live in Hawaii. In addition, they presented a new voting pattern. As George Hong, an astute observer of political affairs who was attorney for several of the Chinese land development groups, pointed out, "The Filipinos have almost no recognized leaders, yet they vote as an ethnic bloc." Clarence Ching, one of Governor Burns's strongest backers among the Chinese entrepreneurs, said the Filipinos were the "most sought-after voting group in Hawaii" because they still were in a "formative state," many of them naturalized citizens; and no one seemed to be able to analyze their voting habits, except that they all appeared to vote for the same candidates.

Bob Schmitt, chief statistician for the State Department of

Planning and Economic Development, had compiled some fairly fantastic long-range figures on Hawaii's potential growth, leading up to the year 2000. The population in the 1970 census was 769,913, and in A.D. 2000 it was estimated that it would be 1,379,000. Using a straight-line projection, if student enrollment at the University of Hawaii, which was 35,000 in 1970, increased at the same rate it did in the first decade of statehood, there would be a total of 416,000 students in the year 2000— more than the entire population of the Islands in 1930. The statistics quite obviously were intended as an unrealistic caricature of purely mathematical projections, and not as estimates.

Even more interesting tidbits could be extrapolated from Schmitt's figures by the Governor's task force on economics for Hawaii 2000. The average annual wage in the Islands, which was $6,320 in 1969, would increase to $51,000 by the end of the century. Assessed valuation of all real property, $6.6 billion in 1969, would be $127 billion thirty years later. The number of automobiles in highways of the State would rise from 37,000 to 2,126,000. Perhaps the most astonishing estimate was in the so-called visitor industry. If the rate of increase from 1940 to 1960 were extended to A.D. 2000, there would be 78,400,000 tourists traveling to Hawaii—approximately sixty times the projected population of the Islands!

In terms of political conclusions to be drawn from the task force studies and those of two experts from the University of Hawaii, John M. Dingman and Daniel Tuttle, Jr., who compiled an analysis of voting patterns in the State for the Journal of Social Psychology (1961), the primary influence in voting in Hawaii was not by racial blocs but party affiliation. Nearly 50 percent of the voting could be traced to partisan feelings, and less than 20 percent was due to the factor of ethnicity. Japanese Democrats usually supported Democratic candidates who were Japanese rather than *haole,* but they seldom broke party lines merely to vote for candidates of Japanese racial origin. The *haoles,* on the other hand, gave support to *haoles* even when it required crossing party lines.

The study of racial matters was further complicated by the method of census-taking developed by the United States Census

Bureau, which went into effect with some unusual curves when Hawaii became a state. On the Mainland the racial divisions were basically white (or Caucasian) and nonwhite, which meant Negroes. The latter were so minimal in Hawaii that they were lumped together in the "All Others" category in earlier Hawaiian census figures. Except for those in the military establishments, there were only a few hundred up to 1940. When the war broke out the NAACP attempted to establish a chapter in Hawaii to support complaints of Negro defense workers, but there were so few complaints the chapter did little business. Later, when the confrontation of blacks and whites began to increase tensions on the Mainland, the NAACP was asked by the local Negro community to stay out of Hawaiian affairs, since their efforts might create tensions that did not exist in the Islands. Yet when the Census Bureau took over in 1960, the only racial division in which they seemed statistically interested was whites versus blacks, which had little relevance in Hawaii.

A second problem that intruded itself was a change in the classification of all mixed racial groups by their nonwhite parents. Prior to 1960, when most Island residents of mixed blood were part-Hawaiians, as they had been since Kamehameha III ordered the first official census of the Islands in 1849, the part-Hawaiian classification was used. This was the practice of the Census Bureau during Hawaii's territorial period. But in 1970 two changes were made. The part-Hawaiian category was deleted entirely, and persons who would have been in that group were classified by the race of the father, which usually was either *haole* or Chinese. Secondly, all persons of mixed white and nonwhite blood were also classified by the father's racial origin rather than by the nonwhite parent. Following these changes there were only about 10,000 "Hawaiians" in the Islands, as against a total of more than 100,000 part-Hawaiians who no longer were classified in that category. The result was a serious overrating of the white and Chinese population and underrating those of Hawaiian blood, as well as affecting comparative figures in all other ethnic classifications.

The one factor that seemed to support Hawaii's claims to having achieved racial harmony, the heart of the melting pot theory, was the large number of interracial marriages. This was perhaps the most sensitive indicator of relationships that crossed racial and cultural lines. Marriages between *haoles* and Hawaiians had been common during the period of the monarchy, when many *kamaaina* families had mixed blood. The term "half-caste," which the missionaries had first applied to those of mixed white and Hawaiian parentage, was abandoned in favor of the Hawaiian term *hapa-haole.*

The number of men of pure Hawaiian blood who married women of other races was less than 20 percent of all marriages during the early years of the Territory, while Hawaiian women —both pure blood and part-Hawaiian—ranged from 40 percent in 1910 to 85 percent in 1960, due primarily to the dearth of Hawaiian males of pure blood. Japanese showed little tendency to engage in interracial marriages at first, but by the 1960s they had increased this ratio from less than one percent to 15 percent for Japanese males and 25 percent of Japanese women among all marriages within the Japanese ethnic community.

These figures present a statistical basis for one of the most pertinent aspects of Hawaii's traditional claims that it was a melting pot of races. It has been previously noted that the mixtures of fractional ethnic groups—the Thai-speaking and Hakka immigrants through the Canton outlet from China; or the indiscriminate mixing of Ilocanos and Visayans from the Philippines —was an unnatural lumping together of diverse ethnic backgrounds in labor camps, due either to ignorance or indifference on the part of the plantation managers. It was also a fiction of Hawaii Tourist Bureau propaganda, before that agency became officially and more euphemistically named Hawaii Visitors Bureau. Yet the record of interracial marriages indicates that the melting-pot theory was actually proving itself, in spite of the inept attitude of the planters or the crass propaganda of the tourist bureau. Andrew Lind, who studied this factor in racial integration in Hawaii, writes:

> The expectation in some quarters that the influx of Caucasians to the Islands following statehood would bring a significant reduction in the ratio of outmarriages [that is, crossing ethnic barriers]

or even a reversal of the upward trend, obviously has not been borne out.[42]

In spite of all obstacles, Hawaii seems actually in the process of proving itself to be a melting pot of races, and this point has considerable significance in assessing the new state's position as "diplomatic representative to half the population of the world."

Among the ten broad areas that the task forces for Hawaii 2000 had to deal with, the most important—aside from racial mixtures and population—were land use and Hawaii's relation to the Pacific community. It was evident that ecology would play a decisive role in determining physical possibilities; but the diplomatic aspects of Hawaii's position in the Pacific, together with the developing life-style in the Islands' political and social system, would become the basic ingredients in Hawaii's role in Pacific affairs. Exactly what did Hawaii have to offer? This was the least tangible, yet the most vital of all the questions.

What the task forces digging into land use found was that there was adequate land on Oahu, where the population was concentrated most heavily, to support an estimated 1,000,000 persons projected for A.D. 2000, but that the pressure to urbanize agricultural lands on the island upon which the City of Honolulu was located would become intense, particularly if the dislocation of Hawaiian people from the small farms they had built up for agricultural purposes were carried out. The anger of Kokua Hawaii and other groups, such as The Hawaiians, over the efforts to resettle residents of Kalama Valley, and the even more controversial Banana Patch project on Maui, in which a synthetic Garden of Eden set aside to lure people back to the simple life resulted in reported orgies of free love and hard drugs, were examples of the dislocation of many indigent groups.

The land use program which Dan Inouye and the freshman legislators of 1954 set in motion had turned up a few thorny patches. It was the opinion of many members of the task force studying this problem that forcing land into use by taxation and

other methods—such as land development by the Chinese tycoons—needed to be handled with great care or it would boomerang into a counterrevolt of Hawaiians, once again
dispossessed of their land.

When the Governor's Conference on the Year 2000 convened in the grand ballroom of Chinn Ho's Ilikai Hotel on
August 5, 1970, it was already evident, as a result of the six
months of intensive study and investigation by members of the
various task forces, that many of these problems were smoldering and about to burst into fire.

The most controversial question of all was the final item on
the agenda—"Hawaii and the Pacific Community." Dr. Kanahele, who had voiced the first of many dubious views of the
usefulness of the Governor's Conference, was chairman of this
task force. As Conference delegates met in the final plenary
session of the working group at the Kennedy Theater in the
Federally financed East-West Center, on the campus of the University of Hawaii, he confessed that he had "repented" his first
impression "with a vengeance."

"It may be an inefficient device," Kanahele said, "but this
conference is a remarkable demonstration of democracy at
work."

He announced bluntly that his task force report would "un-
derscore the intensity of criticism and the sincerity of this criticism" that its members had experienced in their investigations
and interviews. The chief dissenters were young people; and
their chief concern, he said, was that Hawaii was "not qualified
to become the center of anything, except geographically in the
middle of the Pacific Ocean."

Youthful elements, in fact, had stirred up most of the controversy. The day before, in the session on Hawaiian life-styles,
several young men representing various groups, such as the
Students for a Democratic Society (SDS), Youth Action, and a
few merely voicing dissent, had stood up in the middle of the
conference and demanded that the conferees quit talking about
the future and concern themselves with the problems of today.

One young man, giving the name of Tom de Waele, had
demanded that Chairman James Dator of one of the workshop

meetings give up his microphone and turn the meeting over to people who wanted to "do something besides talk." Another representative of Youth Action introduced a resolution calling for an investigation of the Kalama Valley project, where Hawaiians were being displaced to make way for land development. A member of SDS asked the conference to go on record favoring a law making "all politicians legally responsible for their actions." A Young Republican spokesman called for Hawaii to secede from the United States.

During all this progressive confusion, an unexpected sense of awakening seemed to develop. As Kanahele put it, "Ultimately we are dealing with the question of survival. Unless we do something now, our future may be that of a community bypassed. I would like to forestall that eventuality. I don't want to end up in Kalama Valley or Banana Patch."

On the closing day of the Conference, in the Kennedy Theater at the East-West Center during what was scheduled as an open session, a stately Hawaiian woman, Mrs. Pilahi Paki, who was not a scheduled speaker or Conference delegate, arose from the audience and put into words what the central theme of "Hawaii 2000" seemed to be.

The tall, gray-haired woman, dressed in a flowing *muumuu* with a red-and-white flowered pattern, stood in the middle of the group and said, "I am Mrs. Pilahi Paki, and I think I would like to explain to all of you what the Hawaiian word *'aloha'* really means to the Hawaiian people."

Chairman Chaplin, who was presiding at the last plenary session of the Conference, immediately recognized her. The name "Paki" has historic significance for Hawaiians; it was the surname of Princess Bernice Pauahi Bishop, the granddaughter of Kamehameha the Great, who founded the Bishop Estate for the purpose of providing funds for the education of "children of Hawaii."

In a low, unconsciously dramatic voice, Mrs. Paki said, "I would like to offer an explanation of this word. It is the coordination of the heart and mind, and it exists within the individual —not outside. It brings you down to yourself."

She then read from a paper what amounted to an acronymic interpretation of the most widely known word in the Hawaiian language—*aloha*.

" 'A' stands for *akaha'i*, a Hawaiian word meaning kindness, to be expressed with tenderness.

" 'L' stands for *lokahi*, which means unity, to be expressed with harmony.

" 'O' stands for *olu'olu*, a Hawaiian word meaning agreeable, to be expressed with pleasantness.

" 'H' stands for *ha'aha'a*, meaning humility, to be expressed with modesty.

" 'A' stands for *ahonu'i*, the word for patience, to be expressed with perseverance.

"These are traits of character that express the charm,

23

"Aloha"

warmth, and sincerity of the Hawaiians. It was the philosophy of my ancestors."

There was silence in the auditorium as Mrs. Paki finished speaking. She turned gracefully and took her seat. Then the room broke into applause that lasted for several minutes, and the entire assembly—official delegates and those who had come to listen—rose to their feet and gave her a tremendous ovation as she resumed her chair in the midst of the group.

For a moment—although such moments usually do not last —the story of Hawaii from Revolution to Revolution seemed to have taken its full cycle. Mrs. Paki, a consultant in Hawaiian languages originally from Maui, had spent her adult life tracing and translating Hawaiian words and their meaning. She had described the "spirit of *aloha*" as it existed two centuries before, when the first "strangers" arrived in the Islands.

The real question in the minds of many observers of Hawaii had been: Was this spirit of *aloha* as it had been peddled by the Hawaii Tourist Bureau (later the Visitors Bureau) for fifty years, to be regarded as a factor in the process of change, and in Hawaii's place in the Pacific world, or had it been exterminated by those who came to save the souls of the Hawaiians, and in the course of events may have destroyed what was truly Hawaiian?

In tracing events from the Revolution of 1893 to the second revolution in Hawaii many of the factors have been loosely drawn together to avoid creating an artificial and possibly misleading record of progress. One element not particularly apparent is Hawaii's famed "spirit of *aloha,*" chiefly because it did not play a decisive role except in the fertile minds of tourist advertising agents. Sociologist Lind, discussing this point, says,

> Unfortunately most scholars of the Hawaiian social scene have failed to recognize that the social structure in which generosity and hospitality of this type are a central and essential element could in any way persist in the face of assaults of a highly individualistic and competitive culture introduced from the West.[43]

This is an aspect of Hawaii's future role, not only as a state but as ambassador to half the population of the world, that should be more carefully examined. What role will Hawaii play in the Pacific community in the next thirty years? That was the closing theme of the Governor's Conference on the Year 2000. Will the spirit of *aloha* have any significance in this role, or will it be intrinsically as meaningless as it has been within the scope of tourist advertising? The tendency to assume that the philosophy of the Hawaiian people can be applied to the newly created industrial and political complex of Hawaii has been a critical factor in assessing Hawaii's development and it may be more critical in the future. Again quoting Lind, "The use made by tourist promoters of the Hawaiian term *aloha* commonly translated as love or affection illustrates the possible abuse that may occur when a relationship that is essentially commercial and utilitarian is represented as one of intimate and friendly concern."

The angers and resentment that aroused the virtually disenfranchised elements of Hawaii's people, the Dan Inouyes and others who came on the political scene after World War II were not part of an "individualistic and competitive culture introduced from the West." Except for the *malihini haoles,* and to a lesser extent the Portuguese, they came from the Orient or from Hawaii itself; and they were not motivated by racial hostilities. If they had been, there would have been rioting in the streets, burning of schools and libraries, and perhaps a few political assassinations, as there were on the Mainland of the United States.

It was the combination of many racial groups with varying backgrounds but similar complaints that drove them into the organized effort Jack Burns had initiated to redress the political wrongs of half a century. The fact that it was accomplished without violence, and within the prescribed techniques of a democratic society, may have been because "it happened in Hawaii," where there were no real racial tensions.

This does not necessarily rely on the assumption that in Hawaii there was a special kind of race relations, as suggested in the traditional melting pot theory. What was suggested at the Governor's Conference on Hawaii 2000 was that Hawaii, with its background of Polynesian mores, may be able to contribute an element of racial relations to the Pacific Community that would otherwise be lacking.

Mrs. Paki's explanation of *aloha* seemed to express this latent feeling. Earlier the task force on The Quality of Personal Life-Style, as it may exist in A.D. 2000, presented some historical light on the suggestion raised by the Hawaiian lady from Maui. This group, led by Dr. John McDermott, professor of psychiatry at the University of Hawaii, provided an analysis of the underlying values of Hawaiian (Polynesian) life-styles prior to their virtual extermination by the cultural and religious inoculations of the early missionaries and their descendants during the nineteenth century, as they sought to impart Christian morality to the natives. There were three basic aspects of Polynesian life-style, expressed by three words: *Ohana, Hooponopono,* and *Kokua.* The first of these words—*Ohana*—represented the extended family or tribal community of the Polynesian peoples prior to the arrival of the white man. It was an "acting out of mutual respect that pervades man, nature, and the gods." The second value known as *Hooponopono,* was a problem solving technique within the extended family, not unlike a tribal concept of justice, under which disputes were settled. The third value was known as *Kokua,* from which Kokua Hawaii derived its name; it represented the element of cooperation or living together under which gifts were exchanged, goods traded, and a primitive form of the market place was established. It was both cooperative and competitive.

All three values operated within a coordinated system, based on the principle of *Ohana* or the extended family. It was from these common and interdependent concepts that the word *aloha* achieved its significance. While the task force did not specifically suggest that this would become a basis for complex international dealings on economic, political, and racial affairs within the Pacific community, with Hawaii's ancient culture serving as a catalyst, the elements of that possibility exist within the real framework of what has been garbled and, in Professor Lind's word, "abused" as the *aloha* spirit.

It will be apparent by now that much of the symbolism attributed to Dan Inouye as representative of the new Hawaii was drawn from his participation in two elements of the second revolution. One was youth and the other was a nonracial resent-

290: *HAWAII 2000*

ment against the domination of Hawaii's oligarchy and the rule of the Big Five. These two elements seemed to stand like rocks amid turbulent waters, unshaken by the tides that swirled around them. Both were essential—perhaps the most essential —characteristics of the political revolt wrought upon Hawaii's feudal system. Dan Inouye had been eighteen when he enlisted in the 442nd RCT, and was hardly beyond voting age when he joined Jack Burns's crusade to create a new and viable Democratic Party in Hawaii.

These young Turks of the 1940s were middle-aged men by 1970, however; and the young men of Hawaii 2000 had not been born. There were still a dozen ethnic groups in Hawaii's melting pot who lived together in the broad spectrum of Americanism. They would still face the Western Pacific as the diplomatic representative of the United States. The racial mix might change, as indeed it had in the decade since Hawaii became a state, with 47 percent of the population now Caucasian—mostly *malihini haoles* from the Mainland—compared with 32 percent in 1960. But it was doubtful whether there would be any essential change in Hawaii's position as ambassador to the Asian part of the world.

The real problem that confronted George Chaplin's group studying the characteristics of Hawaii 2000 was youth. What would its stance be in the year 2000? Part of the answer might lie in the position of Hawaii's younger generation in 1970, and particularly the attitude of the young people of Hawaiian ancestry. Were the critics of Hawaii 2000 to be regarded as spokesmen for youth?

A small, informal meeting was held one Sunday evening at the home of Arthur Trask, who had been one of the outspoken members of the ad hoc committee formed to protest the appointment of Matsuo Takabuki as a trustee of the Bishop Estate. The purpose was to get some reaction from the younger generation—to determine, if possible, what basic differences might exist between the youth of Hawaii and the rebellious youth movements on the Mainland. One of those present was Arthur Trask's son, Pepe, and he was asked what, if any, differences he was able to discern, since he had come down to Honolulu for the summer after attending college on the Coast.

"The difference is in openness," he said. "Hawaii is not closed in. We enjoy the kind of things young people do in the open. Rock concerts and things like that. We don't feel hemmed in, as many young people on the Mainland seem to feel." He told of a music festival held in the crater of Diamond Head, where not only younger people but many of the older generations sat in the natural amphitheater formed by the ancient volcano, once called the Gibraltar of the Pacific, and listened to rock music.

Was there much likelihood of violence in the schools of Hawaii, such as burning books, or drug addiction?

The young Hawaiian shook his head. "They smoke pot here about as much as they do on the Mainland. But not hard drugs. Most of that comes from the men who have returned from Vietnam for rest periods in Hawaii. They bring the habit with them. We don't have it here."

The meeting was in some respects a reminder of another meeting, described by Lawrence Fuchs in *Hawaii Pono.* A small group of PTA members gathered at the village of Kaaawa, on windward Oahu, and discussed the meaning of *aloha.* An elderly part-Hawaiian couple had remained silent during most of the talking, which was led by a Mainland *haole;* and finally the man, gray-haired and in his seventies, burst forth in a vehement tirade against both missionaries and the *haoles* who led the Revolution of 1893. He described the ransacking of the house of his royalist father during the abortive counterrevolt of 1895 in which Queen Liliuokalani was arrested. This was now in the early 1960s, seventy years after the Revolution; yet he still retained the anger and the hatred of the *haoles* who had created a virtual police state during the time of the Republic of Hawaii.

Were these earlier hatreds still a factor in Hawaii? The question was put to Pepe Trask, and he shook his head, smiling. "Not so much to us," he said. "We have not lived under those conditions. But we have a deep feeling for our people, and our traditions. Perhaps that is what we want to preserve—what little is left—our identity, and our heritage as Hawaiians."

A slightly different aspect of this was expressed by his fa-

ther, Arthur Trask, in a talk to the congregation of Kawaiahao
Church at the invitation of the pastor, the Reverend Abraham
Akaka. At a Sunday meeting in the church on October 11, 1970,
he said,

"Change is the life-style of youth . . . the constant search for
a new life. Where do we go from here? Kahu Akaka suggested
that I say in a few words, 'What is in your heart?' What is in our
hearts is justice for the Hawaiians . . . Should we recite the
indictment of wrongs unrolling almost two hundred years ago
. . . the trespass of venereal disease? Or should we recite the
litany of misfortune of the Hawaiian today, in contrast to his
heritage?"[44]

He spoke of the isolation of the Hawaiian people on the
islands of the Pacific and their conquest of the ocean by "naviga-
tional skills" when the affairs of Europe were "in the bathtub of
the Mediterranean." When Captain Cook arrived in Hawaii in
1778, he said, there were a half million people, all Hawaiians,
in the Islands. They already had "an economic system that
clothed, fed, and housed" the Islands' people. "Upon admission
to Statehood, Hawaii had a similar half million people, but we
imported 98 percent of the clothing, food, and housing."

How deeply this resentment is still imbedded in the hearts
of Hawaiians is a matter of divergent viewpoints. When the
Reverend Akaka was asked about his reaction to the word *huli*
painted on the doorposts of Kawaiahao Church, he said, "I look
at this word *huli* as being a way of saying, 'Are you being true
to your faith? What are the demands that the church should be
meeting?' For this reason, I do not want to erase that word. I
want it to stay there so that all the members of Kawaiahao can
look at it and think."

The pastor was asked if he viewed the activities of Kokua
Hawaii as "a conflict between young Hawaiians and older Hawaiians." He shook his head. "No. The conflict is not between
younger Hawaiians and older Hawaiians, but between different
points of view."

This belated surge of rebellion on the part of the Hawaiians
themselves has been brought into this account, although it may

appear somewhat out of context, to illustrate the basic effect that seems to emerge from the story of Hawaii's change over a span of less than a century—from Hawaii Nei, or old Hawaii, to the new Hawaii. The melting pot theory of Hawaii's racial mixture has not been displaced, or even changed; it has been reinvigorated by events. The reappearance of Hawaiian ethnic identity, smothered in the profuse literature of tourism and the domination of the oligarchy, may actually provide a symbolism of social and racial harmony that the world—or at least the Pacific community—may well heed over the next three decades, leading to the twenty-first century.

The greatest contribution Hawaii can provide, in its strategic location in the middle of the Pacific Ocean, may very well be the much abused spirit of *aloha*—the concept of an extended family (*Ohana*) with its problem-solving concept of justice (*Hooponopono*) coupled with the spirit of living together (*Kokua*), which was the basic framework of early Polynesian civilization.

Whether this concept of *aloha,* which as Mrs. Paki said "is the philosophy of my ancestors," can ever be applied pragmatically to relations among nations that comprise the Pacific community is something only time will tell. In its basic framework, it appears to be precisely what the United Nations prescribed as a formula for lasting peace in the world. In the mortal contest between the materialistic and highly competitive peoples of today the glow of the ancient Polynesian life-style may not even be noticed, or it may burst into flame.

But as Dan Inouye learned in his first erratic steps through the political labyrinth of Hawaii and Washington, politics—and perhaps international diplomacy—is "'the art of the possible.''

Notes

1. *Hawaii: Restless Rampart,* by Joseph Barber, Jr. (New York: The Bobbs-Merrill Co., 1941), p. 25.

2. *The Hawaiian Revolution (1893–1894),* by William A. Russ, Jr. (Gettysburg, Pa.: Times-News Publishing Co., 1959), p. 95; also in the papers of W. D. Alexander, Archives of Hawaii, quoted from Report of Colonel J. H. Blount to President Grover Cleveland, dated July 17, 1893, Honolulu, Hawaiian Islands.

3. *Thrum's Hawaiian Annual, 1888–1894,* by Thos. G. Thrum (Honolulu: Hawaiian Gazette Company, 1896). Also quoted by Russ, p. 78.

4. Executive Document No. 47, to House of Representatives, 53rd Congress, dated Dec. 18, 1897. (Congressional Record, 53rd Congress, 2nd Session, p. 2238.)

5. *The United States Since 1865,* by Foster Rhea Dulles (Ann Arbor: University of Michigan Press, 1959), p. 164.

6. Papers of Jonah Kuhio Kalanianaole, Delegate to Congress, Archives of Hawaii, File No. 4.

7. *Journey to Washington,* Daniel K. Inouye with Lawrence Elliott (Englewood Cliffs: Prentice-Hall, Inc. 1969), Introduction, p. xix–xx.

8. *Hawaii: Last of the Magic Isles,* by Andrew W. Lind (London: Oxford University Press, 1969), p. 20.

9. *Hawaii Pono: A Social History,* by Lawrence H. Fuchs (New York: Harcourt, Brace & World, Inc., 1961), p. 221.

10. *Pacific Commercial Advertiser,* Honolulu, T. H., September 11, 1924; also quoted in an unpublished manuscript, *Protest in Paradise,* by William L. Abbott, p. 188.

11. Dulles, p. 128.

12. Fuchs, p. 42.

13. Inouye-Elliot, p. 19.

14. Fuchs, p. 128.

15. *Hawaii Hochi,* 10 May 1932.

16. Fuchs, pp. 265, 282.

17. Fuchs, pp. 283–284.

18. Inouye-Elliott, p. 73.

19. Fuchs, p. 308.

20. Inouye-Elliott, p. 62.

21. Inouye-Elliott, p. 191.

22. *The Economy of Hawaii,* by James H. Shoemaker (brochure published by the Bank of Hawaii, Honolulu, 1950), p. 15.

23. Fuchs, pp. 372–373.

24. *The Economy of Hawaii,* by James H. Shoemaker (pamphlet privately published in 1954; Introduction, "Review of Outstanding Developments, 1778–1954"), p. xx.

25. Shoemaker, 1954, p. xx.

26. Shoemaker, 1954, p. xxi.

27. Lind, p. 55.

28. *Hawaii Hochi,* 30 May 1932.

29. *Honolulu Advertiser,* 25 September 1958; also Report of Hearing, Subcommittee on Insular Affairs, U.S. Senate, 86th Congress, Feb. 25, 1959, pp. 101–105.

30. Undated transcript of speech delivered by former Governor Wallace R. Farrington, from files of "Wallace Rider Farrington," *Honolulu Advertiser.*

31. Report of Hearing, Subcommittee on Insular Affairs, U.S. Senate, 86th Congress, Feb. 25, 1959, p. 6.

32. Report of Hearing, Subcommittee on Insular Affairs, U.S. Senate, 86th Congress, Feb, 25, 1959, p. 15.

33. *Honolulu Advertiser,* 4 December 1962.

34. Excerpt from keynote address at Democratic National Convention, Chicago, Ill., Sept. 11, 1968, delivered by Senator Daniel K. Inouye of Hawaii.

35. Excerpt from letter from Senator Daniel K. Inouye to Mrs. Bina M. Chun, dated January 14, 1969.

36. *Monthly Economic Review,* published by Bank of Hawaii, January 1971, edited by W. H. Hillendahl, p. 6.

37. Lind, p. 9.

38. Lind, p. 100.

39. Inouye-Elliott, p. 35.

40. Lind, p. 101.

41. *Monthly Economic Review,* published by Bank of Hawaii, January 1971, edited by W. H. Hillendahl, p. 4.

42. Lind, p. 115.

43. Lind, p. 70.

44. Excerpt from transcript of remarks of Arthur Trask, at Kawaiahao Church, Honolulu, October 11, 1970.

Index

Adams, Ray, 207
Adams, Dr. Romanzo, 135, 168, 223, 224, 255
Advertiser, The, 23, 32, 36, 51, 52, 53, 55, 95, 131, 150, 154, 184, 201, 204, 264, 273
Aka, Rev. Abaraham, 258, 259, 292
Ala Moana Case, 81. *See also* Massie Case
Alaska Bill, 202–205, 210–219
Alexander, Samuel T., xii
Alexander, W. D., 17
Alexander & Baldwin, Ltd., xiv, 207, 249
Allen, John, 258
Allen, Riley, 154
Aloha Airlines, 141, 142
American Factors (Amfac), xii, 34, 75, 219
Anderson, Clinton P., 184
Anderson, Jack, 246
Annexation, ix, xiii, 14, 20, 21, 47, 50, 68, 74, 160, 179–180, 195
Annexationists, 6, 7
Anthony, Garner, 102
Aoki, Dan, 112, 125–126, 145, 158, 172, 187, 199, 211, 214, 216, 244
Ariyoshi, George, 177, 187, 208, 247
Asahi, The Hawaii, 80
Atherton, Frank, 29, 79
Atherton, Joseph Ballard, 29
Atherton family, 75, 153
Awamura, Margaret (Inouye), 144

Baker, Mrs. Ben, 213
Baker, Bobby, 212
Baker, Ray Stannard, 22
Balch, John, 106, 116
Baldwin, Harry, 24, 25, 70, 106, 182
Baldwin, Henry P., xii
Baldwin family, 61, 125, 212
Banana Patch, 283, 285
Bank of Bishop & Co., 29, 76, 128
Bank of Hawaii, 76, 136, 168, 248, 269
Barber, Joseph, Jr., 221
Bartenders Union, 186
Bassett, Willard K., 80, 155, 162
"Bayonet Constitution," xii, 6, 7, 23
Beppu, Tadeo, 236
Big Five, The, xii, xiv, 19, 23, 30, 38, 42, 55, 61–62, 69, 74, 81, 104, 105, 123, 127, 221, 223, 225, 256; economic activities, 76, 79, 135, 137, 167–171, 182, 183, 227; political role, 19, 27, 29, 75, 77, 78, 84, 117, 126, 138, 155, 162, 180–182, 187–188, 206, 220, 234; under military government, 102, 134
Bingham, Hiram, xi
Bishop, Charles Reed, 28, 69, 76
Bishop, E. Faxon, 55, 56
Bishop, Princess Bernice Pauahi, 28, 29, 69, 258, 286
Blaisdell, Neal, 209, 244, 264
Blount, Col. John H., 14–17, 61

Bolte, C., 13, 15
Bond, Rev. Ellis, 48
Borthwick, William, 230
Boston, USS, 8, 9, 10, 16
Bottomley, A. W. T., 75
Bourne, William Olund, 179
Brewer, Capt. Charles, xii
Brewer, C. & Co., xii, 27, 249
Brewery Workers Union, 267
Bridges, Harry, 85, 160, 214
Brown, Kenneth, 236
Brownell, Herbert, 172
Buddhists, xiii, 40, 53, 107, 130, 265
Budge, Alexander, 77, 152, 167, 227, 249
Bulletin, The Evening, 36
Burns, John A., x, 88, 89, 98, 121, 149, 230, 233; as delegate, 188, 196, 197–198, 201–217; as governor, 234, 239–241, 260, 264–267, 272, 277–279; as police detective, ix, 119–121, 125–127, 270; as politician, x, 85–87, 118–119, 122–123, 125–127, 139, 144, 147, 150, 157, 161, 177–178, 185–191
Butler, Jack, 57, 58, 80

Carroll, Sen. John, 214, 215
Carter, Gov. George R., 27–29
Cary, Miles E., 90–92, 95–98, 116, 126, 148, 162
Castle, Samuel N., xii
Castle, W. R., 9, 12, 14, 23, 135
Castle & Cooke, Ltd., xii, 77, 152, 167, 227, 248, 269
Castle family, 19, 153, 264, 265
Catholics, viii, 69
Chang, Henry, 89
Chaplin, George, 240, 277–279, 290
Chillingworth, Charles F., 55–56
Chinese: culture, 257, 263; economic role, 137–138, 172–173; Exclusion Act, 55–56; plantation labor, 39, 172, 222–223; politics, 202; "tycoons," 121, 137–138, 171–172, 223, 233, 267
Ching, Clarence, 121, 138, 228, 265, 279
Ching, Donald, 145
Ching, Hung Wai, 137, 138, 172
Ching, Hung Wo, 137, 138, 172, 265
Chinn Ho, 137, 138, 171, 174, 228, 265, 284

Chun, Mrs. Bina, 247
Chun, Won Wung, 47
Church, Sen. Frank, 185, 213
Churchill, Winston, viii
Clarke, John, 259
Cleghorn, A. S., 8, 10, 16
Cleveland, Pres. Grover, 14, 16–19, 21, 195
Coke, Judge James L., 125, 126, 145, 153
Colburn, John F., 6, 7, 8, 16
Coll, Ray, 205
Committee for Public Safety, 6, 7, 8, 9, 14, 15, 22, 155
Commonwealth Government, 184–185, 193, 214
Communism, 84, 118–119, 140–148, 150–152, 157, 160–161, 169, 193, 199, 207, 214, 234
Confucianism, viii, 130, 184, 192
Cook, Capt. James, 273
Cooke, Amos Starr, xi, 29
Cooke, Charles M., 29
Cooke family, 14, 19, 29, 75, 153
Coolidge, Pres. Calvin, 64
Cooper, Henry E., 8
Cornuelle, Henry C., 248
Cornwall, William, 9
Cravalho, Elmer, 189–190
Crossley, Randolph, 176–177, 184, 236, 244
Crowell, Sheriff William, 58

Damon, Rev. Francis W., 72
Damon, Samuel, 9, 10, 12, 14, 26
Darrow, Clarence, 83
Dator, James, 284
Davies, Theophilus H., xii
Dean, Dr. A. L., 88
DeMello, Adrian, 208
Deschler, Lewis, 203
deWaele, Tom, 284
Dewey, Dr. John, 69, 89
Dillingham, Benjamin F., 28
Dillingham, Benjamin F., 2nd, 234–235
Dillingham, Walter F., 28, 55, 102, 150, 157, 167, 178, 247–248
Dillingham, Mrs. Walter F., 143, 157, 211, 235

Dillingham family, 28, 153, 249
Dingman, John M., 280
Doi, Masato, 145, 159
Doi, Nelson, 145, 161
Dole, Rev. David, 12
Dole, James, 37, 77
Dole, Judge Sanford B., 6, 9, 10, 12, 16, 18, 23, 24, 27
Dorn, William Jennings Bryan, 216
Draper, Herbert, 9–10
DuBois, George, 244
Dunn, Frank, 89

Eastland, Sen. James, 213, 214, 215, 226, 228
Education, 68–71, 87–94. *See also* Public School System
Edwards, Webley, 104
Eisenhower, Pres. Dwight D., 162, 177, 198, 205, 217
Emma, Dowager Queen, xiii, 24
England, viii, x
English Standard Schools, 87–89, 93, 162. *See also* Public School System
Equitable Life Assurance Society, 272
Esposito, Joseph, 126
Esposito, Vincent, 126, 144, 163, 177, 187, 189–190, 206, 209, 230, 237, 245, 267, 270

Farley, James A., 80, 81
Farrington, Elizabeth, 161, 187–188
Farrington, Joseph R., 123, 124, 126–127, 150–151, 155–156, 176–177, 178, 182, 187, 188, 197–198, 214, 230
Farrington, Wallace Rider, 36, 37, 55, 69, 92, 124, 194–196
Farrington family, 93, 176
Farrington High School, 118
Fasi, Frank, 126, 144, 146, 155, 163, 208, 233, 244, 264–265, 267
Federation of Japanese Labor, 52–53
Filipino Federation of Labor, 53, 56
Filipinos: culture, 263; ethnic background, 222; immigration, 59; plantation labor, 53–54, 57–59; politics, 60, 208, 223, 279
Fong, Hiram, 133, 139, 172, 181, 188, 233, 236, 246

Fortescue, Mrs. Grace, 81–82
Foster, John W., 14
Four Forty-second (442nd) RCT, ix, 97, 108–112, 123, 159, 211, 290; Veterans Club, 124–125, 144–145, 190, 199, 246, 257
Frear, Gov. Walter F., 28, 29, 30
Fuchs, Dr. Lawrence H., 35, 69, 74, 91, 97, 157, 223, 291
Fukushima, Judge Yatsutaka, 260

Galdeirs, Pae, 258
Gazette, The Hawaiian, 51
George Washington University: Law School, 144, 147, 149, 158
Gibson, Walter Murray, 7
Gill, Thomas P., 126, 163, 177, 199, 206, 207, 208, 230, 236–239, 260, 265, 267, 270
Glade, H. F., 8
"Go for Broke," 111–112
Good, John, 5, 9, 12, 270
Goto, George, 140
Goto, Lawrence, 202
Governor's Conference. *See* Hawaii 2000
Great *Mahele,* xiii, 6, 35, 233

Hackfeld, Capt. Henry, xii, 75
Hackfeld, H. & Co., xii, 75. *See also* Amfac
Haggerty, James, 211–212
Hall, E.O. & Sons, 5, 9, 76
Hall, Jack, 84, 85, 86, 117, 119, 120–122, 125, 126, 140, 142–144, 146–147, 152, 157, 160, 177, 186–188, 199, 206, 214, 223, 236, 247
Harding, Pres. Warren G., 64
Harrison, Pres. Benjamin, 14
Hartwell, Alfred, 7
Hawaii: economy, 22, 169–172, 227–229, 235–237, 248–250, 268; monarchy, xii, 8, 25–26; Provisional Govt., 12–19; Republic of, 19–21, 39, 78, 90; State of. *See* Statehood; Territory of, 21, 94, 102, 132, 194, 270
Hawaii Equal Rights Commission, 183, 200
Hawaii Statehood Commission, 200–201, 204–205, 212, 213, 232
Hawaii Seven, 152, 186, 265–266

Hawaii Tourist Bureau, 37, 62, 287. *See also* Hawaii Visitors Bureau

Hawaii 2000 (Governor's Conference), 240, 277–285, 280–281, 283–285, 286–289

Hawaiian-born, vii, 41, 69, 79, 118

Hawaiian Homes Commission, 31–35, 36, 127, 177, 234. *See also* Hawaii Rehabilitation Act

Hawaiian Pineapple Co., 77

Hawaiian Sugar Planters Association (HSPA), 33, 37, 53, 54, 55, 57, 59, 92

Hawaiian Teachers Federation, 237

Hayden, Sen. Carl, 195

Heen, Judge William, 123, 125, 126, 153, 199, 230, 231–232

Heftel, Cecil, 246

Herald, The Hawaii, 112. *See also Hochi*

Hewett, Harry, 34

Hickam Field, 104

Hill, William (Doc), 41, 45, 123, 133, 161, 206, 207, 209

Hillendahl, Wesley, 248–250, 268

Hind, Robert, 92

Hochi, The Hawaii, 52, 57, 79, 82, 93, 102, 125, 181

Hollinger, Ben, 83–84

Holman family, xi

Holstein, Henry L., 55

Home Rule Party, 19, 23, 24, 27, 28

Hong, George, 279

Honolulu News, 264

Hopkins, Charles L., 17

Horner, Albert F., 33, 34, 55–56

Hotel & Restaurant Employees Union, 186

Hundredth Battalion (100th Bn), 108, 111, 114, 159, 207, 244

Hunniwell, James, xii

Iaukea, Curtis P., 27, 30

Ickes, Harold, 120

Ikuta, Siunji, 89

Imua, 145, 157, 178, 209–211, 226, 237

Inouye, Asakichi, 40, 45, 46, 71, 72

Inouye, Sen. Daniel Ken, vii, ix, x, 41, 45, 65, 66, 70, 74, 75, 87, 88, 94–97, 101, 103–113, 114–117, 123–125, 144–145, 147–150, 157–162, 185–198, 225, 261–262, 271, 272, 273, 289–290; as Representative (Hawaii), 161, 175–177, 185–190, 269, 283, 293; as Senator (Hawaii), 208–209; as Congressman, 229, 231–234, 241–242; as U.S. Senator, 67, 94, 110, 235, 240–243, 245–247, 250, 272; as war hero, 110–113, 123, 144

Inouye, Hyataro, 45, 72, 73, 104

Inouye, Margaret, 146, 147, 149, 160. *See also* Awamura, Margaret

Inouye, Moyo, 45, 72

Inouye, Wasaburo, 71

Inter-Island Steam Navigation Co., 137, 267

International Longshoremen and Warehousemen Union (ILWU), 84–86, 119, 122, 137–139, 140–141, 146, 147, 150, 160, 186, 188, 199, 214, 223, 230, 234, 236, 245–247

Iolani Palace, 6, 9, 10, 19, 82, 117

Iolani School, 69

Issei: as non-citizens, 103; as older generation, 121

Iwanaga, Kame (Inouye), 73

Izuka, Ichiro, 140–143, 150–151

Jackal, ship, x

Jackson, Sen. Henry M., 206, 209, 215–219

Japanese: culture, 40, 46, 257, 263; education, 130, 138; immigration, vii, ix, 29; language schools, 67, 68, 261–262; plantation labor, 40, 50–52, 129–133; political influence, 46, 78–80, 189, 207–209, 247, 254, 280; strikes, 53–55, 130–133. *See also* Labor

Japanese-Americans (AJA), 115

Jarrett, William P. (Billy), 64, 66, 77, 78, 127, 159

Johnson, Lyndon B., 205, 212

Jones-Costigan Act, 182, 200

Judd, Dr. Gerrit P., xiii, 179, 254

Judd, Gov. Lawrence M., 34, 82

Kahahawai, Joseph, 81, 82

Kahala Plantation, 49

Kahanamoku, Anna, 159

Kahanamoku, Duke, 159
Kaina, Rev. William, 258
Kaiser, Henry J., 168, 171, 173, 174, 248
Kaiulani, Princess, 8
Kalakaua, King David, xiv, 6, 7, 15, 19, 22, 23, 27, 37, 179
Kalama Valley, 273, 283, 285
Kamakawiwoole, Rev. Larry, 271–272, 274
Kamehameha I, xvi, 26, 29, 36, 69, 258
Kamehameha III, xiii, 28, 179, 233, 281
Kamehameha IV, xiii, 23, 179, 233, 281
Kamehameha V, xiii
Kamehameha Schools, 69, 258
Kanahele, Dr. George, 278, 284–285
Kauhane, Charles, 162, 175, 188, 269
Kawaiahao Church, 258, 260, 270–271, 292
Kawananakoa, Princess Abigail, 35
Kawananakoa, Prince David, 23, 35
Kawano, Jack, 126, 141, 151
Kealoha, Jimmy, 209, 233
Kennedy, Sen. Edward, 246
Kennedy, Pres. John F., 122, 229, 232
Keppler, Herbert, 257
Kido, Mitsuyuki, 126, 233
Kidwell, Capt. James, 37, 77
Kimoto, Jack, 141
King, James A., 12
King, Samuel Wilder, 84, 124, 153, 156, 170–177, 181, 187–188, 198, 214
Kokua Hawaii, 271–273, 283
Koloa Plantation, 47
Kono, Russell, 159
Kuhio, Prince Jonah, 24, 25, 26–29, 30–33, 35–36, 55, 64, 159, 180, 182

Labor: contract, 22, 45; plantation, 47–49, 133–134; strikes, 51–55, 57–59, 170
Lee, Herbert, 207
Lehleitner, George, 210–212, 213
Lewers, Christopher, 29
Lewers & Cooke, 29, 76
Ligot, Ceyetano, 57, 58, 59
Liliuokalani, Queen, ix, xiv, 5, 7–9, 10–12, 15, 16–19, 23, 45, 61, 74, 89, 110, 155, 171, 259

Lincoln School, 88, 89
Lind, Dr. Andrew, 61, 121, 138, 209, 223–224, 252, 255, 262, 282–283, 287
Long, Oren, 88, 117, 161–163, 177, 198–199, 207, 231–234
Lum, Herman, 145, 159, 187, 199
Lunalilo, King. *See* Prince Lunalilo
Lunalilo School, 104, 105
Lyman, Richard, 259

Makino, Fred, 52, 57, 79
Manlapit, Pablo, 53, 57, 59
Manoa Valley, 111
Martin, Lloyd, 265
Massie, Mrs. Thalia, 81, 82, 180
Massie, Thomas H., 81, 82
Massie Case, 81–83, 93, 153, 156, 180, 260, 263
Masters and Servants Act of 1853, 48, 62, 256, 273
Matson Navigation Co., 38, 77, 267
Matsumoto, Saichi, 89
Matsunaga, Spark, 74, 145, 151, 162, 217, 244
Matthewman, John A., 59
Mau, Chuck, 126, 145, 162, 197, 199
McCandless, L.L. ("Link"), 31, 80, 83–84, 101, 103, 167
McCarthy, Charles J., 33, 52, 55, 117
McClellan, George B., 30
McClung, David, 207
McElrath, Robert, 141, 265
McKinley, President William, 10, 20, 24
McKinley High School, 66, 73, 87–91, 92, 94–97, 104, 105, 116, 122, 126, 148, 198
MacNaughton, Malcolm, 248
Mead, Royal, 64–65
Metcalf Farms, 249
Metzger, Delbert E. 125–126, 150, 152, 158
Mid-Pacific Institute, 72
Mills, George, 23
Mills College. *See* Mid-Pacific Institute
Missionaries: Congregational, viii; Board of Foreign Missions, xi; missionary families, xi, 28–29, 67, 69, 132
Miyake, Howard, 247

Morgan, John T., 211, 226
Murchison, Seth, 171
Murray, Edwin, 259
Murray, James E., 202

National Association for the Advancement of Colored People (NAACP), 281
Neumann, Paul, 19
Nippu Jiji, The, 52, 79, 102
Nisei, vii, viii, 73, 80, 81, 82, 92, 95, 96, 103, 105, 106, 107, 108, 115, 121, 123, 124, 143, 145, 150, 158, 192, 199, 206, 208, 209, 233, 254, 257
Nixon, Vice-Pres. Richard M., 122
Nuuanu Y.M.C.A., 109, 110

Oahu Sugar Company, 133
O'Brien, Rep. Leo, 211, 213, 215, 226
O'Connor, Leilani (McClellan) 216–217
Oligarchy (missionary-sugar planter), 22, 25, 27, 49, 75, 90, 92, 102, 126, 129, 132, 134, 167, 183, 192, 222–223, 255, 261, 267, 293
Olney, Richard, 21
On (Japanese), 107, 111
One Forty-first Infantry (Texas), 112
Oneha, Captain, 58
Organic Act, 20, 22, 24, 32, 181, 187

Pacific Club, 25, 66, 67, 71, 114
Pacific Heights, 38, 111
Paki, Mrs. Pilahi, 285, 286–287, 289, 293
Palmer, A. Mitchell, 75
Parker, Dr. Francis, 69, 89
Parker, Samuel, 9, 15, 18
Pearl Harbor, ix, 78, 82, 95, 101, 104, 107, 134, 136
Peterson, Arthur P., 7, 9
Phelan, Sen. James, 78
Phillips, L. G., 210–211
Pillion, Rep. John, 213, 216–217
Pinkham, Gov. Lucius E., 30, 117
Poindexter, Gov. Joseph B., 81, 101–102, 117
Poindexter, Sen. Miles, 33
Polynesians, viii, xiii, 22; culture, 286–288, 289, 293; kings, xiv

Porteus, Hebden, 207
Porteus, Dr. Stanley, 131
Prince Cupid. *See* Kuhio
Prince Lot. *See* Kamehameha V
Prince Lunalilo, xiii
Prosser, Charles E., 92–93
Prosser Report, 92–93
Provisional Government (proposed), 9, 10, 11, 12. *See also* Hawaii, Provisional Govt.
Public School System, 67–71, 88–91, 129, 133–134, 223. *See also* Education, English Standard Schools
Punahou Academy, 12, 69, 89

Quinn, Gov. William, 188, 204, 207, 233–234

Rayburn, Rep. Sam, 175–176, 205, 212, 234, 241–242
Reciprocity, Treaty of, 14
Reform Party, 6
Reinecke, Dr. John, 118, 141, 186, 266
Reynolds, Jack, 248, 265, 277
Revolution of 1893, vii, ix, x, xi, 6, 11, 12, 23, 63, 74, 89, 102, 127, 146, 195, 200, 263, 287
Rice, Charles, 31, 84
Rice, Harold, 106, 213
Rice, Philip L., 64, 127
Rice family, 61, 206
Richards, Atherton, 77
Richards, Rev. William, xi, xii, 254
Richardson, William (Bill), 80, 88–89, 98, 145, 177, 187, 199, 257, 259, 265
Robinson family, 61, 232
Roosevelt, Pres. Franklin D., 101, 108, 117
Roosevelt High School, 101, 108, 117
Russ, William A., 10
Russell, Sen. Richard, 202, 203, 212
Rutledge, Arthur, 186, 246, 265–267

St. Andrews Priory, 69
St. Louis College, 69, 121
Schmitt, Robert, 279–282
Schofield Barracks, 104, 109, 110
Seaman's Union, 85

Second Revolution, viii, x, 40, 62, 63, 74, 80, 129, 147, 225, 235, 237, 238, 239, 287
Shafter, Fort, 120
Shelby, Camp, 111
Shintoism, xiii, 40, 130, 183–184, 192
Shipman family, xi, 61
Shoemaker, Dr. James H., 136, 168–170, 171, 227, 248, 268
Silva, Charles, 233
Sinclair, Dr. Gregg, 163
Smith, Emma Louise (Dillingham), 27
Smith, Howard W., 216–217
Smith, Hutton, 249
Smith, W. O., 6, 7–8, 12, 13, 21, 150
Smith Act, 152
Soga, Yasutaro, 52
Soper, Col. John H., 9, 10, 16
Spitz, Dr. Allen A., 35
Stainback, Judge Ingram, 117–118, 162, 183–185, 192, 201, 214–219, 227
Star, The, 36
Star-Bulletin, The Honolulu, 36, 55, 92, 93, 119, 124, 153, 259, 260
Statehood, 14, 21, 46, 74, 83, 155–157, 173, 178–217, 232, 256
Stevens, John L., 6, 8, 9, 12, 15, 16
"Sugar is King," 5, 22, 70, 138, 154, 227
Sugar Planters Experiment Station, 70
Suhr, Ed, 13
Summer, George, 249

Takabuki, Matsuo, 120, 143, 145, 159, 162, 177, 187, 199, 257–260, 264–265, 271, 290
Takahashi, Sakae, 97, 114–115, 123, 145, 162, 177, 189–190, 199, 207, 244–245, 264
Taoists, viii
Taylor, Herbert (Yabo), 89
Teamsters Union, 267
Tenney, E. D., 30
Territorial Hotels, 267
Thaddeus, brig, xi, 6, 258, 270
Theo. H. Davies & Co., Ltd. xii, 58
Thiessen, Wayne, 244
Thompson, Duke, 89
Thurston, Rev. Asa, xi, 6

Thurston, Lorrin A., xi, 6, 7, 13, 14, 18, 22–24, 27, 52, 55, 61, 93, 131, 132, 160
Thurston, Lorrin P., 102, 154, 200–201, 204–205, 213
Times, The Hawaii, 102. *See also Nippu Jiji*
Titcomb, Frederick, 233
"Tokyo High," 90, 148. *See also* McKinley High School
Tong, Fook Hing, 89
Tongg, Rudy, 137
Townsend, Henry S., 69, 89
Toyo Kissen Kaisha (N.Y.K. line), 99
Trask, Arthur, 258, 290, 292
Trask, David, 207, 258
Trask, Pepe, 290–291
Truman, Pres. Harry S., 117, 161
Tsukiyama, Wilfred, 73, 74, 78, 107, 115, 142, 207, 209, 233
Turner, Farrant, 207, 209, 249
Tuttle, Daniel, 280
Twain, Mark, 174, 273

Un-American Activities Committee, 146, 151, 152
United States Army, 113, 141
U.S. Military Government (Hawaii), 101–103, 133, 177
University of Hawaii, 70, 73, 108, 109, 123, 131, 133, 141, 163, 172

Vitousek, Roy, 120
Von Hamm-Young Company, 267

Waialua Plantation, 77
Waianae Planation, 34
Waimanalo Plantation, 34
Waipahu Plantation, 77
War Department, 108
Watase, George, 109
Waterhouse, Henry, 8
Waterhouse, John, 54
White, Oscar, 10
Whitney family, xi
Wilcox, George, 248
Wilcox, Robert, 19, 23, 24, 27
Wilcox family, 61, 75
Wilder, W. C., 8, 13, 14, 155
Wilder Steamship Co., 8

Willis, Albert S., 17–19
Wilson, Marshal C. B., 8, 9
Wilson, Mayor John H., 79, 80, 82, 83, 98, 101, 117, 125, 146, 152, 153, 155, 162, 244, 248
Wise, John H., 32, 34, 35, 64, 89
Wise, William (Dog), 89
Wist, Benjamin, 95
Wood, Gen. Leonard, 57

Woolaway, Arthur, 207
World War I, 75
World War II, xii, 45, 61, 65, 68, 70, 73, 97, 101, 111, 117, 122, 129, 134, 138, 152, 167, 168, 182, 190, 225, 227, 253, 288
Wright, George W., 56, 57, 82, 93, 135

Zoroastrians, viii